Regaining Excellence in Education

Mario D. Fantini

Professor and Dean
School of Education
University of Massachusetts at Amherst

Merrill Publishing Company
A Bell & Howell Company
Columbus   Toronto   London   Sydney

To my family

Published by Merrill Publishing Co.
A Bell & Howell Company
Columbus, Ohio 43216

This book was set in Palatino.
Cover Design: Cathy Watterson
Production Coordination: Anne Daly

Credits: **p. 20.** Extract from *School Power: Implications of an Intervention Project*, by James Comer,
copyright © 1980 by The Free Press, a division of Macmillan, Inc. Reprinted by permission. **pp. 28–29.**
Extract from *The Adaptive Corporation*, by Alvin Toffler, copyright © 1985 by McGraw-Hill Book
Company. Reprinted by permission. **p. 30.** Extract from *In Search of Excellence: Lessons from Amer-
ica's Best-Run Companies*, by Thomas J. Peters and Robert H. Waterman, Jr., copyright © 1982 by
Thomas J. Peters and Robert H. Waterman, Jr. Reprinted by permission of Harper & Row, Publishers,
Inc. **p. 116.** Extract from *Schools of the Future: How American Business and Education Can Cooper-
ate to Save Our Schools* (New York: McGraw-Hill Book Company, 1985), by Marvin Cetron, copy-
right © 1985 by Marvin J. Cetron. Reprinted by permission. **pp. 142–143.** Figures from *Action in the
States: Progress Toward Education Renewal*, A Report by the Task Force on Education for Economic
Growth (July 1984). Used with permission. **p. 187.** Figure from "R & D in the Remodeling of Education" (*Phi Delta Kappan* 51, no. 6 [February 1970], p. 301), by Francis S. Chase. Reprinted by permission.

Library of Congress Catalog Card Number: 85-63035
International Standard Book Number: 0-675-20501-8 (paper); 0-675-08224-2 (case)
Printed in the United States of America
1 2 3 4 5 6 7 8 9 — 91 90 89 88 87 86

Preface

One of the fundamental aspirations of developed civilizations is the quest for excellence. The search for ever-expanding attainment appears to be a basic instinct of humankind. The United States has set excellence as one of its ultimate goals ever since the dawn of its own history. From time to time events in history conspire to remind the society of its unfulfilled aspirations and to jolt the national psyche into assessing where it stands in relation to its stated goal of excellence. Mature societies enter into these diagnostic periods with an openness to debate and emerge with a commitment to the quest for a new level of achievement.

This desire for excellence pervades every aspect of our lives. It is our nature to reach far beyond our present stage into ever-expanding visions of opportunity. Targeting high expectations for ourselves carries with it enormous responsibilities, and low achievement leads to frustration in both the individual and society. The twentieth century has been replete with high expectations coupled with more modest achievements. In those moments of peak experience, society may perceive itself as having the internal capacity to move forward and realize its highest ideals. However, we have also experienced moments of high expectations and lower fulfillment. And in these moments, the inner nature and strength of our society and its most sacred values are tested.

Once having embraced a vision of excellence, the society becomes vulnerable to the verdict that it has not yet attained it. During such periods, society and the entire social infrastructure may undergo serious review and engage in a sometimes bitter debate. If the society survives, it will carry out a careful assessment, recommit itself to the goal of excellence and redefine and restructure the means by which it can best be attained. Without the standard of excellence, the society retreats into a posture that is less than outstanding. While there may be moments in history in which the reality of the situation indicates reduced expectations and more modest goals, it is the nature of advancing societies to reach for ever-expanding standards.

We are in such a period at the present time. Excellence is the call word. As we reembrace the goal of excellence, it rekindles anew our deepest aspirations for its attainment.

However, this has also been a period of critical reassessment in which certain institutions of the society have been jolted. Certainly this is true for business and industry, which have found a challenge from other advanced societies in this century. The unexpectedness of the challenge and our lack of preparedness to meet its implications shook the confidence of many citizens. Eras of shaken confidence test an institution's strength, nature, and mission. While many institutions do not survive such crises, others do, and their success can teach us valuable lessons. Many recoveries are spectacular, such as that of the Chrysler Corporation, which turned itself around after fierce realignment and now feels that it has adjusted to a period of new opportunity, a process highly unlikely without an ultimate goal of excellence.

Similarly, we have seen a recommitment to excellence on the part of our educational institutions. Running almost parallel to the bumps and wobbles experienced by the private sector, the public sector and especially the public school became the subject of intense criticism, analysis, and review. A virtual bombardment of national reports concluded that while the public schools may have embraced a goal of excellence, they have fallen far short in practice. Further, unless there is a serious mid-course correction, the consequences will be dire indeed not only for the students but the entire nation. As one report dramatically phrased it, without the achievement of excellence, the public schools put the entire "nation at risk."[1] There is no more important topic than the regaining of excellence in public schools; there is no more important agenda item for the nation. John Dewey warned us in the early decade of this century:

> It is necessary to prepare the coming generations for a new and more just and humane society which is sure to come, and which, unless hearts and minds are prepared by education, is likely to come attended with all the evils that result from social changes effected by violence.[2]

As we will see, the public schools are not merely self-contained agencies that serve local communities. As a strategic institution in society, the public schools represent our most fundamental social infrastructure. The public schools develop the human capital of the nation, dealing with nearly 85% of the populations that will compose the next generation—clearly a critical mass. It is a truism that the public schools are the basic agency in the transition of the young to mature adults.

---

[1] The National Commission on Excellence, *A Nation at Risk: The Imperative for Educational Reform* (Washington, D. C.: U. S. Government Printing Office, 1983).

[2] Reginald Archambault (ed.), "My Pedagogic Creed," *John Dewey on Education: Selected Writings* (New York: The Modern Library, Random House, Inc., 1964), 9.

In that crucial sequence are laid the building blocks for the future. It is an awesome responsibility, and unless there is a fundamental reaffirmation of reformation, the studies almost unanimously forecast serious consequences for our entire society. A society that embraces excellence embraces a first-class view of itself; a society that accepts less than excellence accepts a second-class view of itself. Yet all human beings are entitled to a first-class view of themselves, and this is the end towards which we must strive.

This book is being written at a time when almost every state in the nation has accepted responsibility for the reexamination of its public school system. Each state has rightfully rededicated itself to the ultimate goal of excellence for its commonwealth. Unfortunately, merely stating the belief in excellence does not attain it. Herein lies the pervasive problem: defining excellence in modern times together with the means for its achievement. Consequently, this book is dedicated not only to the necessity for excellence, but to the goal of achieving it. Pervasive as this theme is and as preoccupied as we appear to be with excellence, definitions of excellence do not come easily, and the delivery mechanisms that are necessary for the achievement of excellence are even more elusive. At the very least, this book and its discussion of excellence should contribute further to the national debate on the topic, which shows no signs of abating. At the most, the pages that follow can help formulate the framework for the educational reforms which are being planned and developed, and on which the future of society may well rest.

ACKNOWLEDGEMENTS

That this book is published at all is a tribute to my many colleagues who assisted in one important way or another toward its preparation. I am indebted to Merrill Publishing Company for their endorsement of this project; Helen Schneider and Debra Smith, for their careful review and editorial assistance; Cynthia Gala and Nancy Burnett, for their secretarial support and patience in typing draft after draft; Luvern Cunningham (Ohio State University), for his thoughtful review of the manuscript; and most especially, Laura Holland, for her exceptional research and technical assistance. An unusual debt of gratitude is extended to Nancy Kaminski, for her adept administrative and organizational talents. Her cooperation, review of the manuscript, and devotion to the project have been instrumental in bringing the work to completion.

Contents

and Evaluation as Diagnostic and Helping Tools | Research and Development | Lifelong Learning in the Educative Community | Toward a More Adaptive School Structure That Models What It Teaches

6
Modernization and Excellence 121

7
Modernization In Action 141

Introduction

American public education is in desperate need of regaining excellence. This book is dedicated to this task. The 1980s can be characterized as the decade in search of excellence in all fields, especially in the fields of business, industry, and education. The economic woes of the 1970s and early 1980s brought attention to the problems of productivity in the United States. The Chrysler Corporation bankruptcy case and the competition with Japan and other developed countries began to raise our national consciousness and standards of excellence. The popular book, *In Search of Excellence: Lessons from America's Best-Run Companies* by Thomas Peters and Robert Waterman, Jr.,[1] summarized the lessons learned relating to excellence from America's most successful corporations. John Naisbitt's *Megatrends*,[2] another best seller, presented a framework for guiding excellence in the future. Another popular book, *The One Minute Manager*, by Kenneth Blanchard and Spencer Johnson,[3] suggested that excellence in corporations depends on the ability of leaders to deal sensitively with the human side of organizations. In the field of education, a Report of the National Commission on Excellence, *A Nation at Risk: The Imperative for Educational Reform*,[4] led a score of reviews that not only triggered a national debate but concluded that unless *excellence* replaced *mediocrity* as the standard in our schools, American society would face irreversible damage.

The search for excellence is not a theme of recent origin. Several decades back, for example, John Gardner devoted an entire book to the subject.[5] The call for excellence seems to follow events or crises that shake our national consciousness. Some of us recall the launching of the Russian Sputnik in 1957, which sparked intense national debate about the shortcomings of our public school system. The conclusion was that the Soviet system of education must be superior to ours, for it produced the scientists who engineered the first space satellite. That national debate resulted in a rededication to excellence and an unprecedented involvement of the federal government in public school improvements as evidenced by well over one hundred federally-funded education acts.[6] It is noteworthy here that American public policy clearly established a functional relationship between education—especially math and science education—and national defense. In 1959, the Congress passed the National Defense Education Act, which launched extensive federal aid to our professionals.

Our current crisis is rooted in economic concerns. Our national consciousness has been jarred by the challenges posed to United States' business by Japan. The automobile business in particular became the catalyst for a new crisis, and the near collapse of the Chrysler Corporation became a lesson to many Americans. Other manufacturing areas have also seen the Japanese emerge victorious. In a technical age, Japan was outdoing the United States in productivity. How could this happen? Once again came the urgent call for excellence. Once again, there appeared an array of national studies on the public schools. This time, the involvement of government in school improvement efforts comes not at the federal but at the state level. A functional link has been clearly established between our public education system and national economic development. In less than a quarter century, our public school system became central to American national defense and economic survival. Little wonder that school reform has become a national priority, and that excellence has become a codeword in school reform.

As we shall see in this volume, part of the problem is that both reform and excellence are difficult to achieve. At times, we have come to believe that reform has been realized following a period of activity conducted in its name. Merely to claim reform or excellence is no guarantee or substitute for actual realization. The fact that we are falling victim to increasing national crises points out the lack of excellence in education and reveals the depth of the issues. This realization prompted the National Commission on Excellence in Education to proclaim:

> If an unfriendly foreign power had attempted to impose on Americans the mediocre educational performance that exists today, we might well have viewed it as an act of war. As it stands, we have allowed this to happen to ourselves. . . . We have, in effect, been committing an act of unthinking, unilateral educational disarmament.[7]

Such language was needed to convey the seriousness of the situation. The report's conclusion was deceptively simple—mediocrity has replaced excellence in education. The consequence is so imperative that it became the title of the report: *A Nation at Risk*.

The legacy of mediocre education is painful, dangerous, and often hidden. In *Illiterate America* Jonathan Kozol suggests that 60 million Americans cannot read the words in his book because they are functionally illiterate. The United States ranks 49 out of 158 nations in literacy, and Kozol estimates that over $100 billion annually is lost in earnings and expenses arising directly from this degree of illiteracy.[8]

John Goodlad, in his book *A Place Called School: Prospects for the Future*, stated that

> American schools are in trouble. In fact, the problems of schooling are of such crippling proportions that many schools may not survive. It is possible that our entire public education system is nearing collapse. We will continue to have schools, no doubt, but the basis of their support and their relationships to families, communities, and states could be quite different from what we have known.[9]

The issues involved in regaining excellence in education are deep-rooted, well beyond simple or monetary solutions. Regaining excellence in our schools will necessitate systemic remedies—a new contemporary model of education developed democratically and based on state-of-the-art knowledge. We cannot expect a 20th century model of education to work for a society approaching the 21st century. All the studies conducted on our public school system reveal the growing symptoms of nonproductivity—low achievement, high dropout rates, discipline problems, poor attendance, public loss of confidence, and low morale of education professionals.

If these are the symptoms, how do we define and cure the disease? Excellence can be achieved only if there is a fundamental restructuring of our present model of education in favor of a state-of-the-art model that can provide a clear agenda for both policy and practice. Reform efforts for the most part seem to fall into two general categories: strengthening the present school structure or restructuring schools by introducing competition and choice in education. Both of these proposals have their own logic and merit. Yet ultimately they fall short of the goal of attaining excellence unless each is somehow integrated into a new vision of public education. The test is how we convert a school system into an educational system.

Much depends on our definition of excellence. The essential ingredients of excellence are defined from the dynamic nature of our contemporary world. This definition then serves as a yardstick for assessing the major reform efforts being proposed in the name of excellence. This book attempts to present a clear, logical, and sequential statement on regaining excellence in education, drawing equally from theory and practice in the past, present, and future. The intent is to present an ultimately optimistic blueprint for reforming one of America's most important institutions.

NOTES

1. Thomas J. Peters and Robert H. Waterman, Jr., *In Search of Excellence: Lessons from America's Best-Run Companies* (New York: Warner Books, Inc., 1984).

2. John Naisbitt, *Megatrends* (New York: Warner Books, Inc., 1982).

3. Kenneth Blanchard and Spencer Johnson, *The One Minute Manager* (New York: William Morrow and Company, Inc., 1982).

4. The National Commission on Excellence in Education, *A Nation At Risk: The Imperative for Educational Reform* (Washington, D. C.: U. S. Government Printing Office, 1983).

5. John W. Gardner, *Excellence: Can We Be Equal and Excellent Too?* (New York: Harper and Brothers, Publishers, 1961).

6. *1984 Catalog of Federal Domestic Assistance* (Washington, D. C.: Superintendent of Documents, U. S. Government Printing Office, 1984), pp. AEI–19–20.

7. The National Commission on Excellence in Education, *A Nation At Risk: The Imperative for Educational Reform* (Washington, D. C.: U. S. Government Printing Office, 1983), 5.

8. Jonathan Kozol, *Illiterate America* (New York: Anchor Press, 1985).

9. John Goodlad, *A Place Called School: Prospects for the Future* (New York: McGraw-Hill Book Company, 1984), 1.

PART I
What is Excellence?

The Changing Context: Implications for Education and Excellence

1

THE CHANGING WORLD VIEW

Discussion of a topic as important as excellence must be viewed in the context of the times. If we were living in the 19th century, we would develop a 19th century concept of excellence. In each century and each era, people attempt to mold a concept of excellence. The term *excellence* has not always been used. Sometimes the word *quality* appears as if it were synonymous with excellence. Sometimes the word is *best* or *superior*; other times it is *noble* or *first class*. The label is not as important as the intent—to reach for an ideal state. This ideal state is fundamentally tied to human motivations, values, dreams and aspirations; it represents the fundamental drive of the individual, the community, the institutions, and society. Lacking the energy to build a future world view, the individual becomes developmentally arrested and the society becomes stagnant.

Consequently, leaders of all nations proclaim the goal of excellence. The founding fathers of this nation had their own view of excellence. Politically, excellence would be achieved when the fundamental rights of citizens were realized, when the government created the conditions to promote these rights essential to a free and just society. While these appear to be elusive goals, they do constitute the intangible but real directional map of our society against which we evaluate ourselves, our institutions, and our civilization. At times, we are rudely awakened by the distance we have yet to travel in order to realize the promise.

Each era is influenced by the major events and the prevailing philosophies that shape the collective perceptions of a society. Sometimes these discoveries or theoretical propositions are so fundamental that they create a world view with encompassing ideas that provide us with a new concept of ourselves and the universe.

Two giant thinkers who influenced our world view, Sir Isaac Newton and Albert Einstein, developed theories of the universe that affected every phase of human experience. Newton saw the universe as a fixed, closed system, while Einstein described the universe as an open, dynamic, and relative system. The differences between the Newtonian and Einsteinian models represent two entirely different views of how to organize schools for productive learning. Ira Gordon[1] has delineated the fundamental differences between these two models in Table 1–1.

The Newtonian view of a mechanistic universe defines the world as a big machine, with a fixed purpose, general discoveries, and definable rules. Applied to the school, the closed, static view leads to such fixed notions of intelligence as measurable I.Q. and a fixed age-graded sequence. The school resembles the factory model and is organized like a machine based on uniform principles to which all must adjust, standardized testing, academic tracking, and standardized human classifications. In this, each part of the bureaucracy synchronizes with the others to result in maximum effectiveness and efficiency. The factory model, adapted to the public schools, deals with masses of students by processing them through a type of assembly line tied to standardization and a normative structure.

However, these concepts are giving way to the more open, dynamic, and relativistic theories of the new world view developed by Albert Einstein and others. Under the Einsteinian view, flexibility becomes more desirable than a fixed state. Since the world is not static but dynamic, flexibility becomes one of the conditions for discovery and for adapting to the changing nature of the environment. Applied to organizations, this flexibility becomes one of the hallmarks of successful adaptation in pursuit of excellence. The bureaucratic structure, with its emphasis on standardization and uniformity, needs to be modified, restructured, and reformed to keep pace with this changing concept. In addition, the static concept of I.Q. has been replaced by more dynamic notions of intelligence and talent.

Other major theories also contribute to a changing world view. Charles Darwin's notion of the "survival of the fittest" has had an enormous impact. In this

TABLE 1–1

Newtonian Model Man	Einsteinian Model Man
A mechanistic, fixed closed system characterized by:	An open-energy, self-organizing system characterized by:
1. fixed intelligence	1. modifiable intelligence
2. development as orderly unfolding	2. development as modifiable in both rate and sequence
3. potential as fixed, although indeterminable	3. potential as creatable through transaction with environment
4. a telephone-switchboard brain	4. a computer brain
5. steam-engine driven motor	5. a nuclear power plant energy system
6. homeostatic regulator (drive reduction)	6. inertial guidance and self-feedback motivation system
7. inactive until engine is stoked	7. continuously active

Source: I. J. Gordon, "The Task of the Teacher," *Studying the Child in School* (New York: Wiley, 1969), 2–3.

view, the environment selects those who are well-adapted to the environment and are more likely to survive. Ralph Tyler suggests that when this view was applied to the school structure, the norm became that those who succeed do so because they are more "fit" to survive.[2] That is, the scholastic environment selects those most intellectually fit from those who are not. The work of Sigmund Freud triggered a revolution in psychology that continues today. Freud's definition of the psyche and the subconscious has changed our view of who we are, how we got that way, and how we may become more than we are. Freud and others forced us to look deeper into the individual psychological inner world. For the schools, this meant a much closer look at the *individual learner* and the emotional forces that impinge upon *individual* personality development. John Dewey's philosophy of education also had an impact on schools. Dewey saw the school as a social institution, which was both a part of the community and a miniature democratic society. Education was the process of living, not a preparation for future living. Many schools interpreted Dewey's view as "learning by doing," emphasizing a child-centered, experiential style over the fixed, subject-matter centered, didactic approach. Major thrusts such as these alter our perspectives and are essential to an age of change.

A CENTURY OF RAPID TRANSFORMATION

We must begin any contemporary debate on a vision of excellence with the major reality of the late 20th century—its rapidly changing nature. If, as in the tale of Rip Van Winkle, we were to go to sleep and wake up twenty years later, we would not see the same society. Given the dynamics of changing conditions, it is likely that our definition of excellence will also change significantly. Yet many believe there are transcendental features associated with excellence that should cut across time and place. Certainly the Declaration of Independence, the Bill of Rights, and the United States Constitution have attempted to maintain principles throughout time. Even though changing times have posed real strains on our interpretation of these principles, the principles have remained the same. They became open to review as new understandings surfaced. We could not have lived through the 20th century without realizing that our commitment to freedom for all and equality under the law were goals that had not been realized. The human and civil rights movements of the 1960s and 1970s were attempts to redress the difference between the stated goal of political equality and the unequal achievement of that goal. It may be useful to review some of these forces as we come to grips with the important concept of what excellence means for the late 20th and 21st century. What is its nature? Can we formulate a concept of excellence that is rooted in the real world?

We have to review what we mean by excellence in public education given the context of the period in which we live. How do we then get a clear view of that context?

While we are well aware that things are changing, sometimes most of us may be too close to see things objectively. For instance, we all know about the horse and buggy days and the old tin lizzy. These modes of transportation came and went, replaced by a new generation of automobiles which, in turn, have also been replaced. This process seems to go on for most things, including our social institutions. Home, church, workplace, and marketplace have all changed dramatically with the times. So, too, have our schools. We can recognize how much change has really taken place when we see the one room schoolhouse compared with today's comprehensive schools. As we change, we try to retain what we value. We accept change more readily if in fact change can help us realize further those things we care about. Yet some changes collide with our values and are resisted—sometimes successfully, sometimes not.

MEGATRENDS

John Naisbitt's best-selling book, *Megatrends*, identifies these forces of change in a different way. The popularity of the book revealed the need for a better understanding of the changing nature of our existence. In *Megatrends*, Naisbitt defined ten pervasive directions in which the society appeared to be moving, based on item analyses of newspapers throughout the nation. The interrelated megatrends were identified as the following shifts from

Industrial	to	Information Society
Forced Technology	to	High Tech/High Touch
A National Economy	to	A World Economy
Short-Term Planning	to	Long-Term Planning
Centralization	to	Decentralization
Institutional Help	to	Self-Help
Representative Democracy	to	Participatory Democracy
Hierarchies	to	Networking
North	to	South
Either/Or	to	Multiple Option[3]

In essence, these are the major patterns emerging in our society that affect our lives. In particular, they affect the functioning and behavior of our institutions and are of paramount importance for the schools. If we consider these directions or trends and understand forces shaping our world, perhaps we would be better able to deal with them. It may be useful to review these trends with an eye toward their possible implications for schools and educational reform.

From an Industrial to an Information-based Society   The *first megatrend* is the movement of society from an industrial to an information-based society. The public schools as we know them today were organized and developed during the industrial revolution, and the structure that we now have is still geared to an industrial-based economy. However, we are now moving toward an information-based economy, and the existent school structure may not be able to keep pace. On the day-to-day level, the teachers who are performing inside the industrially based educational structure still use books, still assume that information accumulates at a rate with which educators can keep pace, and in essence expect to be the main dispensers of that information to their students. However, we now know that it is virtually impossible to keep pace with all the changing information and constantly evolving theories of the information age. Therefore, the role of teachers under an information-based system changes dramatically. Instead of dispensing information directly, they teach their students how to retrieve information and how to gain access to new tools of technology and telecommunication. Many teachers who are socialized under different information retrieval systems—namely, the print medium—will have to undergo retraining so that they will be able to use electronic means of retrieving information.

This has significance in terms of how they teach as well as what they teach. The new electronic information systems can update themselves much more quickly than textbooks can be updated and revised. It is an enormous waste of time to have the periodically out-of-date textbook and the teacher as dispensers of knowledge when students could have new modes of information retrieval at their fingertips.

The information age also means that we have a new experience of time. Electronic time is of a much different order from the so-called manual time that we find in school. Today's young people are being weaned on electronic communication. Television, the home computer, and video games have given them a different internalization of time and place, a concept of a world that can be traveled in a matter of seconds via telecommunications. However, when students move into the schools, they move into a time mode that came out of an industrial transportation period when the printed word was still the major mode of communication.

The schools were once primarily the major agency for acculturation. With the advent of television and telecommunication, we have acculturation modes that are vastly more powerful than the manual system that still exists in the schools. Therefore, we have discontinuity and conflict between the socialization that takes place outside of school and the socialization that takes place inside the school. Many students who cannot adjust become bored because of the slower pace and the linear nature of experience within the schools. Transcending distinctions of middle class or working class, electronics is a major socializing force of contemporary society.

From a Forced Technology to High Tech/High Touch The *second major trend* takes us into the newer modes of automation, in which machines do increasingly more of what human beings used to do, and do it more effectively and efficiently. In this high technology/high touch environment, the ability to deal with the human side of the organization becomes extremely important. People have certain needs and aspirations, and unless there is corresponding attention to the human side of the organization, it is unlikely that high tech alone can provide the productivity and excellence that we all seek. As we automate the schools and as computers find their way into the classroom, the human organization that had been put into place during the industrial period may feel challenged. As human beings begin to see computers do more of what they used to do, and do it better, they lose a sense of their own identity, which leads to resistance to the introduction of computers on the one hand and the loss of professional confidence on the other.

In concert with automation, teachers could be very useful in terms of achieving certain kinds of tasks. Teachers and others who have been inside the institution, trying to make it work, are still there. Many of them have been socialized in the ways of the earlier environment and now face the invasion of their environment by the new technologies. The ability of leaders to provide the kind of high touch that can counter high tech will signal in very real ways that the human side of the organization is still paramount, and that people are still indispensable parts of the organization. Managers, superintendents, and principals have to understand the importance of both high tech and high touch in the schools. Otherwise, there may be conflicts and misdiagnoses of teachers' frustrations with what is taking place in the name of reform, as well as a lack of fulfillment of the goals of excellence.

From a National to a World Economy   The *third megatrend* identified by Naisbitt is the movement from a national economy to a world economy. No one who has lived in the past decade can escape the fact that we are living in an interdependent world. At one time, our economy was primarily a nationally oriented economy, and we dominated the world market. The situation has been changed by advancing technology and by the economic development of many other countries. Many American industries are now multinational, and they are concerned with global markets, with the cultures of the different nations in which they operate and with which they do business. Multicultural understanding takes on a greater importance, since it makes good business sense to understand with whom you are doing business.

The school curriculum has to reflect multicultural understandings. Multilingual and multicultural education are no longer frills but major necessities, especially for those who are going to deal with the global aspects of our economic structure. Such programs, which have been on the margins of schools, are now more central, and we need to cultivate people who have multicultural and multilingual talents. Instead of just teaching Latin, French, and German, because of growing international markets, we now have Arabic, Chinese, Russian, Spanish, and Swahili. Those who are able to speak these languages and understand these cultures will be at an advantage in international marketing. Sensitive leadership also requires an understanding of different cultures and an ability to communicate people to people, nation to nation. These needs have clear implications for what we teach, when we teach it, and even how we teach it.

From Short-term Planning to Long-term Planning   A *fourth trend* identified by Naisbitt concerns the shift from short-range goal setting to long-range goal setting. The public schools have been oriented to short-range planning, as has business and industry. As new needs arose, the schools added appendages to a structure that came out of an earlier era. When jobs became more specialized and training was important, we created vocational education; when we became an automotive society, we created driver education; when we discovered poverty in our midst, we developed compensatory education and supported lunch programs. A whole host of services arose that were cognizant of short-term needs and quick solutions. The problem with short-term, quick fix solutions is that they do not remain as an integral part of the organization—they deal primarily with symptoms rather than causes. Ultimately, they make the institution more complicated, more unwieldy, and more dysfunctional. This means that the people inside the organization are confused about all of the things they have to do. It also confuses the consumers, because they are not sure what it is the schools do best. Accountability becomes diffused. The schools are expected to do almost everything, and they are criticized because they cannot do what they were never designed to do.

The so-called band-aid approach, associated with the short-term, quick solution, can be counter-productive in the long term. The irony of this is that the more institutions resort to short-range solutions, the more crises they have to deal with, and the more short-range solutions they have to develop in response to the new crises. The cycle becomes increasingly unproductive. The chain reaction that can be set in motion ultimately ends in a political process, such as the one we are in now, with a series of national reports pointing out the problems, even the crises, in the schools. Admittedly, long-range solutions are more difficult, more politically vulnerable, and they pose severe strains on existing personnel. It is easier to develop short-range add-ons than to look at long-range institutional renewal and redefinition of the organizational structure.

In the case of the school, existing structures have become unwieldy. Each of the short-term solutions becomes part of the ongoing operation, which leads to costly and duplicative efforts that cost the taxpayer. These considerations are particularly appropriate when considering school reform. School reform, in one sense, means taking a long look at the schools, determining what their goals should be, and how the schools can best achieve these goals. People may enter into reform with the intent of taking a long-term view, but in all too many cases, they fall victim to the apparent expectancy of short-term, quick fix solutions.

We have seen in business and industry that the quick fix solutions are no longer appropriate or productive. If organizations want to maintain their competitive edge, they have to keep pace with change, and they have to develop their organizations in terms of long-range goals. Effective managers have to look at long-range restructuring and its implications for people. For the public schools, it means that the present structure is simply no longer appropriate to the needs of the information-based economy, and that no amount of add-ons will help. A totally new system is needed—one that is able to deliver the necessary services effectively and efficiently. It takes some imagination to develop a vision of a new structure in which the people presently in the schools are part of the process of modernizing the schools. This transformation of an old structure to suit contemporary needs is best done through enabling legislation on the part of state and federal government and through partnerships between the schools and other private and public agencies.

From Centralization to Decentralization The *fifth megatrend* suggests a shift from centralized to decentralized structures in our society. This bottom-up trend is transforming how we carry out the major functions of our society. Centralization is one of the patterns that followed our industrial period. Now, under the weight of the knowledge-based economy, centralizing forces are giving way to the local initiatives of a new entrepreneurial clientele, further stimulating our pluralism and diversity.

Our public schools have also been highly centralized organizations. The "downtown central office" became a phrase that many school board staff used to refer to "power headquarters." All of the real power and decision-making was viewed as taking place in a distant central headquarters far removed from the front lines. Moreover, this centralization included a board of education who purported to represent the public. Yet many central boards were also viewed as distant from parents whose primary relationship was with the school their children attended. During the 1960s and 1970s, community discontent with schools often led to conflicts with central school boards, and contributed to the decentralization of the public schools.

Big city schools especially become targets for decentralization. Major decentralization plans were implemented in New York City and Detroit which established community school systems of autonomous school districts, each with its own governing board. The Mayor's Advisory Panel on Decentralization of the New York City Schools summarized the perceived advantages of their plan:

☐ increase community awareness and participation in the development of educational policy closely related to the diverse needs and aspirations of the city's population;
☐ open new channels and incentives to educational innovation and excellence;
☐ achieve greater flexibility in the administration of the schools;
☐ afford the children, parents, teachers, other educators, and the city at large a single school system that combines the advantages of big-city education with the opportunities of the finest small-city and suburban educational systems;
☐ strengthen the individual school as an urban institution that enhances a sense of community and encourages close coordination and coopera-

tion with other governmental and private efforts to advance the well-being of children and all others;

☐ all with the central purpose of advancing the educational achievement and opportunities of the children in the public schools of New York City.[4]

This trend continued with proposals calling for decentralization to continue to the level of the individual school and to individual students and families. For example, Theodore Sizer,[5] in his book *Horace's Compromise*, recommended that individual schools be freed from mandated curriculum, offering teachers, principals, students, and parents the opportunity to experiment based on the unique conditions of the school and community. This decentralization has included the establishment of schools within schools, alternative forms of education collaboratively planned within the larger school by parents, teachers, and students based on choice. Many school districts are promoting school-based management policies that move more authority to the individual school level. Several states—among them, Massachusetts—have established policies mandating school-based councils in which each school would have its own board of trustees composed of teachers, parents, other community residents, and representatives from business and industry. With the advent of new educational technologies, this decentralization trend should continue to offer learners and their advisors more options.

From Institutional Help to Self-help   A *sixth trend* involves the movement from institutional help to self-help. We see this in the do-it-yourself movement in terms of diet, health care, home improvement, and more entrepreneurial activities in which the individual assumes responsibility and feels in control, independent of institutions. This transition has a special significance to the schools because of their role in socializing individuals to be independent learners. Yet the present school is structured to make students dependent on adults, grades, and discipline. The self-help approach means that students have to gain control of their own learning at an early age, identify the resources they will need to enrich their individualized learning experiences, and orchestrate those resources to gain control over the learning process.

This trend makes the school's role in the educative process particularly important. It also, however, makes the use of the new technology important, because if teachers can be released by the new automation from teaching the old basics, they can then move into the newer basics, such as helping individuals learn how to learn. This is obviously related to being able to retrieve information—knowing where to look, when to look, and how to look. These processes are important, as is the ability to think analytically and to ask critical questions. People who are trained to think for themselves can raise questions about their rights as well as their responsibilities. Naisbitt establishes that over one million families educate their children at home. This phenomenon has been explored more fully by home schooling advocate John Holt in this book, *Teach Your Own.*[6]

Self-help does not imply a sense of narcissism. Part of the new responsibility of the schools would be to help people gain a sense of connection with others while pursuing self-help, developing support groups, identifying needs in the community, and trying to assist others who may be in difficulty. Part of the self-help trend is the need to develop a sense of caring about those in the community who may not be able to perform certain kinds of functions. For example, there are many citizens who are unable to perform certain tasks, such as shoveling the walk, taking out the garbage, or walking on icy pavements. The school curriculum might reflect (and the school might support) efforts to perform community service, in which teams of people from the high school reach out to help needy citizens.

From Representative Democracy to Participatory Democracy A *seventh trend* is the shift from representative democracy to participatory democracy. This represents the notion of elitist versus classical democracy. At one time, direct participation of every citizen was considered to be extremely important. As society became more complicated, we delegated participation to representatives, who then were in a position of speaking for their constituents. Tied to the growth in self-help, this trend means that each person is a political agent, and that citizens begin to exercise individual power. In the schools, this implies more direct participation of students, teachers, parents, business and industry, and the arts—more participation of all of the elements of the community. Direct participation may involve students teaching each other, teachers serving as resources to one another, parents coming in as volunteers and tutors, and university students coming in as mentors, tutors, small group instructors, or teacher aides. The arts community can participate directly in enriching the curriculum in the schools. People in business and industry might like to assist in making some of their expertise available. Schools will have to develop more options for people acknowledging that there are different styles of teaching and different styles of learning.

From Hierarchies to Networking The *eighth trend* concerns the movement from hierarchical structure to networking. Instead of the institution having a vertically "top-down" flow, it moves "laterally" to connect with other institutions and agencies to form a horizontal network. This network becomes a way to deliver services that are appropriate to contemporary realities. It improves the flow of organizational communication and the delivery of services.

Instead of becoming isolated and linear in its organization, the school becomes an integral part of the human service network, collaborating with others in the task of improving learning. This concept of the school is based on the realization that parents, human service agencies, media, the peer group, the workplace, and museums and libraries all teach, and these multiple linkages become part of the new fabric that ensures a broader education. Teachers and principals may have to move out of their classrooms and offices into the community to develop these networks and linkages with the legal, scientific, arts, and business and industrial communities. These networks expand opportunities for learning and provide many more options than can possibly be offered in a linear institution with a hierarchical management structure. This suggests more emphasis on cooperation, collaboration, and facilitation for the schools and for professional educators. To achieve these very complex goals, educators need to learn complex skills requiring more inservice training.

There are further fundamental implications for schools. The basic unit of education is no longer the classroom or even the school, but the entire community. Further, the licensed and certified teachers in the school are not the only educators; our concept of teachers must expand to encompass networks of people who educate informally and non-formally, as well as formally. This will require a complete redefinition of roles and responsibilities and will impose severe strains on our abilities to organize and utilize people. Such a shift represents a type of deinstitutionalization, moving away from rigidly hierarchical structure into more dynamic collaboratives.

From North to South As society becomes more information-based, more decentralized, and more globally oriented, there is a corresponding tug on how our population is distributed. During the industrial era, the migration went towards the Northeast. For the first time in American history, the 1980 census reported that there were more people in the South and West than there were in the North and East. The rise in leisure time coupled with the increase in retirement communities has given the "sunbelt" states an added attraction.

These mobility patterns clearly affect the public schools. Urban centers, once the home of the major industrial sites, are affected by a changing economy and shifting populations. Urban schools are left with decaying central cores, deflated tax bases, and increasingly poor and minority populations. With the decline of the North and the East as economic centers, the national influence of school systems in those regions also declines. Conversely, the West and South pick up both school-age population and increased financial support. New schools need to be constructed and more staff hired. The growth in such states as Florida, California, and Texas increases their influence. We have already seen the rise in political leadership in the southern states, particularly in reference to improving the public schools. The governors of such states as Mississippi, Florida, South Carolina, Arkansas, North Carolina, and Texas were among the first to address school improvement issues.[7]

The challenges caused by the growth of the South and West present special opportunities for public education. Urban school districts in the Northeast should get special financial consideration in state legislation, given the growing concern of business and industries for the educated labor pool and the growing inequality of finance associated with urban settings. In addition, many city residents concerned with quality of life issues are asking their elected officials to give greater priority to improving their schools. Many Northeastern cities are engaged in a renaissance that includes greater attention to the public schools.

From Either/Or to Multiple Option The *final trend* identified by Naisbitt has to do with movement from an either/or dichotomy to an array of options and choices. People want more options in all areas, including places to go, television channels to watch, places to eat, part- and full-time employment, family forms, and architectural styles. With options come more individual choice and more individual control.

In the schools, the structure that we currently have in place provides very few options. We either move in this direction or that; we may substitute one monolithic bureaucracy for another; we have one standardized program or another to which all must adjust. It is clearly evident that some people learn better in one environment than in another. When any single option is imposed on a group of people, resentment arises, dysfunction occurs, and effectiveness is compromised. The more options the school can provide, the more the school can provide for human variability. There is no one best approach. There may be goals and destinations that we all hold in common, but the means to achieve these goals are diverse.

OTHER DEMOGRAPHIC TRENDS

Another component in the context in which educational excellence is being pursued involves dimensions of our changing demographics. Demographic trends reveal that we are a mobile society. One-fifth of the entire population moves each year. Changing career patterns, relocation of business and industry from one region of the country to another, the movements of population from urban, suburban, and rural areas all influence our schools and their traditional assumptions about the stability of neighborhoods and communities. As Naisbitt indicates, the 1980 U.S. Census Bureau statistics revealed for the first time in American history that the South and West had more people than the North and East. Demographic trends have significant impact on the schools.

As a nation, we are getting older. By the year 2000, about half of us will be 65 years or older. For the schools, this means an aging professional staff, and in the coming decade many will consider retirement. Attracting new professionals to public education offers both challenge and opportunity. In the light of the changes being contemplated in the name of school reform, the new personnel can assume roles that are more accurately tailored to the changing nature of the educative process.

Further, as the United States population grows older, fewer families have school-age children. "Today, although 90% of American children attend public schools, only 27% of adult Americans have kids in school. Thus . . . 73% of adult Americans who relate to the schools are primarily taxpayers who have no direct stake in the quality of education being offered."[8] Most Americans do not have firsthand relationships with the schools or a firsthand investment in the quality of the schools. The traditional base of support for public education came from parents who had children in school. During the baby-boom of the post World War II period, parents represented support for the schools. Fewer students and the public's concern over the lack of productivity in education has now placed the schools and educators on the defensive, affecting professional morale at the very time school reform legislation is being proposed and debated.

Demographers forecast a second baby-boom period of more modest proportions over the next decade. This will mean that teacher shortages will again appear with the retirement of senior professional personnel. The teacher shortage may be profound; we already see major teacher shortages in math and science which have prompted the federal government to initiate emergency legislation to help relieve the problem.[9] Once again, this is both a challenge and opportunity since new personnel who have not been conditioned by years of work inside traditional schools can be attracted into the profession and schools.

It is also becoming clear that America, given the increasing Hispanic population, is increasingly a bilingual nation.

> Estimates of the number of Latinos residing in the United States run as high as 20 million according to *The Hispanic Almanac*. The 14.6 million Latinos represented a sixty-one percent (61%) increase from 1970 to 1980, compared to a nine percent (9%) growth for the non-Latino population in the United States. Latinos now constitute 6.4% of the total United States population. The largest portion of this population is made up of Latinos of Mexican, Puerto Rican and Cuban descent, although there are significant numbers of persons from Central and South America as well as the Caribbean and Europe.[10]

The impact on schools has led to legislation in bilingual education. This trend continues to make our society more pluralistic. We continue to be a nation of immigrants. This growing diversity can be viewed as an asset or as an unfortunate barrier to homogeneity. Again, the schools make certain assumptions about the kind of learner that best fits the school programs. The more diversity in the student population, the more the schools must adapt to human variation. Once again, we have challenge and opportunity as we attempt to reshape our schools in pursuit of excellence.

Another trend that has direct bearing on the public schools is the changing nature of American families. Dr. Katharine Kersey, Director of Early Childhood Education at Old Dominion University, estimates that "less than 10 percent of all households include the wage-earner husband, homemaker mother, and dependent children." Yet traditional public schools are organized with the expectations that such a family structure is pervasive. Conventional public schools depend on the home and family for all kinds of support that single families or working families cannot adequately provide. Kersey concludes, "The reality is that there are fewer support systems, less family networking, and fewer extended families than ever before in our history."[11]

Moreover, this increasing isolation and the aging population make even more visible the generational isolation that is operational in the schools. Our public schools have kept youth separated from the adults in the community. Urie Bronfenbrenner has noted the relative paucity of situations in which children and adults freely interact and the increasing extent to which television viewing and peer group activities seem to crowd out adult-child interactions. Bronfenbrenner observes:

> . . . Both from our own research and that of others, we cannot escape the conclusion that, if the current trend persists, if the institutions of our society continue to remove parents, other adults, and older youth from active participation in the lives of children, and if the resulting vacuum is filled by the age-segregated peer group, we can anticipate increased alienation, indifference, antagonism, and violence on the part of the younger generation. . . .[12]

Our traditional bases for authority have been eroded; the sense of a community sharing a common culture, values, and ethics has virtually collapsed. We are now in transition, unsure what the new bases for authority are or should be. A new individualism has replaced the old sense of membership in a community or belonging to a neighborhood. In this, the traditional authority figures have been stripped of their power. As James P. Comer illustrates in his study:

> In 1952, during my first year in college—enacting the "look at me, I made it" ritual—I returned to my elementary school. One of my favorite teachers, Miss Cross, whom I and my classmates all respected, was being "sassed" by two ten or eleven-year-old children. She noticed my surprise and discomfort and said to me in a resigned tone, "Things have changed since you were here." Indeed they had, but that was only the beginning. The disrespect for authority in the 1950s escalated to the serious authority problems, violence, and vandalism in the schools today. Many school staffs appear powerless in the face of troublesome student behavior.
> . . . Why did these problems not exist in yesterday's schools? Largely because principals and other authority figures had more power than they have today. Prior to the late 1940s, a school principal was often an autocratic ruler—powerful and feared. Teachers were on the second tier in the hierarchy of school power and authority. Principals and teachers together could establish and reinforce desirable student behavior. Most parents, students, and teachers accepted absolute principal power as the way things were and should be.[13]

The habits of the young have also changed. This is a generation weaned on television and telecommunication. School-age children on the average watch television for at least as many hours as they spend in school. For many, television is the means by which they learn the culture. This new modality has affected reading and study habits and perhaps influenced how children process information. Although we do not yet know the full implications on the young, it is clear that their socialization is different from that which the schools have been built upon and which the schools continue to expect. The results of this disparity in orientation may well contribute to the growing sense of learner boredom in schools. After all, television is an entertainment medium that many school-age viewers can turn on and off by choice. Schooling is not an entertainment medium, and students cannot easily turn teachers on or off in the same way. This conflict may be a factor to consider in student motivation, attention span, and expectations.

SOCIALIZATION OF THE MODERN YOUNG LEARNER

If learners are central to our quest for a new education that embraces excellence, what can we say about them? Children born today will graduate from high school in a new century. Children are being socialized in dramatically different fashion from their parents. Today's young, as a generation, are exposed to some common overarching influences. The family structure is more diverse, with no prevailing family model and no well-defined roles of mothering, fathering, and grandparenting. The majority of the young are maturing faster physically, and in turn, emotionally. As a generation, many youngsters are immersed in telecommunications—electronic tools that provide instant replay, instant information, and virtually instant global communication.

They have grown up in an era of human and civil rights and assume that the pursuit of these rights is just and natural. Unlike many of their parents and grandparents, who were brought up to respect the *privilege* of living in an affluent and democratic America, they assume their *right* to live in this society. Some social observers contend that overly permissive and indulgent parents have produced a generation of narcissistic children.[14] Comprising the so-called "Me Generation," these children may appear to be more concerned with their own needs at the neglect of others than previous generations have been. This is also the generation that has spent its lifetime living under the threat of nuclear annihilation and the reality of daily violence. They have become far more oriented towards living in the here and now, and are less likely than previous generations to delay gratification.

Today's young represent a major consumer market, spending billions on cosmetics, fashions, and records and tapes. Mass communication exposes them to styles, tastes, and values that differentiate them from their elders. This, coupled with the growing isolation of the young from adults, has created a youth culture. Schools, structured as places for the young, have exacerbated this intergenerational isolation, which has also contributed to more premarital sex, more venereal disease, more pregnancies, and more suicides than with previous generations.

The moral climate has also shifted. The phenomenon identified as "Watergate" led to a lack of trust in political leaders. Youth no longer identify with traditional political or business leaders. Instead, the role models of this new generation are increasingly those who possess high visibility as a result of some exceptional talent. Rock stars, professional athletes, movie and television celebrities have all become the electronic super-teachers. Obviously, such celebrities can show caring behavior, as many popular musicians did in the dual Live Aid Concerts for African Famine Relief.[15] However, such celebrities and superstars can also exhibit greed, pettiness, and violence. The demise of the close-knit community as a source of moral and ethical role models has caused a greater reliance on alternatives. Some youth have accepted responsibility for their own actions, some identify with superstars, and others are confused and fall victim to quick and easy escapes.

Contemporary forms of socialization are producing a generation of learners that is qualitatively different from previous generations. The schools, however, retain structures that are based on socialization patterns associated with earlier generations. While it is dangerous to generalize, it may be safe to say that the percentage of students who are socialized along the lines of earlier generations is dropping quickly under the weight of the powerful forces associated with what Alvin Toffler calls the "super-industrial age."[16]

Public schools cannot be productive unless they adapt to the changing nature of the learner. In addition to increased diversity in the learner population, there are these increasingly common influences that combine to form—or at the very least, influence—a new generation of learners who find the environment in traditional schools out of step with their own broader orientation. For the schools to expect these larger psychosocial forces to vanish is unrealistic. For the schools to expect the present generation of learners to adjust to a school structure designed for previous generations is similarly unrealistic. Instead, the schools must modify and change to establish compatibility with this and succeeding generations. Such adaptations are a realistic basis for reform and the restoration of excellence to public education. In fact, ongoing adaptations of the school to the society are a long historical tradition.

HOW SCHOOLS RESPOND TO CHANGING CONTEXT: SCHOOLS AND THEIR COMMUNITIES OVER THE YEARS

In the United States this historical connection between the schools and their communities dates back to the earliest colonial times. In the period prior to the birth of our independent nation in 1776, there were two basic classes in the colonies—the rulers and the workers. The rulers were expected to complete an education befitting their status, while the workers were viewed as not needing formal education, since they could carry out their responsibilities without it. However, the founding fathers put forward the idea that every citizen ought to be both a ruler and a worker. Thomas Jefferson, who warned that "a society that expected to be both ignorant and free, expected what never was and never will be," also envisioned a general education that enabled every citizen to judge what served or endangered a person's freedom. Formal education, therefore, was necessary for everyone in a democracy, and thus emerged the notion of *universal public education.* As noted historian Henry Steele Commager put it, "We're still so new to the concept of universal public education that we have not achieved it, although we have used the term for a very long time."[17]

Within the strongly decentralized United States of the early federal period, local control of the schools—and other social institutions—grew out of a strong agricultural tradition. The agricultural period created a community framework with a cohesive system of community expectations. The newly created schools, as an institution, were viewed as an integral part of the community. The school was responsive primarily to the home and to the church—the two major educational institutions of that period.

In the larger social fabric, a type of division of labor took place. The primary responsibility of the school was to teach reading, writing, and arithmetic, some view of citizenship, and certain cultural values. For the most part, spiritual and moral needs were viewed as the responsibility of the entire community, to be implemented through the agencies of the church and the family. Because children were expected to continue in their parents' trade or business, the family was closely linked to vocational needs. This model of education connected the school to nonschool environments and formed a total system of human learning that was prominent roughly from the 17th through the 19th centuries.

According to Henry Steele Commager, two trends later transformed the model that evolved during this period: (1) the concept of universal public education and (2) the view of the public schools as the universal coordinator of education for the society.[18] The 19th century moved into an industrial period, shifting from a rural to an urban population, from farming to factories, and from hand tools to industrial machinery. The advent of mechanized transportation facilitated the formation of the industrial base. Great waves of immigrants provided the labor that was necessary to run the new factories. We began to form a different social model, with a different set of relationships between school and nonschool settings. The transition from agricultural to industrial society, the impact of that transition on basic family patterns, and the need of immigrants to acculturate and assimilate all imposed demands on the school that were unlike those of the agricultural period. Instead of the one room schoolhouse and a division of responsibility for the socialization process, there was much more delegation of responsibility to the school. There was also an increased emphasis on and attention to formal learning, with set standards. Many more people were in need of an education, i.e., in acquiring literacy, a sense of citizenship, and vocational preparation and training compatible with the newly emerging marketplace.

The industrial age in America was the era of the comprehensive high school, with standardized curriculum, uniformity, and more professionalization and unionization of workers, including teachers. The school as an institution appeared to be the central agency empowered to carry out the ever-increasing number of functions needed to keep pace with the myriad changes caused by industrialization. School curricula appeared to be continuously expanding.

By the 1960s, however, heavy industrialization began to give way to high technology. The information age and a global economy was beginning to take form and shape. But also beginning in the 1960s and continuing through the 1980s, the transition from one economy to another caused serious budgetary cuts of many of the resources that traditionally accompanied the comprehensive school. In this period, the public began to review what it expected from the schools. There were strong indications that the schools had tried to achieve too much, and there had to be realignment between what the schools could do and what the other educative agencies in the community would do.

The family, as well as other community agencies, had undergone a series of transformations. In addition, the process of democratization led groups that had previously felt disenfranchised—minorities, women, handicapped, the aged—to claim equal rights as citizens. These changes had profound effects on the capacity of the educative agencies to perform their roles as they had in earlier periods. The call arose for more coordination and more partnerships between the school and other agencies. Partnerships emerged between the workplace and the school, between higher education and the school, between parents (and families) and the school, between the arts community and the school, and between health agencies and the school. All such partnerships were forced to do more with the resources already available in the community and to avoid duplication of services and facilities. The model that emerged during this period was one of coordination, establishing and extending a partnership between the school and the surrounding community.

During this period, we have witnessed the advent of telecommunications. Computers, interactive television, cable television, public educational television, and telephone connections combine to make the home a much more powerful learning environment than ever before. Similarly, these technological developments have given learners much more control over their own learning. These changes have fostered a new model for human learning, coordinating the school and nonschool environment, in which the learner can become much more self-directing and in which all of the resources of the community, including the school and educators, are recognized as learning resources. The new model will take us into the 21st century, which in many ways will be an age of lifelong learning.

To reiterate, historically there have been four overlapping stages of human learning in America. These stages may be charted as follows:

Shared Stage   The first stage was the division of labor model, which grew out of the colonial agricultural period in which the family, the church, and the school all performed various functions decided upon by the community (Figure 1-1).[19] This model, however, gave way under the weight of the industrial socioeconomic period, in which the school grew from one room schoolhouses into very comprehensive facilities.

Delegative Stage   In the process of expanding its services, the school also expanded its role in society and took on a newfound authority. This led to the need to professionalize those who were in the business of delivering these expanding educational services. This delegation of responsibility model (Figure 1–2) [20] strengthened

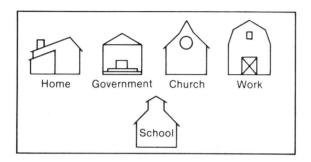

FIGURE 1–1
Shared Stage: Division of Educational Responsibility.
(Source: Reprinted, by permission, from Mario D. Fantini, "Changing Concepts of Education: From School System to Educational System," Community, Educational, and Social Impact Perspectives, Donna Hager Schoeny and Larry E. Decker, eds. [Charlottesville, Virginia: Mid-Atlantic Center for Community Education, University of Virginia, 1983] 32–33.)

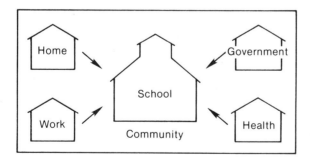

FIGURE 1–2
Delegative Stage: Delegation of Educational Responsibility.
(Source: Reprinted, by permission, from Fantini, Community, Educational, and Social Impact Perspectives, *32–33.)*

the school and weakened the other community institutions, making the school dominant in the relationship between school and nonschool environments.

Coordinative Stage The period after world War II was a transition from an industrial-based to a post-industrial society. During this period, the school began to lessen its dominance as a comprehensive school and began to return to a number of community agencies whose multiple responsibilities had been delegated to the schools (Figure 1–3).[21] This occurred primarily because of economic constraints, but also because of the growing perception that the schools had been overloaded and were not in a position to deliver the multifaceted quality education that was needed.

Facilitative Learning Stage By the 1980s, the advent of educational technology and telecommunications had begun to revolutionize modes of acquiring information potentially leading to a new model (Figure 1–4).[22] The individual in the home will become the primary center of the educational process, and the resources of the entire community, indeed, the entire world, will be increasingly available to the learner. With parents, professional educators will be the primary advisors of the young as they begin to gain more and more control over their own lifelong education.

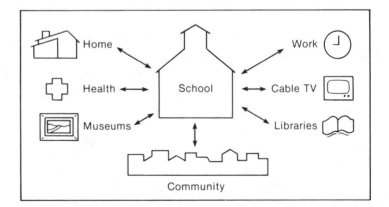

FIGURE 1-3
Coordinative Stage: Coordination of Educational Responsibilities.
(Source: Reprinted, by permission, from Fantini, Community, Educational, and Social Impact Perspectives, 32–33.)

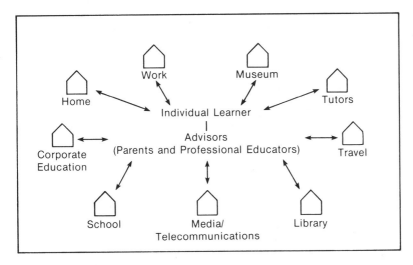

FIGURE 1–4
The Facilitative Learning Stage: Facilitation of Community Learning Educational Resources and Services.
(Source: Reprinted, by permission, from Fantini, Community, Educational, and Social Impact Perspectives, *32–33.)*

LEARNING ABOUT CHANGE AND EXCELLENCE FROM PRIVATE ENTERPRISE: IMPLICATIONS FOR EDUCATION

In our free market economy, the private sector is usually the first to be affected by the major trends in the society. While transformations have affected all of our institutions—family, church, neighborhoods, workplace—perhaps the one sector that has had to adapt faster or perish is the private sector. It has become clear to most Americans that business and industry are redefining how they function. In so doing, they too rededicate themselves to excellence.

THE NEXT AMERICAN FRONTIER
Robert B. Reich's *The Next American Frontier* examines how economic growth has changed in the United States and abroad. The high volume, mass production model that Americans pioneered has been taken over successfully by Japan and other countries with lower labor costs, natural raw materials, and new developing markets. As with other advanced industrial nations, the United States needed to regain its competitive edge by restructuring business and industry. Reich sug-

gests that in this necessary transformation we invest heavily in people and merging the goals of economic growth (America's business culture) with those of social justice (America's civic culture).[21]

Certainly, business and industry have had to address the problem of regaining excellence as a matter of survival.

THE ADAPTIVE CORPORATION

Alvin Toffler, one of the first social observers to warn of the impact of change on our future, has attempted to prepare some of America's largest firms for the new erra. In his book, *The Adaptive Corporation,* Toffler reminds us of his earlier warnings:

> Two decades ago, when I (and a very few others) warned that the end of industrial civilization was in sight, it sounded melodramatic. Today, as the smokestacks crash around us, more and more sociologists, historians—and managers—are reaching the same conclusion.
>
> One has to be blind to be unaware that something extraordinary is happening to our entire way of life. The swift spread of microprocessors . . . biotechnology . . . the electronicization of money . . . the creation of startling new materials . . . the move into outer space . . . artificial intelligence—all such technological advances are accompanied by equally important social, demographic and political changes. These run from the transformation of family life to the "graying" of the population in affluent countries (while median age plummets in the Third World), from conflict over transborder data flows to the global diffusion of lethal weaponry.[24]

Toffler reminds the private sector especially of yet another level of specifics in the changing world order:

> The international economy has been fundamentally (but only temporarily) restructured by the Arab oil embargo, the rise of Japan as a world-beating competitor, and the emergence of South Korea, Taiwan, Singapore, and Brazil as newly industrialized countries. The collapse of major banks and the mushrooming cloud of unregulated Eurodollars have destabilized the world banking system, and today's global debt crisis threatens to knock the remaining props out from under it. The condition of the world economy is anything but equilibrial.
>
> Meanwhile, technological breakthroughs, deregulation, stagflation, plus volatile interest rates and other erratic forces subvert the strategic assumptions of even the best-run firms. Of course, one is tempted to ask, if companies have so far managed to survive all this, what else can happen to them?
>
> The answer is: plenty.[25]

In the first page of *The Adaptive Corporation,* Toffler sets both the survival and the excellence agenda for business and industry:

This is a little book for those who intend to survive—for managers prepared to initiate change. It is about every company faced with the need to rethink its goals and restructure itself.

Some firms are already beyond rescue; they are organizational dinosaurs. These are non-adaptive corporations, many of which will disappear between now and the not-too-distant turn of the century. Companies with household names and famous products; companies with assets in the billions; companies with tens, even hundreds of thousands of employees; companies with enviable reputations on Wall Street, and seemingly unassailable positions in their markets—all are at risk.

For many of these firms 1955–70 were years of almost uninterrupted, straight-line growth in an equilibrial environment. In such a period, the formula for adaptation is relatively simple. Managers look smart—indeed, they very often *are* smart—if they simply do "more of the same."

Since then this straight-line strategy has become a blueprint for corporate disaster. The reason is simple: instead of being routine and predictable, the corporate environment has grown increasingly unstable, accelerative, and revolutionary. Under such conditions, all organizations become extremely vulnerable to outside forces or pressures. And managers must learn to cope with non-linear forces—i.e., situations in which small inputs can trigger vast results and *vice versa*.

The adaptive corporation, therefore, needs a new kind of leadership. It needs "managers of adaptation" equipped with a whole set of new, non-linear skills.

Instead of constructing permanent edifices, today's adaptive executives may have to *de-construct* their companies to maximize maneuverability. They must be experts not in bureaucracy, but in the coordination of ad-hocracy. They must adjust swiftly to immediate pressures—yet think in terms of long-range goals. And while in the past many managers could succeed by imitating another company's strategy or organizational model, today's leaders are forced to invent, not copy: there are no sure-fire strategies or models to copy.

Above all, the adaptive manager today must be capable of radical action—willing to think beyond the thinkable: to reconceptualize products, procedures, programs and purposes before crisis makes drastic change inescapable.

Warned of impending upheaval, most managers still pursue business-as-usual. Yet business-as-usual is dangerous in an environment that has become, for all practical purposes, permanently convulsive.[26]

IN SEARCH OF EXCELLENCE

Perhaps the book that best reveals the experience of the private sector, especially the ways in which business and industry have begun to recapture excellence, is *In Search of Excellence* by Thomas Peters and Robert Waterman. In this work, the authors identified eight attributes associated with successful companies that they studied:

One   A bias for action: a preference for doing something—anything—rather than sending a question through cycles of analyses and committee reports.

Two   Staying close to the customer—learning his preferences and catering to them.

Three   Autonomy and entrepreneurship—breaking the corporation into small companies and encouraging them to think independently and competitively.

Four   Productivity through people—creating in all employees the awareness that their best efforts are essential and that they will share in the rewards of the company's success.

Five   Hands-on, value driven—insisting that executives keep in touch with the firm's essential business.

Six   Stick to the knitting—remaining with the business the company knows best.

Seven   Simple form, lean staff—few administrative layers, few people at the upper levels.

Eight   Simultaneous loose-tight properties—fostering a climate where there is dedication to the central values of the company combined with tolerance for all employees who accept those values.[27]

The popularity of this book along with the authors' actual findings have had a pervasive effect on private sector thinking as companies attempt to regain excellence. Peters and Waterman found that those companies that were able to change in accordance with changing societal realities were most successful. The forces shaping our world impinge on the public sector institutions such as the schools as much as they do on the business and industry of the private sector. If the ingredients identified by Peters and Waterman work for the private sector, can they also work for the public sector? If we were to relate the eight characteristics of successful companies to the public schools, what would happen?

A Bias for Action   Public schools are by their nature conservative—that is, they conserve the values and traditions of the nation, state, and locality. They have come to establish a normative set of operating procedures. Because the school is accountable to the state and to a local school board and community, it does not always have autonomy of action to depart from established practice. Policies must be adopted by the state and local authorities before change can be contemplated. Given the differences among communities, deviation from tradition is not easily attained.

Public schools belong to the public, not to professionals. It is the public that must enable the schools to change and adopt a "bias for action." To be sure, there are individual schools and school districts that have been given this sanction, but on the whole the schools change very little. John Goodlad found in his comprehensive study of public schooling in the United States that while schools may differ, schooling is everywhere very much the same.[28] However, we are now in the midst of a school reform movement in the United States, with nearly every state involved in school reform legislation. This is tantamount to a mandate for change that legitimizes a bias for action. Consequently, the time may be ripe for schools to move in the direction of more action rather than to continue to maintain the status quo.

Close to the Customer   Theoretically, the public schools exist to help all children learn. To do this, the schools and schoolpeople need to keep close to the learner. Once again, this depends a great deal on individual schools. However *en masse*, the public schools have not assumed the stance that parents and their children are customers. At best, the schools may view learners and their families as clients. It is one thing to say that the customer is always right; it is another thing to say that the client is always right.

These different orientations are more than a play on semantics. In the private sector, customers are the lifeblood of the enterprise—without customers, there would not be business or industry. Staying close to the customer is, therefore, crucial if not critical to success. The public schools view learners as clients who are mandated by law to be under their supervision. The responsibility of the school is to work with these clients in terms of certain learning prescribed by law. To be sure, there are philosophically based attitudes that influence this major client-centered orientation. For example, the elementary schools may be more "child-centered" than the secondary schools, which may be more subject-matter centered. But these are slight deviations on the same client-based theme.

Staying close to the learner has meaning in the school, but not in the same sense as in the private sector. Staying close to the client has more to do with getting the learner to accept the modes of the school and to keep up with the lessons for which the school is responsible. The school seeks the support of the family and community in getting the client to adjust to the school. In so doing, the school believes the learner will have the best chance of learning what the schools are expected to teach.

Finally, a customer can decide to go elsewhere if, for one reason or another, he or she is dissatisfied with the company. Clients assigned to particular schools cannot easily do the same. Compulsory attendance means enrollment at designated schools. Choice is not a part of the client system of the public schools. Clients who do not keep up with what the school expects are reassigned to other classes and tracks, not by choice but by professional decision-making.

Recently, there have been attempts to alter the client orientation of the public schools in favor of a more consumer-oriented position. Proposals have been made for increasing options and choices for parents and students. Some of the proposals have been based on the experiences of the private sector, with its emphasis on competition and consumer choice. Again, the climate may be favorable for what

Peters and Waterman refer to as keeping close to the customer. If this were to happen, there would be many more individualized programs, more tailoring of programs to fit the unique talents, styles, and interests of learners, more options and choices of different kinds of programs for students and parents.

Autonomy and Entrepreneurship   We sometimes lose sight of the fact that schools are part of a "school system," and there is a central administration to this system that assumes overall responsibility for carrying out the policies of a school board. Such an arrangement may be likened to the corporate headquarters and the board of directors, with school superintendents as the counterparts to chief executive officers (CEOs). The degree of autonomy and entrepreneurship within the school system depends on the degree to which authority is delegated and decentralized. Given the indications of sameness in the processes of schooling reported by Goodlad and others, we are left to wonder what difference this delegation has made.

The notion expressed by Peters and Waterman is that autonomy and entrepreneurship enable smaller units to plan and develop new initiatives based on competition. However, as indicated earlier, the public school system is not based on competition but on uniformity and standardization. To break this cycle will require fundamental restructuring that could not be initiated without enabling policies. There is some evidence that decentralization is on the rise in the public schools, based in part on attempts to improve the performance of individual schools following a sustained period of public accountability. Growing dissatisfaction with schools has focused on the individual school. Community participation has resulted in the creation of school-based councils and administrative attention to school-based management.

Recent studies, such as that conducted by Theodore Sizer, have promoted more experimentation at the individual school level, aimed at breaking the mode of standardization.[29] Similarly, Ernest Boyer's work in high schools suggests that freeing the teachers to innovate at the individual school level may bring about sought-for results.[30] We are left with the problem of how to introduce more "marketplace" conditions in the public school system. The essence of the marketplace is competition, an element thus far alien to our public schools.

Productivity through People   All organizations, private and public, depend on people to carry out the goals of the enterprise. In the private sector, successful companies were able to establish rewards that served to motivate workers in favor of the company goals. Often this meant participation in shaping approaches believed to be more productive. This worker investment in the business of the company, if successful, carried with it tangible rewards. In the Peters and Waterman study, both the intrinsic psychology of human investment through participation and the extrinsic rewards through financial gain worked to increase the productivity of successful companies.

The public school reward system has functioned primarily at the psycho-professional level. School persons are not rewarded financially if the school is successful. They have been socialized to salary schedules, and increments come automatically, regardless of the school's success. Most rewards are those that appeal to the teachers' sense of professionalism. In recent years, the problem of low salaries for teachers has prompted consideration of plans to reward individual teachers on the basis of performance. Those that do well would be recognized and rewarded financially under the so-called merit pay proposals. Other plans have emphasized differentiated roles for teachers—for example, from beginner to master teacher—with each role qualifying for salary differentials.

The standardization in the schools makes this kind of policy fraught with difficulty. Plans to reward the people in public schools differently have been largely opposed by teachers and their professional organizations. Nonetheless, the growing concern with the low status and salaries of public school personnel has encouraged dialogue on this issue.

Hands-On, Value Driven   Companies whose executives are continuously tuned in to the organization's main purposes are most successful. Keeping an eye on the major goals of the business is a central feature of leadership, for the leader is ultimately accountable for realizing these goals. Conversely, if the goals are not attained, productivity is compromised and the leadership is called into question.

Clearly, this applies to the executives within the public schools. Whether we are talking about superintendents or principals, each is an executive officer accountable to the main purposes of the enterprise. It has been true for some time that strong leadership is a key ingredient to effective schools. Most of the research conducted on the question of school effectiveness identifies executive leadership as a central feature of successful schools.[31] Managers who can articulate the goals and inspire workers to work harmoniously towards those goals are the managers who stand out. We have seen a major turnover of educational administrators, especially in urban school districts, with the average longevity of big-city superintendents less than three years. Many school leaders are confused about which goals to emphasize, given the multiple expectations associated with public education. Some states are establishing middle-management training institutes or principals' centers [32] to help combat this problem. Peters and Waterman have identified a characteristic that must be given priority if the public schools are to be productive.

Sticking to the Knitting   Doing what the business is best designed to achieve seems like a self-evident principle, but evidently many organizations fail to practice it. Keeping the company on track can be a serious problem with the public schools. What do the schools do best? Over the years, the public schools have assumed more responsibility, especially as the other agencies in the community changed. The schools have been asked to deal with health, nutrition, career training, moral and ethical development, driver education, home economics, and life adjustment, to name a few—all in addition to the "3 Rs." Training of the intellect, long considered the essential role of our schools, has been augmented by other functions. Dealing with both the intellectual and emotional needs of the young has posed severe strains on the public schools. The schools were designed to promote intellectual development, but have also had to respond to new demands. Some reformers believe that the schools have been asked to do too many things, from babysitting to producing first-class scientists, that are at times conflicting and contradictory.

What schools do best is to promote formal learning in scholastic areas. They may need to return to this function with renewed emphasis, but what of the other needs and goals? Can the schools serve them all without spreading themselves too thin? Do they have the resources to do it all? There are plans underway for the schools to do what they do best, while asking other agencies in the community to assume functions formerly delivered by the public schools. For example, mental health agencies could assume more responsibility with the emotional needs of learners, business and industry could assume more responsibility in vocational education, and health agencies could offer information on sex and drug education and personal hygiene. The debate on school reform is focusing on this issue in particular, with the return to basics and the establishing of core academic requirements as cases in point. The other goals are important, but may have to be delegated to other educative agents and agencies in the community.

Simple Form, Lean Staff The most successful companies are able to streamline their upper-level administrative staffs. Cutting back from a top-heavy administrative structure allows for a more adaptive, flexible arrangement. Reducing the number of levels within the organization seems to improve communication and diminish the distance between management and labor.

One of the steady sources of complaint in the public school system is the organization is too top heavy. Teachers and other school personnel often cite the number of posts associated with central administration as a problem. The more layers, the more bureaucratic the organization. Given the need to adapt to new challenges and opportunities, it makes sense to review the central administrative functions with an eye toward reduction. Reducing a top-heavy, top-level administration also sends a message to the front line personnel that this organization is serious about change. This appears to be happening in some school districts because of budgetary cutbacks. These cutbacks may be a boon in disguise. There are many top-level roles that have built up over the years and surely some of these are no longer as necessary as they once were. The problem, however, is in the politics of change. It takes both courage and agreement on the part of the chief school officer and the board of education to implement any such streamlining. Now that the private sector has begun to demonstrate the benefits of simplification in organizational structure by having fewer top-level roles, perhaps the public sector will follow.

Simultaneous Loose-Tight Properties The last of Peters and Waterman's eight basic principles of excellent management is a synthesis of the others, combining strong central leadership with maximum oppportunity for the rank and file to innovate. This double combination is necessary to establish a central-decentralized balance—a kind of win-win situation. Tight central management keeps everyone geared to central goals, while allowing and expecting individual workers to use their imagination in better achieving these goals.

Similarly, in schools this simultaneous loose-tight style of management would be appropriate. The labor intensive public schools need to capitalize on the individual talents of teachers, counselors, and other school personnel. Yet, their individual creative energies must somehow be mobilized to contribute to the overall goals for which the school is accountable. Strong central leadership, which is able to project these goals, may prove to be the most successful.

Since we are also talking about professionals in the public schools, this loose-tight principle takes on added significance. As professionals, teachers and others make a commitment to hold the best interests of the learner supreme. Yet teachers are also members of collective teachers' associations or unions. The ability of teachers to maintain a *professional* independence as a professional while also connecting as a member of a larger body is important. If the individual identity of teachers is subsumed under the collective weight of the association, then individual initiatives may also suffer. Clearly, this has a bearing on the ability of strong central leadership to inspire collective dedication to the enterprise, while also creating the conditions for independent professional initiatives.

Perhaps the primary lesson derived from this private sector experience with excellence—one that is clearly tied to public sector interests—is identified by Peters and Waterman in the introduction to their book:

> What really fascinated us as we began to pursue our survey of corporate excellence was that the more we dug, the more we realized the excellent companies abounded in such stories and imagery. We began to realize that these companies had cultures as strong as any Japanese organization. And the trappings of cultural excellence seemed recognizable, no matter what the industry. Whatever the business, by and large the companies were doing the same, sometimes cornball, always intense, always repetitive things to make sure all employees were buying into their culture—or opting out.
>
> Moreover, to our initial surprise, the content of the culture was invariably limited to just a handful of themes. Whether bending tin, frying hamburgers, or providing rooms for rent, virtually all of the excellent companies had, it seemed, defined themselves as de facto service businesses. Customers reign supreme. They are not treated to untested technology or unnecessary goldplating. They are recipients of products that last, service delivered promptly. Quality and service, then, were invariable hallmarks.[33]

THE ONE MINUTE MANAGER

Another popular book that caught hold with the private sector, especially at the top leadership levels, is *The One Minute Manager*.[34] Kenneth Blanchard and Spencer Johnson's presentation summarized the following managerial and organizational principles:

☐ People who feel good about themselves produce good results.

☐ Help people reach their full potential—catch them doing something right.

☐ The best minute I spend is the one I invest in people.

☐ Everyone is a potential winner; Some people are disguised as losers; Don't let their appearances fool you.

☐ Take a minute: Look at your goals. Look at your performance. See if your behavior matches your goals.

☐ We are not just our behavior; We are the person managing our behavior.

☐ Goals begin behaviors; Consequences maintain behaviors.

These principles are equally applicable to schools and school leaders. Based on the field of organizational development (OD), they represent a positive leadership style found to be successful with the human side of management—schools included.

Superintendents of schools, central office staff, and building principals are all involved with the management of human resources. Given the rising criticism of public schools, the historically low salaries of many teachers, and the fiscal constraints under which many schools operate, these management principles take on greater significance. They represent a useful summary and reminder that leaders need to keep a constant vigil over the human side of their business, without which the goals that the organization strives to achieve will seldom be realized.

THE USER-FRIENDLY PHILOSOPHY: THE LEARNER AS CONSUMER

There is yet another lesson to be learned from both the private sector and the advanced technological age that we are entering. One of the more intriguing terms to come out of our corporate vocabulary is "user friendly." Primarily relating to computer use, user friendly means an attempt to reassure the customer that the computer and its accompanying software will be easy to comprehend and easy to use. Attempts to de-mystify computers and make them less intimidating have bottom line implications. Obviously, if a product is intimidating, people will be less likely to buy and use that product. Consequently, it is simply good business to develop a product that is easy to use and which gains results.

The user friendly philosophy has important implications for the school. But first of all, how can a computer be friendly? It is friendly in that the program is developed in such a way that it literally guarantees success for the learner. If the learner, for any reason, is not responding and does not understand, then the fault is not with the *learner*, but with the program as *teacher*. It is a kind of no-fault insurance policy. It is up to the program to make the connection with the learner. Therefore, people who are working on these programs bear responsibility to provide opportunities for all learners to experience success.

Another important idea communicated by the concept of user friendly is that the learner is not stupid. In a user friendly implementation strategy, everyone is expected to succeed. There are no learner failures or user failures, only program failures. The program can be on any subject, algebra or history, for example, or literally anything that now takes place in the school. Indeed, programs are coming out now that reflect the school's curriculum, and the subject matter of the school now can become the subject matter of computer programs. This has the potential to empower the learner. It erases stigmatizing labels (such as slow learner, underachiever, disadvantaged, and deprived) and substitutes the idea that anyone *can* learn, given the right program. Compared with the structure that has developed inside the public schools, this is literally a revolution.

There is no way that the public schools can now be considered user friendly. Students come to school, are randomly assigned, and must accept any teacher. If the learner is fortunate enough to connect with a compatible teacher, then he might have a good year. If not, the fault lies with the learner, not with the deliverer. This sets in motion a whole set of problems: Why can't Johnny learn? What's wrong with the learner? The institutional labels—slow, underachiever, etc.—begin to take hold. This is easily transformed into a self-fulfilling prophecy or psychology that is destructive to human motivation. The computer does not promote such a psychology, since it can offer a series of alternate programs until an appropriate one is found. While the computer will never replace the human teacher, because it is user friendly and views everyone equally as a winner, it deals with the problem of achieving quality equally. *Everyone* can learn regardless of background and *everyone* has access to the curriculum that is delivered by computer.

The user friendly school, therefore, would be one in which the student would be valued in the same way that a customer is valued. The customer does no wrong; neither does the student. The basic philosophy is, "If you, the student, are not learning by the way we are teaching, then we will try something else." The constructive optimism of such an approach is dramatically important in our search for educational excellence. The user friendly philosophy opens the door to a new vision of teaching and learning that may lead to a fundamental restructuring of how our schools ultimately do business.

CONCLUSION

How does all this add up for the public schools? In the larger world view, we have moved from a concept of the universe based on Newton's law of mechanics to one defined by Einstein's theory of relativity. From an emphasis on the importance of heredity, we have moved, with such thinkers as Freud, Darwin, and B. F. Skinner, to a concept of the importance of the environment, from the physical universe outside the person to the psychological universe within the person. From an emphasis on the cure of obvious ills and inequities, in health care, education, economics, and other areas, we have shifted to an approach that attempts instead to deal with prevention. From a meritocracy, we move more to a concept of democracy, with concern and concurrent realization that quality education, in order to be truly equal, must be individualized and personalized, rather than standardized.

We can see connections between these concepts and the larger theoretical formulations in the public school, which help explain why the public schools are organized and structured the way they are. There is the belief that not all learners can learn and that those who are more able *will* learn: the "survival of the fittest" theory. The static notion of intelligence and the fixed concept of growth and development are rooted in the structure of the Newtonian universe. Further, the factory model also contributes to the human classification system intrinsic to the schools. Interrelated shifts in world views, educational goals, and means of delivery may all be summarized in Table 1–2.

TABLE 1–2
Shifts emerging in the second half of the 20th century

World View	
From:	*To:*
Newtonian world view closed mechanistic static	Einstein's world view open relativistic dynamic
National isolationist independence	Global interdependence
Heredity	Environment
Meritocracy	Democracy—participation and human rights
Cure	Prevention
Privilege	Right
Physical	Psychological-sociological
Close knit community	Network of groups and individuals
Transportation	Communication

Educational Goals	
From:	*To:*
Adjustment	Development and potentiality
Exclusivity	Inclusivity and equal access
Elitism	Universality
Limited literacies: 3 Rs and civic competence	Expanded literacies: technological, medical, legal, global, etc.

TABLE 1–2, cont.

Educational Goals, continued	
From:	*To:*
Occupational development	Talent development
Individualism and self interests	Cooperation and human caring

Means of Delivery	
From:	*To:*
Uniformity and standardization	Diversity
Chance	Options and choice
Learner failure	Program or institutional failure
Teaching in the classroom	Learning in multiple learning environments: school and community
Teacher as primary deliverer	Teacher as facilitator of self-directed learning in school and non-school settings
Human teachers	Electronic teachers, human educators
Testing as measurement	Testing as diagnosis
Schoolhouse add-ons	Community resources—doing more with what we have
Group norms	Individual norms
Age-based schooling	Lifelong education
Professional control	Public control
Centralized	Decentralized
Standardization	Personalization

If we must summarize an overall direction at this point, it would be that we are moving from a *teaching* system to a *learning* system. This is far more than a neat parallel construction, for it represents a fundamental shift in our view of education and schooling. Education in the future will be perceived as a learning rather than teaching activity. To be sure, teaching is an important route to learning, but it is just that, only *one* route. There are *many* routes to learning, but all center on the learner. It is the learner and learning that become the fundamental pillar for any system of education. Moreover, the concept is built around the learner as *consumer*, not as a client of some monolithic institution. This is another significant feature in the transition to excellence in education. The learners will be customers of a streamlined system that tailors services to fit the learner. The customer will have access to learning options in and out of school.

We will move toward an *education system*, replacing our present *school system*. Schooling is, after all, one part of education, not its total. Education takes place in both school and non-school settings. Increasingly, the conditions that provide maximum learning and development are more readily accessible to all learners regardless of age, class, race or sex. Education is a continuing process of empowering people to become all they are capable of becoming, through increased self direction in the utilization of formal and non-formal educative resources. Who the learner is, when, where, and how learning takes place are all being redefined. This is a process that will go through several phases and into the next century.

The point of this section is to suggest that the larger societal context educates us all. It is like a hidden curriculum that shapes us as we attempt to adapt to it. Schools are currently caught up in a maelstrom of change. In this process, humanity attempts to return to or redeem its most prized values, while at the same time adapting to and acquiring new ones. In our society, *liberty, freedom*, and *justice* are transcendental values that serve as standards for assessing the major implications and developments of change. New values such as *productivity* and *cost-effectiveness* come out of our adaptations to the commercial free market experience. If we are to find the essential features of excellence in education today, it is to the realm of values that we must turn. Values are the ultimate standards that guide our behavior and represent the basics of our belief system.

NOTES

1. I.J. Gordon, "The Task of the Teacher," *Studying the Child in School* (New York: Wiley, 1969), 2–3.
2. Ralph W. Tyler, presentation at the American Educational Research Association 1985 Annual Conference (Symposium: "Responding to Demands for Curriculum Improvement: Starting at the Margins"), Chicago, April 1985.
3. John Naisbitt, *Megatrends: Ten New Directions Transforming Our Lives* (New York: Warner Books, 1982).
4. Mayor's Advisory Panel on Decentralization of the New York City Schools, McGeorge Bundy, Chairman, *Reconnection for Learning: A Community School System for New York City* (New York: Frederick A. Praeger, Publishers, 1969), xiii.
5. Theodore Sizer, *Horace's Compromise: The Dilemma of the American High School* (Boston: Houghton-Mifflin Company, 1984).
6. John Holt, *Teach Your Own: A Hopeful Path for Education* (New York: Delacorte Press/Seymour Lawrence, 1981).
7. Paul Sweeney, "Southern Governors Work for School Improvements," *The Boston Globe*, Sept. 30, 1983, 8.
8. John I. Goodlad, *A Place Called School: Prospects for the Future* (New York: McGraw-Hill Book Company, 1984), 141.
9. Education for Economic Security Act.
10. Juan Rosario, National Executive Director of ASPIRA of America, Inc., "ASPIRA

Institute for Educational Policy Research: A Proposal" (New York: ASPIRA of America, Inc., 1985), 5–7.

11. Katharine C. Kersey, "The Dilemma of a Child," *Community Educational Journal*, Vol. XII, No. 3, April 1985, 11.

12. Urie Bronfenbrenner, *Two Worlds of Childhood: U.S. and U.S.S.R.* (New York: Russell Sage Foundation, 1970), 116–17.

13. James P. Comer, *School Power* (New York: The Free Press, Macmillan Publishing Company, Inc., 1980), 3–6.

14. Christopher Lasch, *The Culture of Narcissism: American Life in an Age of Diminishing Expectations* (New York: Norton, 1978).

15. JFK Stadium/Philadelphia and Wembley Stadium/London, July 13, 1985.

16. Alvin Toffler, *The Third Wave* (New York: Bantam Books, Inc., 1980).

17. Henry Steele Commager, "The Schools Can't Do It All," *Community Education Journal*, Vol. XII, No. 3, April 1985, 8.

18. *Ibid.*, 8.

19. Mario D. Fantini, "Changing Concepts of Education: From School System to Educational System," *Community, Educational, and Social Impact Perspectives*, Donna Hager Schoeny and Larry E. Decker, eds. (Charlottesville, Virginia: Mid-Atlantic Center for Community Education, University of Virginia, 1983), 32.

20. *Ibid.*, 33.

21. *Ibid.*, 35.

22. *Ibid.*, 40.

23. Robert B. Reich, *The Next American Frontier* (New York: Times Books, 1983).

24. Alvin Toffler, *The Adaptive Corporation* (New York: McGraw–Hill Book Company, 1985). 3.

25. *Ibid.*, 2–3.

26. *Ibid.*, 1–2.

27. Thomas J. Peters and Robert H. Waterman, Jr., *In Search of Excellence: Lessons from America's Best-Run Companies* (New York: Warner Books, Inc., 1984).

28. John I. Goodlad, *A Place Called School: Prospects for the Future* (New York: McGraw-Hill Book Company, 1984), 264.

29. Theodore R. Sizer, *Horace's Compromise: The Dilemma of the American High School* (Boston, Massachusetts: Houghton Mifflin Company, 1984).

30. Ernest L. Boyer, The Carnegie Foundation for the Advancement of Teaching, *High School: A Report on Secondary Education in America* (New York: Harper and Row, Publishers, Inc., 1983).

31. George Weber, *Inner-City Children Can Be Taught to Read: Four Successful Schools*; Michael Rutter, et al., *Fifteen Thousand Hours: Secondary Schools and Effects on Children*; Ronald Edmonds, "Effective Schools for the Urban Poor"; Ross Zerchykov, "School Effectiveness: Public Schools for the Urban Poor."

32. North Carolina; Massachusetts.

33. Thomas J. Peters and Robert H. Waterman, Jr., *In Search of Excellence: Lessons from America's Best-Run Companies* (New York: Warner Books, Inc., 1984), xix–xx.

34. Kenneth Blanchard and Spencer Johnson, *The One Minute Manager* (New York: William Morrow and Company, Inc., 1982).

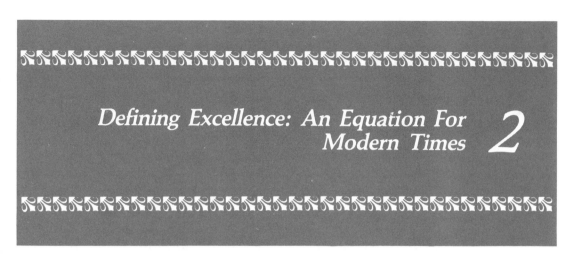

Defining Excellence: An Equation For
Modern Times *2*

IN SEARCH OF A MODERN DEFINITION OF EXCELLENCE IN EDUCATION

As the schools attempt to adapt to changes in society, they also redefine their concept of excellence. Some definitions are so general and vague as to be virtually meaningless. Yet as Daniel L. Duke argues, "It is the pursuit rather than the achievement of excellence that matters most."[1] It is a process of reaching for something that is perceived to be the best possible.

The National Commission on Excellence in Education, whose report, *A Nation At Risk: The Imperative for Educational Reform*, launched a national debate on the subject of school reform, offers this definition of excellence:

> We define "excellence" to mean several related things. At the level of the *individual learner*, it means performing on the boundary of individual ability in ways that test and push back personal limits, in school and in the workplace. Excellence characterizes a *school or college* that sets high expectations and goals for all learners, then tries in every way possible to help students reach them. Excellence characterizes a *society* that has adopted these policies, for it will then be prepared through the education and skill of its people to respond to the challenges of a rapidly changing world.[2]

If we are to reach for an ideal set of conditions that might be appropriate for a social institution such as the public schools to embrace, what would it be? Our public schools are agencies that were created to reflect the noblest values of our nation. Thus, for our purposes, we choose to define excellence in terms of the most basic values of our society. These values are not pie-in-the-sky notions to be acknowledged and then dismissed from real-world considerations. The values central to our emerging definition of excellence are deep-rooted in our tradition as a free and just society and in our practice as an economically productive nation.

AN EQUATION FOR EXCELLENCE

Clearly, everyone is in favor of excellence. Yet, when asked to define the term, educators lack consensus and clear conceptions of what excellence actually comprises. This section will develop a concept of excellence that contains five key ingredients: quality, equality, effectiveness, efficiency, and participation. Excellence will be stated in the form of an equation:

$$\text{Excellence} = \text{Quality} + \text{Equality} +$$
$$\text{Effectiveness} + \text{Efficiency} + \text{Participation}.$$

Excellence will be achieved when we are able to offer quality to the most students, in the most productive and economical form, while utilizing both the substantive and procedural dimensions of democratic participation.

QUALITY

The first component to consider is *quality*. Like excellence, quality is universally acceptable, but elusive in character. We talk glibly of quality, yet we would be hard pressed to define quality comprehensively. It appears safe to say that quality relates to the very best that we have to offer. We recognize quality when we see it, and we miss quality when it is absent. Quality clearly pertains to a selected range of superior activity and optimal standards.

In the field of education, quality assumes its own form and shape. The goal of quality education is to develop the full capacities of the learner and to support the unfolding of individual potential. Unless we are pushed to the limits of our potential, qualitative supports are really not present. Our experiences thus far suggest alternative concepts of quality in education, which we must consider in our search for excellence.[3]

The Nature of the Learner   The first concept of quality is based on the nature of the *learner*. This concept is deep-rooted in our educational experience and is primarily related to formal educational systems. A plethora of testing systems have been developed to try to screen the most capable, the best, and the brightest from the masses, so that they may pursue their identified intellectual talents to the fullest.

In elementary and secondary schools, I.Q. tests, ability groupings, and tracking screen students to determine who shall be eligible for particular types of learning or for eventual advancement to higher education. In higher education, the college or university that best demonstrates quality is the institution that is able to attract the most talented students through a vigorous, competitive screening process. Therefore, those students who score highest on SATs (or other standardized tests) and who have the highest academic rank in their graduating high school class are assembled in undergraduate classes. Similarly, in graduate education, those who score highest on the GREs are considered the most capable of profiting from advanced education.

Based on a premise of intellectual superiority and inferiority, the basic idea is that the very best students get the very best education. To rectify the implicit inequality of this situation, the traditional approach has been to administer competitive qualifying examinations, which are open to all learners, including college and high school dropouts. Thus, supposedly on the basis of proven ability, the best students are singled out from the rest, somewhat like winnowing out the wheat from the chaff. However, certain problems emerge with this attempt to create equality through testing. There is the problem of the nature of the examination itself; the question of what the tests actually measure, what they reveal, and their possible cultural biases; and additional issues of the test makers' and impact on the test takers' identities and expectations. In elementary and secondary schools, evaluation by teachers (including tests) becomes the basis for promotion to the next grade or the granting of a diploma. Only those most able will meet the standard of quality. Not all students are expected to finish; only the most capable will succeed.

We can argue that this concept of quality is effective, but its effectiveness is achieved only with a small number of students. The actual efficiency of such an approach is also debatable, since it may not take into account alternative modes of delivery that may be technologically advanced, pedagogically appropriate, and cost-effective.

The Nature of the Curriculum   A second concept of quality is based on the nature of the *curriculum*. A rigorous, usually standardized curriculum, to which all learners must adjust, is deemed the best way to achieve quality. This belief usually leads to the development of a strong core academic program, taking the form of four years of English, four years of social studies, four years of science, and three years of foreign languages. Knowledge is carefully delineated and delivered. Strict academic standards are not only explicitly stated, but are exemplified by a lack of inflation in grades. Even a class of able students would be subjected to a grade distribution in which a number of students will do poorly. In fact, such standards are most vigorously applied and perceived when there is an expectation that not all learners will pass or even should pass, or when a significant number do indeed fail. Thus, only a few students can earn a rating of excellent. The common or core requirements are unified and systematically reviewed by qualified professional teachers. In other words, the harder the school, the more quality is assumed.

Equality exists in terms of opportunity to take the curriculum, once the learner is judged to be qualified. There were major attempts in the 1960s to reform the curriculum, making it broader in scope, more flexible in structure, and more relevant to students' diverse concerns. These reforms may have had an impact on who was eligible and able to qualify, and thus worked towards increasing equality by making courses and programs more accessible to students. The debate over quality throughout the 1970s and 1980s, however, has reestablished core requirements and revived a more rigorous and traditionally scholastic curriculum in many schools. There has been a renewed emphasis on providing quality only for those deemed most likely to benefit from the traditional curriculum. These trends, in turn, influence who has access to the quality curriculum and thus again affects equality in education.

In terms of effectiveness, the expansion of the curriculum in the 1960s similarly expanded the range of populations for whom the curriculum seemed relevant, appropriate, accessible, and, therefore, for whom the curriculum was effective. However, many have argued that broadening the curriculum beyond the traditional structure has resulted in the diffusion of traditional academic subjects, the dilution of academic rigor, and the decline of effectiveness. A restricted curriculum may be more effective in a strictly academic sense, but only for a limited population. As for efficiency, the new areas of the curriculum were delivered in old ways—through lectures and textbooks, with student achievement measured by tests. Beyond the question of whether new areas are best measured by old means, there is the issue of the use of new technologies in pedagogy, and whether these new technological tools might be most cost-effective.

The Nature of the Professional Staff A third concept of quality depends on the nature of the professional *staff*. The more highly qualified the staff, the more likely that quality will be attained. In higher education, those most likely to be hired and promoted are those teachers with doctorates from the most prestigious institutions, who have published the most significant work, and who are engaged in research. The underlying assumption of this concept is that the more qualified the staff, the more likely they will be able to deliver quality academic services. The quality of the staff will also yield more outside recognition in the form of grants, contracts, academic prestige, and Nobel and Pulitzer Prizes. Thus, those institutions capable of assembling the best staff are judged to deliver the highest quality education.

There are many questions about the effectiveness and the efficiency of this approach to achieving quality education. First of all, Nobel Prize winners are limited in number and expensive to hire. As the most advanced researchers and specialists in their particular fields, they may well prefer to pursue advanced research in specialized areas rather than teach. They may not want to teach basic material to beginners in the field, and they may not be pedagogically equipped to deal with beginning learners. Those who will profit most from these professional staff are those students who are most able or who are already highly prepared. Equality, therefore, is "equality" only for a selected few and is not a true equality of access. For traditional classrooms, it is difficult to expose every student to the best, except through large and impersonal group situations, which in turn may not be effective for some learners. In addition, we have seen a general reluctance to use new modalities, such as cable television, to make the rare instances of excellence universally available to all students.

These three concepts combine to form the basic foundation for the most widely established and accepted theory of quality in education. They have traditionally been woven into a conventional wisdom that is at once both subtle and pervasive. For instance, much of the basis for ascertaining quality is often erroneously based on the perceived prestige that the institution has gained through a generalized image. These institutions are perceived to be exclusive places for better students and faculty, and therefore highly desirable. The ivy league schools and certain private elementary and secondary schools enjoy this generalized perception. In the public schools, judgments of quality are based on similar criteria. Good schools are places where good students attend, and this is usually defined in terms of socioeconomic status; the school is located in a "good" neighborhood or may be a special admissions school where high achieving students dominate. Yet, there are more accessible elementary and secondary schools and community colleges that have developed programs in which *all* students succeed. Many of these schools are not highly visible, often teaching working class students in urban and rural areas.

Based on the psychology and philosophy of exclusivity, the three traditional definitions of quality are elitist. Intriguing and powerful, elitism makes an alternative concept based on inclusivity seem somewhat unacademic and anemic by comparison. The entrance of a different concept of quality, while often posing a serious challenge to established assumptions, is difficult to legitimize.

Educational Outcomes   A fourth concept of quality is emerging, however, that shifts away from the nature of the learner, the rigor of the curriculum, and the caliber of the faculty to focus on *educational outcomes*. Whereas the other definitions of quality rely heavily on *input*—students, faculty, curriculum—the fourth emphasizes *output*. Under this definition, quality is best achieved when all learners attain the competencies for which the educational institution is accountable. These include the old basics—(3 Rs)—academic mastery in the subject matter, and the new basics—computers, telecommunications, critical thinking, application of knowledge, problem solving, caring, and talent identification. In this model, it is not the *means* but the *ends* that are important. Effectiveness is measured by how many learners attain competence. The greater the number of learners who succeed, the higher the quality of the education. Obviously, if the educational agency is responsible for assuring that all students succeed (i.e., achieve the necessary competencies), then the criterion of equality is also met.

Under this fourth concept of quality in education, we must clarify our educational goals and explicitly define what skills and competencies are necessary for an educated person. The aims of education must be made public and be put in measurable terms. Then, the achievement of those skills and competencies will be the major test of quality. Academic standards, under this fourth concept of quality, could be set by the foremost scholars in each field. The means by which people gain access to the material and achieve competency must be varied and diverse, including the use of video cassettes, computers, and a wide range of learning tools, techniques, agents, and environments. The crucial differences in this fourth concept of quality, therefore, will be the diverse modes of delivery used to achieve the desired learning outcomes.

Prevailing modes of delivery in the other concepts of quality rely on standardized modes, such as the qualified person, which undermine efforts to achieve equality in the broader processes of learning and education. Clearly, education takes place in various settings, and people can learn in a variety of ways in school and nonschool settings. The advent of educational technology provides opportunities to redefine when, where, and how learning takes place and is programmed to be user-friendly with built-in, self-pacing instruction, and instant reporting of progress.

In terms of delivery of quality, the current prevailing modes rely on tests to determine achievement. Results from those tests lead to a normal distributive curve, in which students with high test scores are identified as high achievers and those with lower scores are identified as low achievers or "failures." This categorization of students works against effectiveness. In the new mode, state-of-the-art technological tools and pedagogical theory are put into effect in a diversified delivery system, maximizing both effectiveness and efficiency.

With this system of options and choices in the pursuit of quality, the whole psychology of the fourth concept is essentially different from that of the other three. The idea here is to create opportunities rather than obstacles, to find ways to help everybody achieve the necessary skills rather than distinguishing between those who can learn quickly in one particular mode and those who cannot. The focus of the problem shifts away from the learner to the design of the most appropriate and productive programs for each and every learner—matching learner style to teaching style. There are no learner failures, only program failures.

While the first two concepts of quality make assumptions about the validity of grades and standardized tests, and the third concept relies on superior teaching to deliver quality services for those learners reaching certain levels, this fourth concept builds on the third and ties the other concepts together. It recognizes the right of *all learners* to pursue a full and complete education. It insists that the curriculum has to be tailored to fit the *individual differences* among the learners, and that diverse populations ought to be provided with a *range of learning opportunities* from human teachers to electronic teachers, from peer tutoring to experiential learning, from traditional classrooms to alternative schools, and to encourage more and more people to complete the necessary levels of competency.

The real test of quality in education lies with *results.* Quality must be viewed in terms of *outcomes:* The educated person should display specific competencies in specific areas. The list of specific competencies quickly grows long and inclusive—to be literate and have a world view, to appreciate the contributions of civilization, to value freedom and justice, to appreciate aesthetics, to have a commitment to the common good, to be critical and analytic, to have empathy, and to participate politically, economically, and socially in society. The well-educated person is a wise consumer, a caring and competent person, is able to achieve a balance between individual freedom and responsibility to society, has developed a talent that is fully translatable into a self-satisfying career, and has a sense of self-worth and a strong respect for other people and cultures. Such standards help define the content of quality education. This concept of quality must be applied to our next value, equality.

EQUALITY

The second part of the equation, *equality*, has traditionally been one of our cherished ideals. Without equality, we cannot hope to function as a democracy. The subtitle of John W. Gardner's book on *Excellence* written in 1961 is "Can We Be Equal and Excellent Too?" Gardner believed that we could. And this belief penetrated much of the sentiment of the 1960s.

> But the democratic promise of equal educational opportunity, half fulfilled, is worse than a promise broken. It is an ideal betrayed. Equality of educational opportunity is not, in fact, provided if it means no more than taking all the children into the public schools for the same number of hours, days, and years. If once there they are divided into the sheep and the goats, into those destined solely for toil and those destined for economic and political leadership and for a quality of life to which all should have access, then the democratic purpose has been undermined by an inadequate system of public schooling.
>
> It fails because it has achieved only the same quantity of public schooling, not the same quality. This failure is a downright violation of our democratic principles.
>
> We are politically a classless society. Our citizenry as a whole is our ruling class. We should, therefore, be an educationally classless society.[4]

Equality of educational opportunity has been a fundamental tenet of our public school system. In their struggle to implement the goal of equality, however, our public schools have chafed against the norms of scholasticism. The formal structure of education was historically geared to the socially and economically privileged classes. Later, the concept of privilege was extended to those who were deemed to be the best and brightest among us. Both concepts led to exclusion rather than inclusion. Education was for those who were most qualified by virtue of background, intelligence, or superior training. Elaborate systems of assessing the best and the brightest were created to judge who should receive further education and who should not. Often these screening devices denied many people access to quality education.

John I. Goodlad, who conducted a comprehensive eight-year study of American schooling, offered the following observations on the results of testing and tracking in the schools:

> Denial of access to schools, of access to knowledge, and access to effective teaching has been most glaringly apparent with respect to race and defined disability—classified disability if you will. That is, disability defined as feeble-minded and therefore unfit for schools.[5]

Goodlad found that such testing was used to categorize students and that these categories became the basis for tracking students, thus providing a very different sort of education to students on the basis of categories defined and determined by test scores. In efforts to study the extent and nature of tracking in the United States, Goodlad found that tracking was pervasive and that many school principals, guidance counselors, and others denied that tracking did indeed exist. Furthermore, he discovered that the students in the upper track classes—those with the higher test scores and the more academic orientation—were being taught different subject matter, were being encouraged to pursue different values, and were being taught differently from the lower track students. The irony, as Goodlad points out, is that those students who might gain the most from the varied pedagogical techniques and individualized attention (devoted to students in the upper tracks) are the very ones who are least likely to receive it (students in the lower tracks).

Historically, tests have been used to classify persons as intellectually or academically inferior, mentally slow, and unsuitable for scholastic competition. Learners who are classified as slow or inferior too often accept the labels and do poorly because they are expected to do poorly. We have learned that such a method of classifying people leads to a psychology of expectation and self-fulfilling prophecy.[6]

Those classified as bright are expected to achieve more than those not so classified. The brunt of this crude pigeon-holing has unfortunately been borne by minority groups, many of whom have been falsely labelled.

True equality, however, means inclusion: *All* are expected to learn. We now know that every person can learn under the right conditions, which may mean finding the best learning sequence or best learning environment for each person. If one method or approach does not work, another is designed, and still another, until a compatible match between learner and learning system is achieved. Under a contemporary policy of equality, it is no longer sufficient to say that we will give everyone an *opportunity*, but if they fail, it is not our fault. The new philosophy is that all people have the right to learn and to achieve the goals for which the school is responsible. Under this policy, there are no learner failures, only program failures.

When quality and equality are merged, elitism is replaced by *inclusivity*. Quality is not measured by how few students succeed, but by how many succeed. Here is where our public system diverges ideologically from the private system of education. The private schools are based on exclusion; the public schools on inclusion. Quality in the public schools is achieved when *all learners succeed*, not only those considered most able. Such a goal cannot be realized in the present model of schooling, which reflects 19th century exclusionary thinking. Ironically, many current reform efforts aimed at achieving educational excellence also reflect an exclusionary bias, with students denied access to quality based on institutionalized discrimination by class, race, culture, sex, and special needs. *Barriers to Excellence: Our Children At Risk* poses the problem in this form:

> . . . many students, parents, educators, and advocates . . . expressed frustration that . . . school reform paid little attention to issues of educational access and equity. For these witnesses, no talk of reform was set without a commitment to high quality education for students with limited English proficiency and handicapping conditions and without a pledge to promote compensatory education services, desegregation, equitable allocation of resources, and sex equity within our schools.[7]

Effectiveness and *efficiency* have been more recent ingredients in the equation for excellence. Nurtured by a national preoccupation with productivity and economy, these factors are now crucial. A modern definition of *effectiveness* centers on the most productive approach, while *efficiency* looks to the most economical. Quality was expensive, but modern technology has changed much of this economic exclusivity. Almost everyone has a television or radio, and sophisticated calculators and computers are adapted for the common home market. Average people now have access to telecommunications tools that expand opportunities for gaining the kind of knowledge that used to be available only to the privileged few.

EFFECTIVENESS

Finding the most effective or productive method, technology, or procedure by which each person can learn is a major responsibility of the public system of education. Professional educators have an obligation to update their knowledge of both subject matter and pedagogy. As more productive procedures are identified, we may promote learning with all learners, including those who have not been learning by traditional means. Excellence demands that these new tools be fully utilized. If we are ophthalmologists, for example, our goal would be to help everyone's vision. If there are people whose sight could be improved or saved by a new chemical or surgical procedure, we would be obligated by our professional ethics to learn the new approach and to administer it to patients. Similarly, in education, schoolpeople are obligated to develop new techniques that will ensure that more people will *learn.* This includes those learners now considered *slow, underachieving, undermotivated, unready, handicapped,* or a host of other labels that now refer to part of the learning population. If a learner has difficulty learning from a classroom teacher, then alternatives are found. Perhaps a computer or a peer tutor could be used. Tailoring teaching to learning styles is part of the personalized procedure in a reformed school system.

The concept of effectiveness in the public schools has been influenced by developments in the private sector and business and industry. Given the business environment, without continuous improvement, research and development, and state-of-the-art technology, a business would soon lose its competitive edge. A company that is non-competitive in the marketplace could be out of business entirely. Seeking the greatest *productivity* becomes an important feature of excellence.

In human services, this quest for productivity takes on some obligatory features that are tied to professional responsibility to serve the public interest. For example, in the medical field, doctors cannot best serve the patient if they retain procedures that are antiquated. Similarly, in the field of education, if there are more effective ways of achieving quality and equality, then those methods must be utilized. We have found, over the past twenty years, educational procedures that have proven to be more effective than current practice. This type of research and development effort needs to be built into our definition of excellence, with a continuous spiral of improvement in the way we conduct business and in the way we deliver our services.

Many studies on school effectiveness have been conducted over the past years in the light of national concern about declining productivity of public education. These studies have looked at various factors believed to influence effectiveness. For example, in 1970, George Weber studied reading achievement in four successful inner-city elementary schools.[8] These schools were identified as being more productive compared to similar schools in the area. What factors affected their productivity? Weber offers the following conclusion:

> Reading achievement in the early grades in almost all inner-city schools is both relatively and absolutely low. This project has identified four notable exceptions. Their success shows that the failure in beginning reading typical of inner-city schools is the fault not of the children or their background—but of the schools. None of the successes was achieved overnight; they required from three to nine years. The factors that seem to account for the success of the four schools are strong leadership, high expectations, good atmosphere, strong emphasis on reading, additional reading personnel, use of phonics, individualization, and careful evaluation of pupil progress. On the other hand, some characteristics often thought of as important to school improvement were *not* essential to the success of the four schools: small class size, achievement grouping, high quality of teaching, school personnel of the same ethnic background as the pupils, pre-school education and outstanding physical facilities.[9]

Ronald Edmonds also conducted school effectiveness studies and concluded that "the behavior of the school is critical in determining the quality of that education." He found the following school characteristics shared by effective schools:

- ☐ Strong administrative leadership;
- ☐ A climate of minimum instructional expectation;
- ☐ An orderly yet unoppressive atmosphere;
- ☐ Pupil acquisition of basic skills taking precedence over other activities;
- ☐ Redirection of school resources to basic instruction;
- ☐ Frequent monitoring of pupil progress.[10]

In a study of British secondary schools, Michael Rutter and his colleagues reported that "the research showed *which* school variables were associated with good behavior and attainments and which were not. . . . The pattern of findings suggested that not only were pupils influenced by the way they were dealt with as individuals, but also there was a group influence resulting from the ethos of the schools as a social institution."[11]

This study identified a series of secondary school characteristics that positively affected the students' behavior and their academic achievements. Good standards set by the school and good behavior models provided by the teachers both had positive effects. Frequent praise for students and the practice of giving the children responsibility were also effective. Finally, well-conducted lessons and good general conditions within the school were also identified as factors with a positive effect. Rutter and his colleagues similarly were able to identify a series of factors that did *not* significantly affect either the behavior or the achievements of the students: small size and/or a single site for the school, modernity of the physical plant, favorable teacher-child ratio, continuity of individual teachers, a year-based system of pastoral care for students, and severe punishments for unacceptable student behavior.

EFFICIENCY

In attempting to reach all learners, professionals must be mindful of the constraints imposed by costs. Efficiency embraces the most *economical* way of doing things. Since resources are limited, we must make wise choices about using the most effective approaches in the most economical manner. We must seek the most *efficient* procedure or technique that is also effective. Applying the standard of efficiency forces all institutions, including the schools, to do more with existing available resources, while also adding new approaches that are cost beneficial. In other words, it is not a simple matter of adding more to the school budget or taking more from the taxpayers' pockets.

Much of the discourse on efficiency has centered around money—usually in the form of more money to improve the quality of our schools. Too often this means little more than new money added to the old. But what about the old money—that is to say, what are we doing with the resources we already have? Efficiency implies using new money in ways that enable us to use the old, established resources more fully and equitably.

There is growing evidence that more money alone may not produce the hoped for results. Edmonds, in his work on school effectiveness, concluded that the characteristics associated with successful schools "do not result from higher overall expenditures"[12] and are clearly within reach of any school today. A critical review of research on school effectiveness sponsored by the Rand Corporation concluded that "increasing expenditures on traditional educational practices do not lead to substantial improvements."[13] The study went on to suggest that there seem to be opportunities to reduce or redirect expenditures without causing decline in outcomes. Traditional educational practices that do not make a major difference in student outcomes include teacher experience, teacher advanced degrees, and reduction in class size.

In a study for the Institute for Research on Educational Finance and Governance at Stanford University, Henry Levin and his colleagues subjected four different approaches to improving the math and reading performance of elementary school children to cost-effectiveness analysis. These four approaches—or "educational interventions"—included

☐ reducing class size (the most prominent traditional method for improving educational outcomes);

☐ increasing the length of the school day and instructional time (a recent rallying point in educational reform efforts);

☐ computer-assisted instruction (which has been explored for the past two decades); and

☐ peer and adult tutoring (which have a long, but informal history in American education).[14]

Using techniques of meta-analysis of cost-effectiveness, the four approaches were evaluated and compared. The results revealed that peer tutoring was by far the most cost-effective approach. Despite popular expectations and preconceptions, the reduction of class size and the extension of the school day were found to be the least cost-effective. Computer-assisted instruction came in between these two extremes.

Such information is important in our attempt to get the very best for the very least. While many may question these and other results, the main point is that these approaches can have the desired effect while being cost-efficient. Too often, we continue old practices even when we know that other approaches may be superior. The conventional wisdom within the fabric of traditional schools will not easily give way to newer possibilities, even when the evidence challenging the traditional ways is substantial. Policymakers, faced with fiscal responsibilities, will increasingly be on the lookout for effective and efficient practices to replace those that are less productive and more costly.

Matching existing teachers to existing students on the basis of teaching and learning styles is a case in point. Under the present school model and structure, students are assigned to teachers by grade level or on the basis of intellectual classification. However, if students and teachers were assigned on the basis of compatibility between their teaching and learning styles, there would be no new costs to the system, only new patterns within it. If computers prove to be more effective with a number of learners, then business and industry could loan computers to the school. In return, the business would gain excellent public relations for assisting the community in school improvement. If college students were given course credit for tutoring, this would not only be using available resources, but would also benefit the students. Similarly, the school could recruit community volunteers, such as retired teachers, parents, students from colleges and universities, or professionals from business and industry to serve as tutors.

PARTICIPATION

The right of citizens to participate in public institutions is one of the features that makes those institutions public. This is certainly the case with public schools. No definition of excellence in a democratic nation can exclude *citizen involvement.*[15]

Citizen involvement, especially *parent* involvement, in education is deeply rooted in American history. Lay participation has been a matter of policy and practice in our public schools since their founding. Lay boards of education act as school trustees in local systems nationwide. Schools, in turn, have become extensions of the family as teachers, and administration officials find themselves assuming parental tasks with accordant responsibility and, indeed, occasional strain.

That educational personnel serve *in loco parentis* indicates a functional tie between institution and home, affirming a parental element within the educational process at the same time that it transfers parental authority to the schools. As a result, this partial transfer is a matter of opposition as well as identification—the more that schools assume parental obligations, the more parents become removed from direct involvement in the schools.

While historically, elitist theories of democracy have both resulted from and contributed to the rise of professionalization, including concentrating power with the so-called experts, professionalism has not totally eclipsed participatory democracy. Instead, there is an unresolved tension between the individual participant and the specialized representative. This tension is the basis for discussion of political participation in American society. In education, it marks the opposing poles of models of community participation in their present and historic forms.

The growing complexity of American society corresponded with the evolution of political and educational processes toward the representative rather than direct, unmediated participation. This does not indicate a total surrender of parental authority in public education. To the contrary, *in loco parentis* statutes preserve the ultimate authority of parents as participants in establishing school policy and in reviewing the procedures by which services are delivered to their children. It is, therefore, important to emphasize that parents maintain the right to participate actively and effectively in all public matters.

The Contemporary Debate about Citizen Participation: Ends Vs. Means Parent participation in the governing of institutions remains central to democracy. Validated by its practice, participation is an end in itself. But does participation improve the quality of education in our schools? It is one thing to guarantee parents' right to participate in and to govern public institutions such as the schools, but it is quite another to judge the appropriateness or quality of such participation against criteria of specific educational outcomes and goals. A central question emerges: Is citizen participation an end in itself or is it also a means towards chosen ends? In the last analysis, it is probably both.

The concept of accountability expresses the relationship between parents and school officials in which the authority to determine educational objectives lies with the lay community, while the task of realizing these objectives lies with teachers. Citizens and parents expect their children to learn to read, and they hold their children's teachers accountable should their children not be able to read.

During those times in which schools are perceived by the community as fulfilling their charge, schools are allowed to regulate themselves, and the representative approach to lay participation is dominant. However, in periods when public schools appear to fall short of the community's aspirations, direct citizen involvement increases, and parents call teachers into account and charge administrators with organizational failure.

More active citizen participation, stimulated by the post-war baby boom and by calls for educational support to returning veterans, began to emerge in the late 1940s and early 1950s. The 1954 Supreme Court decision concerning segregated school systems further stimulated demands for open access to quality education. In 1957, Sputnik transformed such demands into a virtual furor. Improving education became the answer to the needs of national industry and international competition. The activism of the 1960s demanded more participation in almost every governmental process. Activity begun during the 1960s and continued throughout the 1970s called for further clarification of human rights for minority groups, the elderly, the handicapped, the socially disadvantaged, and women.

All these trends resulted in a range of community participation efforts in the public schools. Parent associations, parent advisory units, parent volunteers, homeroom parents, school councils, home tutors, paraprofessionals, community boards, home education are all types of community participation in the schools. We must distinguish among them as we study effects on students' achievement and concepts of self-worth. Furthermore, we must define and delineate these effects before we can formulate educational policies that are responsive to the current accelerated call for excellence.

A Typology for Parent Participation   Families get involved in the schools in many different ways. Thomas A. Liechty identifies five types of educational participants within a county school district: "Inactives," "Voters," "Parents" (those engaged in elective activities and cooperative endeavors), and "Activists" (those responsible for cooperative activities and dynamic endeavors).[16] There are other typologies of participation as well. Salisbury distinguishes between expressive-supportive and instrumental-purposive participation.[17] The latter corresponds to the political and governance-related aspects of the Activist or Citizen roles as defined by Liechty. Distinctions and typologies may be introduced and refined *ad infinitum*, but what we need is a framework placing participants in differing positions along an overlapping four-part continuum that allows us to see participants as clients on one end and decision makers and governors on the other end.

Parents as Clients   When schools view parents and other community people as clients, they tend to offer participation in school affairs as a privilege, not a right. Parents are viewed only as clients, and the schools mount a campaign of controlled information intended to maintain a favorable image. For example, PTAs may be asked to plan social activities or other events such as a "teacher's day" or a "meet-the-staff night." School administrators may participate in various civic meetings to "inform" the community on the state of education in their schools and "interpret" the school programs to the community. A similar function is served by a school newspaper or newsletter that describes the programs of the school in positive terms. The purpose of public relations is, after all, to control communication and emphasize the good news.

Such public relations activities encourage participation specifically in ways that are acceptable to the school. Under a successful school public relations program, parents feel that the school has the situation under control and that their children are in good hands. If parents and other community residents feel content with and confident about school administrators' handling of the schools, there is usually little reason for any other kind of participation. Parents are invited to the schools only for the regularly scheduled public relations events or for a teacher-parent conference.

Parents as Producers: Participation for Instructional Support   The key term here is support. Parents are involved in the curriculum and in the affairs of schools in a supportive capacity as school volunteers, paraprofessionals, hall monitors, tutors, clerical aides, library assistants, lunchroom assistants, and student club assistants. Parent participants are viewed as producers, and their efforts increase the talent base and human resources of the school.

In some instances, this participation is voluntary and expressive-supportive. In other instances, as in paraprofessional programs, parents are paid participants in school affairs. Under these "new career" efforts discussed by Pearl and Riessman,[18] economically disadvantaged community residents are trained to assume

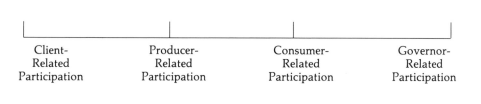

Client-
Related
Participation

Producer-
Related
Participation

Consumer-
Related
Participation

Governor-
Related
Participation

FIGURE 2–1
(Source: Reprinted, with permission, from Fantini, A Two-Way Street, 15.)

roles in the school as paid teacher aides or teacher assistants. These paraprofessionals may supervise lunch-time and recess activities, operate audio-visual equipment, assist children with homework, tutor in specified skill areas, assume clerical functions, prepare materials used in teaching and demonstrations, correct homework, assist students at home in subjects requiring special competency (e.g., mathematics, history, biology), or work with small groups in special technical areas. Paraprofessional programs help community residents earn a living as well as learn something about their schools. In return, the paraprofessionals become important links to the community and are able to reach parents and students who otherwise might not be contacted.

In other instances, schools use institutional resources in the community. Individuals from business and industry may come into schools as visiting teachers. In some schools, much of the education actually takes place in the community itself, outside the four walls of the classroom. Such "schools without walls" (e.g., in Philadelphia, Chicago, Berkeley, Hartford) utilize the resources of the community, such as hospitals, museums, cultural centers, scientific institutions, publishing firms, and insurance firms.

There is evidence that producer involvement does increase student achievement: The more participation relates to actual instructional activities, the more participation increases student achievement. Quite obviously, there are limits in the nature and the number of participants any school system can accommodate. Economic crises, however, can effectively stimulate and may even necessitate volunteer programs, causing reexamination of ways in which community resources may be linked to the educational process. Hence, we may well find participation in instructional support on the rise in future reform efforts.

Parents as Consumers: Participation and Community Service In this, the parents' role consists of being active, intelligent, and informed consumers. The school is perceived as being the center of the community, offering a range of services to all community members in the evenings and on weekends. In support of community service, school officials have extended their afternoon programs for children into evening programs for adults. These programs may be academic, vocational, or avocational in nature: drama clubs, child-care training, or literacy classes.

Such a participatory system makes maximum use of the school's existing structure and available time, transforming the public school into a true community school. A community school can serve more than a social, recreational, or strictly academic function. Parents can use the school to discuss and plan civic programs, while community schools can also serve as forums for solving community problems such as school integration, urban renewal, family relocation, and the organization of indigenous neighborhood leadership.

Parents as Governors: Participation for Accountability and School Governance The role of parents as governors can be seen in terms of the right to hold public officials accountable, the right to choose which institutions may assume the mantle of *in loco parentis,* and the right to organize and express interests. These can be summed up as the rights of accountability, choice, and expression.

1. Accountability. The community acts as trustee of public education by reemphasizing local control, mandating school boards and school committees who set policy, and decentralizing decision making. Schools have attempted to respond to the call for increased accountability in school governance by establishing patterns of consultation with community groups and parents for their opinions. Lay councils can either act in an advisory capacity or assume an actual authoritative function on all policies and all decisions relative to the operation of the school.
2. Choice: Choosing *In Loco Parentis.* The family selects the kind of education most suitable to its members through an educational voucher system. Each family, as a purchaser or consumer of the state's educational services, is granted a voucher equivalent to the cost of a year's education and can shop around for a compatible style of schooling.
3. Expression: Participation for Crisis Resolution. This form of community participation occurs when the school or school system faces a major problem—double sessions, racial conflicts, school busing plans, program cutbacks, or teacher strikes—which triggers substantial community concern. Usually when such issues are discussed, school auditoria fill to capacity with concerned parents whose aim is the immediate resolution of the crisis.

Toward a Broader Concept of Community Participation However, there is far more to the concept of community participation than parent involvement. The democratic process encourages those affected by decisions to participate in the decision-making process. For our purposes, we have looked mainly at patterns of community involvement, but the participation of teachers and other professional educators must also be considered important. Further, as crucial as parents are in the educational process, other community agents and agencies also contribute to learning. Of major importance is the involvement of business and industry, human services, and cultural, civic and recreational agencies. As we define and face the emerging educational conditions and demands of the post-industrial era, this broadened definition of community participation becomes crucial. Community education is the concept that most nearly encompasses what we have been suggesting. Horace B. Reed and Elizabeth Lee Loughran offer this definition:

> The purpose of the community education movement has been to maximize the contact between the school and its community both by facilitating use of the schools by all members of the community and by increasing the school's use of community resources.[19]

John Dewey envisioned this process in 1916 when he granted the school a special role in the community in acting against the inevitable shortcomings of mis-education:

> The school has the function . . . of coordinating within the disposition of each individual the diverse influences of the various social environments into which he enters. One code prevails in the family; another in the streets; a third, in the workshop or store; a fourth, in the religious association. As a person passes from one of the environments to another, he is subjected to antagonistic pulls, and is in danger of being split into a being having different standards of judgment and emotion for different occasions. This danger imposes upon the school a steadying and integrating office.[20]

Community involvement in education is just that—the community participates as educators. Schools are only one of the many learning environments contributing to education. The school may be the most important coordinating agency for linking the diverse educational environments of the community, but the community is essential to the process. Community participation must be broadened to view the entire region as the basic unit for learning. Participants who improve learning are all those who have an impact on the learner. To continue to view community participation only from the perspective of the school is to continue to foster a limited view of its potential. Any attempt to reform schools must include the process of community involvement, the participation of the community. Public schools are integral to community life and, in turn, community participation is essential to the public schools.

After this elaboration on the ingredients that make up excellence, we are ready to conclude with a more abbreviated definition: Excellence in education may be considered more nearly realized when all are learning what they need to become all they are capable of becoming, in the most up-to-date way, using the best available resources in ways that are consistent with democratic procedures and dedicated to the further culturation of a free, just, and compassionate civilization.

NOTES

1. Daniel L. Duke, "What Is the Nature of Educational Excellence and Should We Try to Measure It?" *Phi Delta Kappan*, Vol. 66, No. 10, June 1985, 674.

2. National Commission on Excellence in Education, *A Nation At Risk: The Imperative for Educational Reform* (Washington, D. C.: U. S. Government Printing Office, 1983), 12.

3. Much of the material on pages 65–74 is drawn from an unpublished paper entitled "Alternative Conceptions of Quality Education" (1985) by Mario D. Fantini.

4. Mortimer J. Adler, *The Paideia Proposal: An Educational Manifesto* (New York: Macmillan Publishing Company, 1982), 5.

5. John I. Goodlad, "Conditions for School Reform Related to Marginality," a speech presented at the 1985 Annual Meeting of the American Educational Research Association (Symposium: "Responding to Demands for Curriculum Improvement: Starting at the Margins"), Chicago, April 1985.

6. Robert Rosenthal, *Pygmalion in the Classroom* (New York: Holt, Rinehart and Winston, 1968).

7. *Barriers to Excellence: Our Children at Risk* (Boston: The National Coalition of Advocates for Students, 1985), 4.

8. George Weber, *Inner-City Children Can Be Taught to Read: Four Successful Schools* (Washington, D. C.: Council for Basic Education, 1970), Occasional Papers Number Eighteen.

9. *Ibid.*, 30.

10. Ross Zerchykov, "School Effectiveness: Public Schools Can Teach All Children," *Citizen Action in Education* (Boston: Institute for Responsive Education), Vol. 8, No. 1, April 1981, 1.

11. Michael Rutter, et al., *Fifteen Thousand Hours: Secondary Schools and Effects on Children* (Cambridge, Mass.: Harvard University Press, 1970), 205.

12. Ronald Edmonds, "Effective Schools for the Urban Poor," *Educational Leadership*, October 1979, 15–24.

13. Harvey A. Averch, et al., *How Effective Is Schooling?* A Rand Educational Policy Study (Englewood Cliffs, New Jersey, 1974).

14. Henry M. Levin, Gene V. Glass, and Gail R. Meister, "Cost-Effectiveness of Four Educational Interventions" (Stanford, California: Institute for Research on Educational Finance and Governance, School of Education, Stanford University, 1984).

15. Material in this section is adapted from: Mario D. Fantini, "Community Participation: Alternative Patterns and Their Consequences on Educational Achievement," *A Two-Way Street: Home-School Cooperation in Curriculum Decisionmaking* (Boston, Massachusetts: Institute for Responsive Education, 1980), 9–28.

16. Thomas A. Liechty, "Patterns of Citizen Participation in Education," a paper presented at the Annual Meeting of the American Educational Research Association, San Francisco, California, 1979.

17. R. H. Salisbury, *Citizen Participation in the Public Schools* (Lexington, Massachusetts: D. C. Heath, 1980).

18. A. Pearl and F. Riessman, *New Careers for the Poor* (New York: Free Press, 1965).

19. Horace B. Reed and Elizabeth Lee Loughran (eds.), *Beyond Schools: Education for Economic, Social, and Personal Development* (Amherst, Mass.: Citizen Involvement Training Program, Community Education Resource Center, School of Education, University of Massachusetts, 1984), p. 229.

20. John Dewey, *Democracy and Education* (New York: The Macmillan Company, 1916), 26.

PART II
Major Reforms Aimed at Excellence

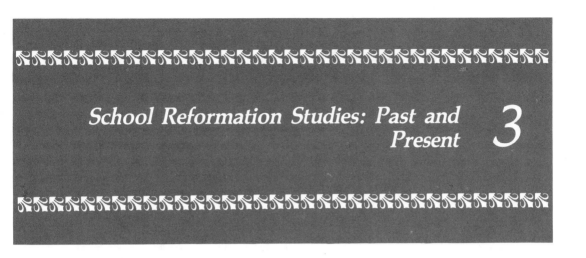

School Reformation Studies: Past and Present 3

NATIONAL STUDIES AND SCHOOL REFORM MEASURES

In order to move toward achieving excellence in public education, the present state of schools needs to be examined. So much has been written about American education that only the central problems identified by this research and the assessment of the studies' recommendations on school reform will be presented here. Headlines from the pages of newspapers and journals exemplify the range of issues and problems in education that have captured the attention of the public and absorbed the energies of researchers in recent years: "Poll Finds Public Endorsement of School Reforms"; "School Discipline No. 1 Worry"; "Public Schools Need an Overhaul, Study Finds"; "Study: Public Schools on Verge of Collapse"; "Severity of California Schools' Budget Crisis Seen in San Jose District Bankruptcy Filing."

PLACING CURRENT REPORT PROPOSALS IN HISTORICAL PERSPECTIVE

The current studies on the state of American education continues an interrupted progression of school reform reports that dates back to the last century. A. Harry Passow's highlights of past reform measures help place current studies in historical perspective:

> For some educational historians, the 1890s are viewed as a watershed, marking the emergence of the high school as an accepted extension of the common school. The Committee on Secondary School Studies (more commonly referred to as the Committee of Ten) issued its report in 1893, asserting that the course of study it proposed was to be the same for all students, whether or not college admission was the goal. In fact, the committee argued that preparation for college was not the main purpose of the high school. . . .
> . . . In 1909, the so-called Carnegie Unit represented an effort to standardize high school credits on the basis of classroom hours and to calculate college entrance requirements quantitatively. It was assumed "that a satisfac-

tory year's work in any major subject cannot be accomplished in less than 120 sixty-minute hours, or their equivalent." For the next half century, the Carnegie Unit exercised considerable influence on standardizing curriculum in American schools.

. . . The Commission on the Reorganization of Secondary Education began its work in 1913 although its influence report, *The Cardinal Principles of Secondary Education,* was not issued until 1918. The commission recognized that enrollments were increasing in high schools but that high dropout rates were continuing. Fewer than one third of those who began the four-year high school were graduated and only a small fraction of the graduates went on to higher education.

. . . Health, command of the fundamental processes, worthy home membership, vocation, civic education, worthy use of leisure, and ethical character—these were the seven objectives of secondary education, and each of the subjects taught was in need of extensive reorganization to contribute more effectively to the attainment of the objectives.

. . . The Commission on the Relation of School and College of the Progressive Education Association was established in 1930 "to explore possibilities of better coordination of school and college work and to seek an agreement which would provide the necessary freedom for secondary schools to attempt fundamental reconstruction."

. . . Toward the end of World War II, the Educational Policies Commission issued a report titled *Education for All American Youth,* in which the commission declared:

> When we write confidently and inclusively about education for all American youth, we mean that all youth, with their human similarities and their equally human differences, shall have educational services and opportunities suited to their personal needs and sufficient for the successful operation of a free and democratic society.

. . . James B. Conant's report on the comprehensive high school in 1959, *The American High School Today,* offered some twenty-one recommendations but concluded that "no radical alteration in the basic pattern of American education is necessary to improve our public high school."

. . . Throughout the late 1950s and 1960s, committees and commissions undertook curriculum development projects in practically all of the subject areas, usually with the support of the federal government and foundations. The so-called era of innovation was marked by new curricula, organization, technology, and staff deployment, but as Charles Silberman observed, "the reform movement has produced innumerable changes, and yet the schools themselves are largely unchanged."

. . . When student dissent and unrest spread to the high schools from the college campuses in the late 1960s, cries of "curricular irrelevance" and "prison-like constraints" were loud and clear. The riots and demonstrations of the late 1960s—surely part of the larger societal framework—together with the developments in the 1970s—triggered another reassessment of the goals, structure, operations, and control mechanisms in the secondary schools. It is in this context that the various diagnoses of the achievements and shortcomings of the high schools and the needed reforms have been advanced.[1]

This overview reveals the developmental struggle this nation has had in preserving our values while adapting to changing societal realities. The 1980s have brought new state and national proposals for school reform.

Of the many recent reports, *A Nation at Risk*, issued in 1983 by the National Commission on Excellence in Education, is credited with wielding the most influence. It captured the urgency which characterized other reports and summarized the indicators of the national problems that necessitated reform and school improvement:

- ☐ International comparisons of student achievement, completed a decade ago, reveal that on 19 academic tests, American students were never first or second and, in comparison with other industrialized nations, were last seven times.
- ☐ Some 23 million American adults are functionally illiterate by the simplest tests of everyday reading, writing, and comprehension.
- ☐ About 13 percent of all 17-year-olds in the United States can be considered functionally illiterate. Functional illiteracy among minority youth may run as high as 40 percent.
- ☐ Average achievement of high school students on most standardized tests is now lower than 26 years ago when Sputnik was launched.
- ☐ Over half the population of gifted students do not match their tested ability with comparable achievement in school.
- ☐ The College Board's Scholastic Aptitude Tests (SAT) demonstrate a virtually unbroken decline from 1963 to 1980. Average verbal scores fell over 50 points and average mathematics scores dropped nearly 40 points.
- ☐ College Board achievement tests also reveal consistent declines in recent years in such subjects as physics and English.
- ☐ Both the number and proportion of students demonstrating superior achievement on the SATs (i.e., those with scores of 650 or higher) have also dramatically declined.
- ☐ Many 17-year-olds do not possess the "high order" intellectual skills we should expect of them. Nearly 40 percent cannot draw inferences from written material; only one-fifth can write a persuasive essay; and only one-third can solve a mathematics problem requiring several steps.
- ☐ There was a steady decline in science achievement scores of U.S. 17-year-olds as measured by national assessments of science in 1969, 1973, and 1977.
- ☐ Between 1975 and 1980, remedial mathematics courses in public four-year colleges increased by 72 percent and now constitute one-quarter of all mathematics courses taught in those institutions.
- ☐ Average tested achievement of students graduating from college is also lower.

    ☐ Business and military leaders complain that they are required to spend millions of dollars on costly remedial education and training programs in such basic skills as reading, writing, spelling, and computation. The Department of the Navy, for example, reported to the Commission that one-quarter of its recent recruits cannot read at the ninth grade level, the minimum needed simply to understand written safety instructions. Without remedial work they cannot even begin, much less complete, the sophisticated training essential in much of the modern military.[2]

Table 3–1, developed by the editors of *Education USA*, National Public Relations Association (1984), profiles 14 national studies conducted during the early 1980s,[3] and analyzes the critical areas addressed by these reports.

An analysis by the Northeast Regional Exchange, Inc. points out common precepts running through eight of these reports:

    ☐ Education is correlated with economic and social development. Improved education outcomes are essential for the economic and social well-being of the individual, and therefore, of the nation. While some reports focus on this broad goal, others focus on personal growth or self-improvement, or on traditionally measured student performance.

    ☐ Quality education as a lifelong process is a univeral right. The assumption is that quality schooling through the secondary years is the right of all youth and only the beginning of education. Colleges and other postsecondary training efforts must be linked to secondary schools. Training and retraining programs should be available throughout the working years. Public schools should, therefore, teach not only content but also the process of learning.

    ☐ Public schools will continue as a mainstay of our society. Despite the pessimistic evaluations of public schools in the reports, none of them gives any serious consideration to alternatives to public schooling. Neither vouchers, tax rebates for private schooling, nor alternative schools with public sponsorship are addressed in any significant depth.

    ☐ Quality teachers and teaching underlie improved learning. The cornerstone of school improvement is quality teachers and teaching. Education as a high intensity human resource "industry" requires that we invest heavily in "human capital." Without this, all other improvement efforts will fail.

    ☐ Accountability and leadership by all must increase. Whereas critiques of public schools of the earlier decades were prone to identify villains or weak links, these reports indict all sectors of society. The task, therefore, requires increased accountability and leadership by all at the federal, state, and local level, and in the public and private sector. Common to the reports is the viewpoint that the federal government has "national interest" responsibilities which are exemplified through targeted legisla-

TABLE 3-1
Major Recommendations of Education Reform Reports

Recommendation	A Nation at Risk	Action for Excellence	Making the Grade	Academic Preparation for College	A Place Called School	High School	Horace's Compromise	Educating Americans for the 21st Century	America's Competitive Challenge	Education for Tomorrow's Jobs	The Paideia Proposal	High Schools and the Changing Workplace	An Open Letter to America	Meeting the Need for Quality: Action in the South
CURRICULUM STANDARDS														
Revise Curriculum	●	●		●		●	●	●			●		●	
Strengthen Requirements: – English	●	●	●		●	●		●			●		●	
– Math	●	●	●		●	●		●			●		●	●
– Science	●	●	●		●	●		●			●		●	●
– Social Studies	●	●	●		●	●		●			●		●	
– Technology/Computer Science	●	●	●		●	●		●			●		●	
– Foreign Languages	●		●	●		●								
– Art, Music	●				●	●	●				●			
– Physical Education					●	●					●			
Revise Vocational/Work Courses	●				●	●	●			●		●	●	●
Begin Education Earlier						●					●		●	
Offer Special Help for Gifted and Talented	●	●			●	●		●				●		
Offer Special Help for Slow Learners	●	●	●		●	●					●		●	
Set Core Curriculum		●	●		●	●	●					●		
Incorporate Outside Learning Opportunities						●		●			●			
Emphasize Reasoning Skills	●	●			●	●		●			●	●	●	●
Upgrade/Improve Textbooks	●	●									●			
STANDARDS														
Eliminate Tracking/Group by Mastery	●	●			●	●	●				●		●	
Raise College Admissions Standards	●	●				●			●		●			
Expect More of Students		●			●	●	●				●		●	●
Test for Promotion/Graduation	●	●			●	●					●		●	●
Increase Discipline	●	●									●	●	●	●
Assign More Homework	●	●									●			

Prepared by the editors of *Education USA*, National School Public Relations Assn., 1984. Reprinted by permission.

TABLE 3-1 (cont.)
Major Recommendations of Education Reform Reports (cont.)

Report	**TEACHING** Raise Salaries	Set Career Incentives	Strengthen Teacher Education	Offer Incentives to Attract Teachers	Recognize Outstanding Teachers	Strengthen Evaluation/Testing	Provide More Control/Fewer Administrative Burdens	Improve Math/Science Training/Teaching	**ORGANIZATION** Improve School Environment/Working Conditions	Improve School Leadership/Management	Lengthen School Day/Year	Use Existing School Time Better	Reduce Class/School Size	Increase Parent Involvement	Increase Business/Community Involvement	Form School/College Links	Governance/Funding Responsibility —Local	—State	Main Federal Role Cited As: —Research	—Equity/Civil Rights	—Funding Specific Projects	—Information/Data Collection	—Identification of National Initiatives	—Teacher Training/Support
A Nation at Risk	•	•	•		•	•	•	•		•	•	•		•	•	•	•	•	•	•	•	•	•	•
Action for Excellence	•	•	•	•	•	•	•	•		•	•	•	•		•		•	•	•	•	•	•	•	
Making the Grade	•	•		•	•			•									•		•	•	•	•	•	•
Academic Preparation for College																•								
A Place Called School		•	•				•		•	•		•	•											
High School	•	•	•	•	•	•	•	•	•	•		•	•	•	•	•		•	•		•			•
Horace's Compromise	•						•																	
Educating Americans for the 21st Century	•	•	•	•	•	•	•	•	•	•		•	•		•	•	•	•	•	•	•	•	•	•
America's Competitive Challenge																					•			
Education for Tomorrow's Jobs								•							•	•					•			
The Paideia Proposal	•		•	•			•			•													•	
High Schools and the Changing Workplace														•	•									•
An Open Letter to America	•		•		•	•			•	•			•		•				•	•	•	•		
Meeting the Need for Quality: Action in the South			•		•	•				•						•								

Prepared by the editors of *Education USA*, National School Public Relations Assn., 1984

tion, regulation, and financial support. State governments shape educational policy through establishing priorities, legislation, regulations, and financial support. Neither of these roles is to be confused with the strong and traditional responsibilities of local school districts to implement programs and deliver educational services which must be accompanied by local financial support.[4]

This overview demonstrates the seriousness of the school improvement movement. All the reports have been moved by the dangers of inaction and the challenge of reaching for excellence.

LEGAL AND LEGISLATIVE REFORM

Establishing excellence in education as a legal right has become a major concern of the courts, starting with *Brown v. Board of Education of Topeka* (1954) in which the Supreme Court established that:

> In these days, it is doubtful that any child may reasonably be expected to succeed in life if he is denied the opportunity of an education. Such an opportunity, where the state has undertaken to provide it, is a right which must be made available to all on equal terms.[5]

By the 1970s, the courts had extended this right to populations with special needs. In 1972, the U.S. District Court in Washington, D.C. ruled that all children had a constitutional right to a publicly supported education, without exception *(Mills v. Department of Education of District of Columbia)*. This decision led in November 1975 to PL94-142, the Education for All Handicapped Children Act, which assured every special needs child of an individualized program and a "least restrictive environment." With the 1980s came the emphasis on state-sponsored school reform and excellence became the new standard. Prompted by national studies and reports, virtually every state in the country has been involved in school improvement legislation. Table 3–2, shown on the next page, provides an overview of this involvement.[6]

The heart of the problem cited by the reports is the decline of productivity in schools, and attention is therefore on how to improve the means of delivery used by the schools.

TABLE 3-2

A Summary of State Programs to Improve Education

	A.	B.	C.	D.	E.	F.
Alabama	■	■	■			
Alaska	■	□	■			
Arizona	■	■	□		□	□
Arkansas	■	■	■	■	■	
California	■	■	■		■	■
Colorado	□	□	□		□	□
Conn.		□	□			□
Delaware	□	■		□		□
D.C.	■	■	■	■		□
Florida	□	■	■	■	■	■
Georgia		■	■	□	□	
Hawaii	□		□	□	□	
Idaho	□	■	■	■		■
Illinois	□	■		□		■
Indiana	■	■	■			
Iowa	■					
Kansas	□	■	■			□
Kentucky	■	■	■			□
Louisiana	■	■	■	■		
Maine		□	□			□
Maryland	□	□	■			□
Mass.	□		□		□	□
Michigan	■	■	■	■	■	
Minnesota	□	□	□			
Miss.	□	□	■	□	□	□
Missouri		■	■	□		

	A.	B.	C.	D.	E.	F.
Montana	■	■	□			
Nebraska	□	□		■	■	
Nevada	□	■	■		□	
N.H.	□	□	□			
N.J.	□	■	■			□
N. Mexico	■	■				□
New York	■	■	■		■	□
N. Carolina	□	■		■	■	□
N. Dakota		■		■		
Ohio	□	■	■	□	□	□
Oklahoma		■	□			
Oregon	□	■	□	□	□	□
Penn.	■	■	□			□
R.I.	□	□	■			
S. Carolina	□	□	□	□	□	
S. Dakota	□	■	■			
Tenn.	■	■	■		■	■
Texas	■	■	■		■	□
Utah	□	■	■	□		■
Vermont	■	■	■	□	□	□
Virginia	■	■	■			□
Wash.	■	■	■			□
W. Virginia	■	□	■			□
Wisconsin	■	■	■	□	□	□
Wyoming	□	□				

Source: U.S. Education Department

Here are some of the steps states are taking to improve education standards. Categories in the chart correspond to the letters for the reforms listed here. An empty box means a reform has been proposed, a blacked-in box means a reform has been enacted.

A. Curriculum reform: Toughening the number or type of courses offered at all grade levels.

B. Graduation requirements: Strengthening the number or type of classes required for high school graduation.

C. Student evaluation: Systemwide student testing for promotion or graduation or to assess strengths and weaknesses within a district.

D. Longer school day: Increase in the number of hours a student must be in class.

E. Longer school year: Increasing the number of days in the school year. Michigan did so by requiring that schools make up any days missed as a result of snow or other conditions.

F. Master teachers/career ladders: Providing promotions and extra pay for teachers who stand out as a result of experience, talent or expertise.

STANDARDIZATION AND LOW PRODUCTIVITY: HOW THE SCHOOL PRESENTLY CONDUCTS ITS BUSINESS

THE SCHOOL AS A FACTORY MODEL SYSTEM

It may be useful to look at the public school as a system or organization with its own set of goals, its own delivery mechanisms, and its own claim to goal attainment or productivity. The goals are assigned by the public and deal with the universal preparation of fully educated citizens capable of assuming adult roles in a democratic society. We have had and continue to have problems with our ability to achieve that goal of universal education. Sixty million Americans are considered functionally illiterate; school dropout rates range anywhere from 20–50 percent; there is growing vandalism, absenteeism, boredom, and a loss of public confidence in the schools—all symptoms of major system problems. Such problems indicate a chronic lack of productivity that no organization can endure.

The structure of the public school's delivery system was established during America's agricultural and early industrial period. The summer vacation months, still present in most school systems, is a carry-over from the agricultural period when most children were needed to help with the summer harvest. This sometimes obsolete, fixed standardization is the dominant mode of the school's delivery system. This standardization is based on Newtonian mechanistic thinking, in which the school system is viewed as a big closed machine with all the parts meeting certain predetermined standards supervised by a top-down administrative arrangement in order to run smoothly. Since deviation places the machine in danger, standardization becomes the overarching value. There is only one right way to run the machine.

As suggested in Chapter I, Einstein's Theory of Relativity changed the American world view to include flexibility and openness. However, the schools are still operating under the old assumptions, with results that fall far short of excellence. The system may have produced many winners, but it also produced too many losers. The schools' delivery system continues to generate underdeveloped learners.

Standardization in the schools in the late 19th and early 20th centuries led to a factory-type structure with age-graded classrooms and an emphasis on conformity. Mass schooling became necessary given the numbers of European immigrants needing to be assimilated into mainstream American society. The dominant psychology of the time was normal/abnormal, with an emphasis on the concept of adjustment. Learners were expected to conform to prevailing norms, and those who could not adjust suffered.

Just as there was a mass production emphasis in Henry Ford's new assembly line, so too was there a mass production emphasis in the schools of that era. Immigrants who were encouraged to relocate in America to provide labor for a growing industrial society also needed to have their children educated. The schools became large, comprehensive, uniform—an assembly line factory.

Students progressed through the age-graded structure in much the same way an automobile would be processed through an assembly line, with one worker performing one function and passing it along to another until at the other end a complete product was created. At the other end of twelve grades of schooling, there would be a totally schooled person. Teachers functioned as the assembly line workers, supervisors as inspectors, principals as managers, superintendents and staff as central headquarters. The public both accepted and supported these roles and the standardized process of schooling.

To increase efficiency and effectiveness, the factory system opted for standardization, and any deviation from the standard was suspect. Standardization peaked before World War II, when children sat is rows according to size and there was a *correct* way for both student and teacher to stand in a classroom, a *correct* way to speak in a classroom, a *correct* way to use the chalkboard, and a *correct* way to order the window shades. Even the school buildings tended to resemble factories. Successful management and supervision were judged by the degree to which the norms of the system were carried out.

Some people thought this kind of uniformity in the public schools eased the transition and adjustment of students to the workplace, which in many cases was a factory. Students were drilled on multiplication tables, authoritarian discipline, and demeanor and manners expected of the children (and teachers) toward their supervisors. Much attention was paid to lateness and absenteeism. Students were divided up not only by age, but by ability as determined by tests. Since diversity was viewed as an unfortunate barrier to homogeneity and thus to productivity, the schools were the major agencies for promoting homogeneity.

This factory-like procedure seemed acceptable to many immigrants of the 19th and early 20th centuries. Many had not had formal schooling in their own countries, and they tended to view the public schools as an opportunity for their children and going to school as a *privilege*. Consequently, many immigrants not only accepted the procedures of the school, but also believed the school could do no wrong. If their children had problems in school, the children had to adjust.

Many public schools still resemble the factory system developed earlier in this century. Although the factory did advance productivity given the needs of industrialization, there are now newer and better ways of increasing productivity. The psychology of privilege associated with access to school which made parents important allies of the schools' procedures and norms has given way to a different set of expectations based on a psychology of *rights*.

CHANGES IN CONSUMER ATTITUDES TOWARD THE FACTORY MODEL

Children born in the post-World War II baby boom began to look at America differently, taking advantage of opportunities that their parents had only begun to tap. During human and civil rights struggles, people who were previously disenfranchised and oppressed began to demand their rights. Schools were also affected by these attitudes. In the late 20th century, Americans perceived first-class education as a *right*. Unlike their parents, today's educational consumers blamed the school more than the learner for failure. This new psychology created slogans such as "Why can't Johnny read?"—meaning "Why can't the school teach Johnny to read?" The shift was increasingly toward the problems of the schoolhouse, the organization, and the system.

The new mobility patterns of the post-industrial era also affected the nature of the school structure. Ethnic background became less important. As Depression-based scarcity gave way to affluence and civil rights, people began to legitimize diversity. Homogeneity as a value gave way to diversity as an asset. The factory model of school is not responsive to these changes. Students identified as losers are labeled and assigned to specific tracks that determine not only *what* they are taught but *how* they are taught. Treated as losers, they may well become losers. Children identifed as academic "winners" also have a labelling problem. Encouraged and expected to do well, winners receive extra attention and may do well; however, these children may have special talents or abilities that are neither identified nor developed.

This classification system is hardly infallible; Albert Einstein was, at one point in his schooling career, identified as a slow learner:

> He only started to talk at age three and his parents were so worried by the slow development that they consulted a doctor. He was a solitary and quiet child who disliked games and sports, and even when the children were present he tended to play alone.[7]

Both human beings and the process of learning are too subtle and too complex to be fully, adequately, and appropriately encompassed by any classification system. This type of factory-originated standardization is what the private sector has now identified as a key problem and what many reformers believe must be restructured. This standardized structure has had a major impact on the human side of the school's organization. The same school structure that limited the full and individual development of students also restricted teachers and administrators. Under the factory model, those students and teachers who attempted to deviate from the established and accepted norm were suspect. A teacher might be called a "maverick," while labels for students might be "underachiever," "slow learner," and "disadvantaged," but all such labels conveyed a sense of marginality to the school's mainstream.

MARGINAL STATUS OF INCREASED NUMBERS OF LEARNERS[8]

The pervasive standardization and normative structure of this now outmoded factory structure pushes too many people to the margins. John Goodlad, among others, has commented on the pervasive nature of tracking in the American school system and its insidious effects both inside and outside the school. Students are tested and evaluated on the basis of tests as early as first grade. Using those test scores as criteria, students are assigned to different tracks within the school. Tracks designed for students deemed less academically able are intended to lead to vocational training. Curriculum content, style of the classroom teaching, and nature of the learning experience are all geared toward that end. Other tracks are geared to college preparation, and the climate of the classroom—including the teachers' expectations and the students' self-concepts—reflect that goal. Students are assigned to a track on the basis of single test results, influenced by racial identity, ethnic background, and socioeconomic class. As Goodlad points out:

> Minority students and those from the lowest socioeconomic groups have been found in disproportionate numbers in classes at the lowest track levels, and children from upper socioeconomic levels have been found to be consistently overrepresented in higher tracks.[9]

Once assigned to a particular track and given a particular label, students find it very difficult to change tracks to alter their preassigned classification. This is due both to the underlying faith in labeling and to widespread pedagogical practices within the school. Again, as Goodlad observes:

> One of the reasons for this stability in group membership is that the work of the upper and lower groups becomes more sharply differentiated with each passing day. Since those comprising each group are taught as a group most of the time, it is difficult for any one child to move ahead and catch up with children in a more advanced group. . . . It is not uncommon for a child in the most advanced group to have progressed five times as fast as a child in the least advanced group over the course of a year.[10]

Thus the uses and abuses of tracking and ability grouping are both a result of and a way of perpetuating standardization and discrimination in the schools.

In such a situation, the potential development of human beings is thwarted and human talents are wasted. Too many individuals are not being well or even adequately served by our educational system, which is a tragic loss for those individuals and for the entire society. The stigma of being "marginal" in the classroom all too easily extends from the learner's identity in the school to the individual's role in society.

The report, *Barriers to Excellence: Our Children at Risk*, identifies the various elements of discrimination and differential treatment in the schools that form effective barriers to quality education for all children: class, race, cultural background, sex, and special education or learning disabilities.[11] There is no denying that racism, sexism, classism, handicapism, and other so-called "-isms" are forms of discrimination that are institutionalized by the school's normative structure. Learners identified and categorized by such forms of institutionalized discrimination often feel unempowered and fail to gain the skills and competencies they need to fulfill their own potential or to contribute to society. They remain outside society, forming an educational underclass. They may even become wards of society rather than contributing to it, and both suffer accordingly. Preventing such a situation in the first place is far easier and far less expensive both in human and economic costs than curing it. While it may cost $3,000 a year to provide a quality education for a youngster, it may take $50,000 or more each year to "rehabilitate" an unsuccessfully educated adult. The human cost is incalculable.

There are many indications that people pushed to the margins have valuable talents that are undeveloped or underdeveloped and that they possess capacities that go both unrecognized and untapped. The alternative school movement begun in the 1960s proved that those "losers" in one educational setting may well become "winners" in another. A "marginal" learner is one who, for one reason or another, simply does not fit the dominant pattern of the educational environment and is in conflict with the standardized structure and expectations. *Barriers to Excellence: Our Children at Risk* identifies the inflexibility of the school structure, the use of tracking and ability grouping, and the misuse of testing in the present model of schooling as forming significant barriers to quality education for *all* children.[12] With adequate allowances for human diversity within the school structure, there would be less perceived marginality.

Even so-called "mainstream" learners may be short-changed by the normative structure of schools. An individual extremely talented in music may study several instruments, practice diligently, and even form her own band. In high school, she may begin playing semi-professionally in local clubs and lounges and perform until one o'clock in the morning. This productive experience, reaffirming years of practice and giving her the opportunity to develop talents in a professional situation, puts her in conflict with the school's standard expectations. If she performs until the early hours, she is not fully alert for seven o'clock classes. Unless the school can be flexible enough to accommodate this special situation, this particular learner is forced to choose between developing her talent in music and acquiring the basic skills she will need to further her formal education. While this talented youngster is not considered a "problem learner," she may be pushed to the margin by the inflexibility of the school structure.

The elementary school-age child who is uncomfortable in the highly competitive atmosphere of his classroom must either adjust to that competitive mode or suffer. The child may be identified as a slow learner with no recognition or support for his particular learning style, and he may thus become alienated and disaffected and also forced into marginality.

Similarly, an extremely shy child may need special recognition, support, and encouragement in the realm of social learning before she may comfortably proceed with academic achievement. Learning, with all its affective as well as intellectual components, is a social process. In creating and supporting compatible educational environments for all students, this social aspect of learning must be recognized. For the extremely shy child, a lack of self-confidence in social situations may lead to a sense of being unable to control her own destiny that eventually negates her mastery of academic as well as social skills. A sensitive teacher in a flexible school situation could devise a program designed to support and encourage the shy child's personality, but without flexibility within the school system and structure, the child's legitimate needs will go unmet. Factors contributing to the learner's marginality include the structure of the school program, the components of the curriculum, and the teacher's own personality and teaching style as they relate to the child's abilities and personality.

Standardization in the public school structure has resulted in standardized tests, such as the Scholastic Aptitude Test (SAT), which were designed to reward merit objectively and to determine entrance into colleges and universities fairly. Yet as David Owen in his critical review of the SAT[13] reminds us, those who developed the SAT during the 1920s and 1930s probably believed in racial and ethnic differences.

Leon Botstein, President of Bard College, offers the following observation:

> The use and popularity of SAT tests has done nothing to improve schooling for those populations that need it most. It has merely reinforced the educational advantages possessed by high-income white Americans by placing a respected "scientific" measure on those advantages and redefining them as signs of "aptitude." The performance of students over a 15-year period in New York State's Equal Opportunity Program and Higher Education Opportunity Program (college and university programs designed for low-income students who score poorly on such tests) indicates that the poor and minorities with low SATs can do perfectly well, tests or no tests. As Bowdoin College, which pioneered dropping SAT scores as part of the admission process, has demonstrated, educational excellence in the classroom and high standards in admissions do not need validation or help from ETS. [Educational Testing Service][14]

Standardization in student evaluation and in the school's expectations have unnecessarily pushed many learners to the margins of the school. Students pushed to the margins may often be merely instances of human variability that remain unaccommodated by the prevailing educational environment. Flexibility within the school structure is necessary to accommodate the varied and individual needs of *all* learners. As Sinclair and Ghory explain:

> Youth who do not succeed in school become marginal learners. The strained relationship that they develop with the educational environment leads others

to view them as deviant individuals, either temporarily on the fringes or more permanently out of the mainstream. The environment for learning starts to disconnect from these students who are having difficulties. As marginal learners, they fail to achieve full and satisfying involvement in the life of the school.

Too often educators identify lack of personal effort and weak academic potential as reasons that marginality persists and is seldom overcome. Yet, the assumption that the cause of the problem lies only inside the learner is counter-productive because it releases the school from the responsibility of creating an educational environment that reaches all students. In fact, the reasons for marginality are not always inside the learner. Rather, they often lie in the lack of quality in the interaction between the learner and the environment. We think that by looking closely at this interaction it is possible to gain an understanding of why so many learners are becoming marginal. Further, we believe that this understanding is a necessary beginning for action that will increase learning for all youth, including those who have not been successful in the past.[15]

Imperfect as it may have been, the factory model with its emphasis on standardization and mass schooling was appropriate to its times and needs. Now we are living in a different era, looking toward new social, economic, and educational demands of the 21st century. It is difficult for students and teachers to rise above the restrictions set by the environment of the uniform factory model. A different, more flexible structure might well allow the full creativity and capabilities of both students and teachers to flourish.

All reform-oriented reports agree that change is necessary to improve American education. What kind of change? What is the direction of that change? In critiquing the rising tide of school reform reports, K. Patricia Cross of the Harvard Graduate School of Education concludes that:

> The school reform movement of the 1980s focuses on mechanical solutions that were imposed from the top and that can be implemented quickly.
> We must begin to question whether the ancient structures of education can cope with the diversity that is inherent in university education.[16]

A Nation at Risk, credited with the most urgency and influence, does not develop a model of schooling that could truly provide quality education. While "equity" is mentioned as "a public commitment," very little is suggested in the way of actual implementation, there is almost no mention of pedagogy, or the most promising instructional methodologies for delivering excellence to all. Thus, in significant dimensions, the recent report fails to direct us toward reforms that will lead to a contemporary concept of excellence.

In the end, this report falls back on more of what we already have—more of what has already caused the problem in the first place. In short, this report retains the very schooling that is in need of reformation. While these studies agree that the present school system is not delivering excellence, they believe that more of what is already there will give us our goal. It is this basic assumption—adding on to the present school will restore excellence—that constitutes the tragic flaw in these otherwise well-intended propositions. Perhaps the most telling summary of the plethora of national and state studies is the following commentary:

> Despite the recent avalanche of proposals to fix our public schools, none confronts the basic issue: we expect the schools to accomplish so many tasks at once that they cannot do a job very well for very long. Band-Aid solutions proliferate: a longer day and year, more required subjects, more homework, higher pay for teachers. But more of the same is not necessarily improvement. Nor do the schools need more special programs, layered one on top of the other, each with its requisite administrators, procedures, and paper work.
>
> Because current efforts attempt to patch the present system, they are not likely to bring fundamental reform. Perhaps novelty will account for some initial success, but one need only remember mini courses, new math, values clarification, and the emphasis on math and sciences after Sputnik to see that a ride on any such bandwagon is likely to be a short one.
>
> We have the knowledge and expertise to redesign our public education system. We also have thousands of talented, dedicated educators to carry out the needed changes. Most important, we have hundreds of thousands of students and their parents who deserve a better system than they have now, one that is stable yet responds to change. Now is the time to implement the new design.[17]

As society changes and as the schools continue their long tradition of adapting to serve society's changing needs, the present normative model of schooling must give way to a newer model more attuned to contemporary realities. Assessments of the schools and school reform proposals that focus only on the old model and offer only more of the same solutions cannot yield excellence as we have defined it, an equation of quality, equality, effectiveness, efficiency, and participation. To achieve excellence in education, we must make best and fullest use of state-of-the-art knowledge and technology in the field of education, as well as drawing on lessons learned from its history and from the experience of other sectors.

NOTES

1. A. Harry Passow, "Once Again: Reforming Secondary Education," *Resources for Improving Education: A Study Guide for Educational Administrators*, edited by Mario D. Fantini and Anita Moses (Fort Lauderdale, Florida: National Ed.D. Program for Educational Leaders, Nova University, 1976), 114–119.

2. National Commission on Excellence in Education, *A Nation at Risk: The Imperative for Educational Reform* (Washington, D. C.: U. S. Government Printing Office, 1983), 8–9.

3. Marvin Cetron, *Schools of the Future: How American Business and Education Can Cooperate to Save Our Schools* (New York: McGraw-Hill Book Company, 1985), 148–151.

4. Northeast Regional Exchange, Inc., *Education Under Study: An Analysis of Recent Major Reports on Education*, developed by J. Lynn Griesemer and Cornelius Butler (Chelmsford, Massachusetts: Northeast Regional Exchange, Inc., 1983), 4.

5. *Brown vs. Board of Education of Topeka*, 347 U.S. 483 (1954). *The Courts and Education*, The Seventy–Seventh Yearbook of the National Society for the Study of Education, edited by Clifford P. Hooker (Chicago: The National Society for the Study of Education, 1978), 43.

6. Metropolitan Affairs Corporation, *Dialogue for Change: Options for Restructuring K–12 Education*, A Report of the Education Committee of the Metropolitan Affairs Corporation (Detroit: Metropolitan Affairs Corporation, 1984), 68.

7. James Sayen, *Einstein in America* (New York: Crown Publishers, 1985).

8. This section is adapted from "The Human Side of Marginality," a paper presented by Mario D. Fantini at the American Educational Research Association Annual Meeting, Chicago: April 1985.

9. John I. Goodlad, *A Place Called School: Prospects for the Future* (New York: McGraw-Hill Book Company, 1984), 152.

10. *Ibid.*, 150–166.

11. National Coalition of Advocates for Students, *Barriers to Excellence: Our Children at Risk* (Boston: The National Coalition of Advocates for Students, 1985), 1–31.

12. *Ibid.*, 33–49.

13. David Owen, *None of the Above: Behind the Myth of Scholastic Aptitude* (Boston: Houghton Mifflin Company, 1985).

14. Leon Botstein, "New Book Attacking SATs Has Right Message, Wrong Tone," *The Christian Science Monitor*, 5 July 1985, B8.

15. Robert L. Sinclair and Ward J. Ghory, "Becoming Marginal," a paper presented as part of the Symposium, "Responding to Demands for Curriculum Improvement: Starting at the Margins," American Educational Research Association Annual Meeting, Chicago: April 1985.

16. K. Patricia Cross, "The Rising Tide of School Reform Reports," *Phi Delta Kappan*, Vol. 66 (3), November 1984, 167–172.

17. Anne Westcott-Dodd, "A New Design for Public Education," in *Dialogue for Change: Options for Restructuring K–12 Education*, A Report of the Education Committee of the Metropolitan Affairs Corporation (Detroit: Metropolitan Affairs Corporation, 1984), 69–70.

Improving or Restructuring? 4

Almost all recent school reform efforts geared towards improving the present education system are concerned with the many "pieces" at virtually every level that make up the school system. However, an understanding of and approach to the entire educational *system* often appears to be lacking.

PIECEMEAL OR HOLISTIC REFORM

The problems of reforming public education can be looked at from either a *piecemeal* or *holistic* perspective. The first approach attempts to isolate the problem or problems in one small component of the system. The other examines the system as a whole. John A. Scileppi discusses the difference:

> In the piecemeal approach, an innovator might seek to remove a certain teacher, to change a particular textbook, or to improve a new form of teaching. Such an approach was very prevalent in the 1960s and 1970s, a time of great turmoil in American education. Yet the main effect of these interventions tended to cancel each other out or to fade from existence. Many change agents became frustrated and began to believe that changing the status quo in education was impossible.
>
> Social scientists, however, have come to take a different approach to the problems of American education. They observe that education, similar to other institutions, can be viewed as a social system. . . .
>
> To understand why various attempts at change in education have failed, we need to first understand the systems theory approach. The most basic concept of this approach is that no one element exists in a vacuum, but that it always relates to other components of the system. Thus, if one element is altered, the relationships between it and the other factors are potentially affected. This modification places a stress on the entire system. If all the interrelated components can be made consistent with the reformed element, the change is accepted, the system restabilizes, and a type of synergy or affective directed smooth function-

ing of the system results. If, however, the reform in one element in the system is inconsistent with all the other components of the system, the change is rejected as the system strives to regulate itself to reestablish a steady state following the disruption.[1]

John Goodlad put it this way:

Significant educational improvement of schooling, not mere tinkering, requires that we focus on entire schools, not just teachers or principals or curricula or organization or school-community relations but all of these and more.[2]

There are many levels or elements in the system that influence the learning of children in school. S. S. Boocock (1980) identified these levels as follows:

1. the attributes of the individual child, such as family background, intelligence, achievement motivation, and ambition;
2. the qualities of the classroom, such as teacher expectancies, peer group influence, value climate, style of teaching and theories of learning;
3. the factors of the school itself, such as teacher-teacher and teacher-principal relationships, and the type and quality of facilities in the school;
4. the interface between the school and the community, such as composition of the school board, the nature of parental involvement in the school, and the degree of ethnic diversity within the community; and
5. the forces operating at the level of the national educational system, such as the effect of mass media on the popular image of what quality education means, national legislation affecting education, and the types of learning resources distributed by the major publishing firms.[3]

To bring about systemic reform, all these levels must be considered.

Mario Fantini and Gerald Weinstein, in *The Disadvantaged: Challenge to Education*, advanced another systems view of the public school: it has a *purpose*, a *process* for achieving that purpose, and a *product*—the results. If the purpose and the product are compatible, then the process is *effective*.[4] Analogous to the model of private enterprise, if the goals of the organization are achieved through an assessment of results, then the procedures used in that organization are effective. Thus, if a company's goal of selling a new product line is successful, then one could say that the methodology used—the one that yielded the results—has been effective.

Applied to the public schools, if the public schools exist to deliver quality to everyone, and a process is developed for achieving that goal, then an examination of the results shows that the goal has not yet been met. Reforms seek rectification by dealing with either the *purpose*, the *process*, or the *product*. For example, if the public schools do not try to be "all things to all people," then the goal of universality is really unattainable. Since quality cannot be delivered equally and there always will be winners and losers, we should therefore abandon the goal and become much more realistic about what we can achieve.

The alternative goal could be that the public schools exist to serve the greatest number of people. Some will succeed and some will not. Given this goal and judging the results, the public schools are doing extremely well. However, since *excellence* precludes tampering with the noblest goals of equality in our society, efforts toward quality education for all students in the United States should be redoubled.

Many reforms intervene on the product (the learner) so that the product can more easily fit or adjust to the existing programs. In this way, the learner is reshaped so to take fuller advantage of the established process. Many remedial and compensatory programs attempt to do this. The results of this approach lag behind the goals; they are not fully effective. Other reforms focus on the delivery system and attempt to make the process more effective in achieving the goals and gaining the results associated with those goals. Emily Feistritzer addresses this issue:

> Education is a 240 billion dollar business in this country serving some 46 million elementary and secondary students and about 12 million college and university employees. The organization of the delivery system of these services—the school districts, schools, and colleges and universities—hasn't changed much. Neither have the people delivering the services—teachers and administrators. Nor has what they are selling—the curriculum.[5]

The Rand Corporation, studying school effectiveness in the United States, concluded that "increased expenditures on traditional practices is not likely to improve educational outcomes substantially."[6] Corporations have had to develop their own system of education. According to John Naisbitt and Patricia Aburdene:

> Corporations spend nearly 60 billion dollars a year on education and training. . . . Training and education programs within American businesses are so vast, so extensive, that they represent, in effect, an alternative to the nation's public and private schools, colleges and universities.[7]

Either the pieces of the system or the entire system can be dealt with. It is much easier to deal with one part of the total system than to attempt a fundamental and comprehensive reform of the entire system. It is unrealistic to try a complete transformation of an entire operating system. A system in motion cannot be brought to a halt while we introduce a totally new system.

All school reforms act on the existing system and, of necessity, deal with subsets of the larger system. The central issue involves determining which subsets are most important and why. Most reform measures have been aimed at improving the school *system*. If we attempt to affect the system, *which* system are we talking about? If we are addressing the present school system, then what constitutes a desired change?

An analogy may be useful here. An automobile, for example, is a whole system. Sometimes the automobile does not perform as it should, so we begin to examine its parts. We examine the spark plugs, the battery, the generator, the voltage regulator, and the fuel pump. At times, checking and repairing (or replacing) one piece of the system does not restore effectiveness in the total system. Further, say the automobile is a 1930 model. Replacing the pieces so that the entire system works better may result in an improved 1930 car, but sometimes a completely new car, a completely new model, may be far better.

This may be the case for the reform of the public schools. Even if improvement in various pieces within the present school system is successful, what would result? An improved old model, an improved old system, or a new model, a new system? It is possible to improve the system as it now exists, but all these efforts might only make a 20th century system work better when a 21st century system is needed. This dimension is often missing from the discussion of reform and from the piecemeal and holistic approaches to change. It is time to take a closer look at the structure of present-day schooling to determine the basis for needed change.

MAJOR REFORM DIRECTIONS

For our purposes, we shall categorize the many proposals aimed at the restoration of excellence into those aimed at *strengthening* the present system and structure of schooling and those aimed at *restructuring* the present system of schooling.

STRENGTHENING THE EXISTING SYSTEM AND STRUCTURE OF SCHOOLING

The assumption underlying these proposals is that the present school system and structure are adequate but need to be strengthened. Advocates of this position accept the present pattern for delivering scholastic services: the present age-graded hierarchy, certain student-teacher ratios, classes divided into periods, standardized testing, tracking of students, and 180 or so days of schooling per year for five and one-half to six hours a day.

Many school improvement efforts can enhance the operation of the present model of formal schooling. (See Chapter 2.) A major pattern in legislative proposals involves strengthening the present system through a mandated rededication to scholastic standards and to the tried and true methods of the past. The schools are perceived to have deviated from such standards as they tried to be "all things to all people." Therefore, in an attempt to restore excellence, there is a need to limit what the schools attempt to do, emphasize what the schools do best, and sharply focus existing resources on these tightly delineated goals. This currently popular point of view is the most pervasive route for reform considered and followed by individual states.

This approach asserts that excellence can be achieved if present procedures in the schools are improved and strengthened, which usually means more homework, more discipline, more tests, more money. If students are not learning, create remedial or compensatory programs; if class sizes are large, lower them; and if students do not adjust, create separate programs with special teachers.

REFORMS AIMED AT RESTRUCTURING PUBLIC SCHOOL SYSTEMS

The second route to reform defines the problem as the nature of the structure which attempts to deliver the services that would yield excellence.

Svi Shapiro of the University of North Carolina at Greensboro puts his observations on the reports aimed at restructuring the schools this way:

> Despite the attention generated by the 1983 reports, what marks them most, I believe, is their overwhelming ordinariness and conventionality. They actually provide no new departures from the fundamental character of the existing school system. What we see in the reports is little more than a set of proposals for schooling as usual: for technical training to meet industrial needs, for scientific preparation to combat the communist threat, for socialization to ensure discipline in the office or on the shop floor. What they advocate, more than anything, is more of what already exists rather than something profoundly different.[8]

Reforms aimed at restructuring are geared to a fundamental redesign of the present school model. Given the serious shortcomings identified with schools, the remedies must of necessity be dramatic. Consequently, these reforms call for a structural change of the basic foundations of the entire system. Advocates of this position reject the additive concept because it leaves the existing structure intact. The system itself causes a lack of productivity and a compromise with excellence. While the "add-on" strategy may be safer and politically more expedient, in the long run the situation will worsen.

Most state-initiated school reform legislation aimed at systemic improvements attempts to strengthen the existing structure, and may improve the total operation of the *present* system. Yet the present school system may be outmoded and strengthening it may add up to little more than an *improved old system. Accordingly, we end up with improving the very system that needs to be reformed.*

Those who claim the banner of systemic reform have in mind the creation of a new and hopefully more viable system to replace the old. Suppose that a similar call to excellence was made by our nation in relation to space flight and that a challenge by a foreign power makes this urgent. Such a call for excellence would no doubt include an invitation to those who fly conventional planes to suggest what they would need to fly existing vehicles into space. It is doubtful that a DC-10 or 747 airplane could embrace this new call for excellence. To be sure, the DC-10 or 747 could claim its own commitment to excellence given its nature and design, but to expect a DC-10 or 747, with improvements, to have the capacity for space travel would appear foolish.

It is just as far-fetched to expect an improved school system to meet demands of a new century. Just as in the case of a DC-10 or 747 attempting flight into space, even with extra engines and additional staff it could not yield the desired goal. A *new* school model is needed to achieve excellence in public education for a post-industrial nation. The schools, as the primary social infrastructure of society, is being asked to develop fully all the talents of the people and thus develop fully the human capital of the nation.

One proposal for restructuring the schools deals with deregulation in education, while another proposes a reconceptualized and comprehensive system of education linking together school and nonschool learning.

Deregulation A major policy initiative coming out of Washington in recent years concerns deregulation, which attempts to remove federal controls from business and industry in keeping with the principle that competition is the best stimulant for growth, effectiveness, and efficiency. Transportation and communication have been recently deregulated, no longer subject to federal rules and regulations but instead controlled by the free market system. This has caused increased competition among companies, price wars, and the development and proliferation of options and choices for the consumer. It has also resulted in considerable confusion for customers—for example, consumers in the New York metropolitan area are faced with the choice among eleven companies offering long distance telephone services. There have been a number of casualties—many airline companies now face bankruptcy.

The policy of deregulation can be expanded to include public education. Despite a tradition of local control of public education, the federal government has wielded considerable power and authority since the late 1950s, starting with the passage of the National Defense Education Act. Now, however, recent discussions about the lack of excellence in the public schools has lent impetus to considerations of decentralizing and deregulating education. The hope is that deregulation will help weed out mediocrity, reward effectiveness and efficiency, and restore excellence in the arena of public education. This new deregulatory emphasis offers a possibility for improving the public schools, returning power to localities, and restoring authority to parents.

The Voucher Plan Deregulation policy leads inevitably to an educational voucher plan, which has been gaining increased recognition in recent years with its emphasis on the free market principles of competition and choice in public education. Under this plan, the public schools are seen as part of "government," as state schools. This government style operation is one of the reasons for the bureaucracy and uniformity associated with them.

Under the voucher proposal, the cost of a year of education is determined and given to households with school-age children. Each child would be eligible for a voucher to be redeemed at a school of choice. It works something like the G.I. Bill, in which returning servicemen who qualify for admission to a school or college of choice have the cost of education fully or partially covered by the voucher.

This voucher system would eliminate what Dr. James R. Rinehart, Professor of Economics, considers education's primary problem:

> The primary problem appears to stem from a structural weakness in the public school system, namely, the absence of competition in the purchase, production, and delivery of education.[9]

Milton and Rose Friedman, often associated with the free marketplace scheme for education, believe that the public schools are controlled and regulated by government, which restricts the freedom of citizens to choose. The Friedmans suggest that competition and choice are the two forces around which to construct a new system of education. Since these forces have worked in the economic sphere, why not in the educational arena as well? In *Free to Choose*, the Friedmans provide their rationale and proposal for restructuring the public schools:

> At first, schools were private, and attendance was strictly voluntary. Increasingly, government came to play a larger role, first by contributing to financial support, later by establishing and administering government schools. The first compulsory attendance law was enacted by Massachusetts in 1852, but attendance did not become compulsory in all states until 1918. Government control was primarily local until well into the twentieth century. The neighborhood school, and control by the local school board, was the rule. Then a so-called reform movement got under way, particularly in the big cities, sparked by the wide differences in the ethnic and social composition of different school districts and by the belief that professional educators should play a larger role. That movement gained additional ground in the 1930s along with the general tendency toward both expansion and centralization of government.
>
> . . . Unfortunately, in recent years our educational record has become tarnished: Parents complain about the declining quality of the schooling their children receive. Many are even more disturbed about the dangers to their children's physical well-being. Teachers complain that the atmosphere in which they are required to teach is often not conducive to learning. Increasing numbers of teachers are fearful about their physical safety, even in the classroom. Taxpayers complain about growing costs. Hardly anyone maintains that our schools are giving the children the tools they need to meet the problems of life. Instead of fostering assimilation and harmony, our schools are increasingly a source of the very fragmentation that they earlier did so much to prevent.
>
> At the elementary and secondary level, the quality of schooling varies tremendously: outstanding in some wealthy suburbs of major metropolises, excellent or reasonably satisfactory in many small towns and rural areas, incredibly bad in the inner cities of major metropolises.
>
> . . . Public education is, we fear, suffering from the same malady as are so many of the programs discussed. . . . More than four decades ago Walter Lippmann diagnosed it as "the sickness of an over-governed society," the change

from "the older faith . . . that the exercise of unlimited power by men with limited minds and self-regarding prejudices is soon oppressive, reactionary, and corrupt, . . . that the very condition of progress was the limitation of power to the capacity and the virtue of rulers" to the newer faith "that there are no limits to man's capacity to govern others and that, therefore, no limitations ought to be imposed upon government."

For schooling, this sickness has taken the form of denying many parents control over the kind of schooling their children receive either directly, through choosing and paying for the schools their children attend, or indirectly, through local political activity. Power has instead gravitated to professional educators. The sickness has been aggravated by increasing centralization and bureaucratization of schools, especially in the big cities.

. . . Education is still another example, like Social Security, of the common element in authoritarian and socialist philosophies. Aristocratic and authoritarian Prussia and Imperial France were the pioneers in state control of education. Socialistically inclined intellectuals in the United States, Britain, and later Republican France were the major supporters of state control in their countries.

The establishment of the school system in the United States as an island of socialism in a free market sea reflected only to a very minor extent the early emergence among intellectuals of a distrust of the market and of voluntary exchange. Mostly, it simply reflected the importance that was attached by the community to the ideal of equality of opportunity. The ability of Horace Mann and his associates to tap that deep sentiment enabled them to succeed in their crusade.

. . . Schooling, even in the inner cities, does not have to be the way it is. It was not that way when parents had greater control. It is not that way now where parents still have control.

The strong American tradition of voluntary action has provided many excellent examples that demonstrate what can be done when parents have greater choice.

. . . One way to achieve a major improvement, to bring learning back into the classroom, especially for the currently most disadvantaged, is to give all parents greater control over their children's schooling, similar to that which those of us in the upper-income classes now have. Parents generally have both greater interest in their children's schooling and more intimate knowledge of their capacities and needs than anyone else. Social reformers, and educational reformers in particular, often self-righteously take for granted that parents, especially those who are poor and have little education themselves, have little interest in their children's education and no competence to choose for them. That is a gratuitous insult. Such parents have frequently had limited opportunity to choose. However, U.S. history has amply demonstrated that, given the opportunity, they have often been willing to sacrifice a great deal, and have done so wisely, for their children's welfare.

No doubt, some parents lack interest in their children's schooling or the capacity and desire to choose wisely. However, they are in a small minority. In any event, our present system unfortunately does little to help their children.

One simple and effective way to assure parents greater freedom to choose, while at the same time retaining present sources of finance, is a voucher plan. Suppose your child attends a public elementary or secondary school. On the average, countrywide, it cost the taxpayer—you and me—about $2,000 per year in 1978 for every child enrolled. If you withdraw your child from a public school and send him to a private school, you save taxpayers about $2,000 per year—but you get no part of that saving except as it is passed on to all taxpayers, in which case it would amount to at most a few cents off your tax bill. You have to pay private tuition in addition to taxes—a strong incentive to keep your child in a public school.

Suppose, however, the government said to you: "If you relieve us of the expense of schooling your child, you will be given a voucher, a piece of paper redeemable for a designated sum of money, if, and only if, it is used to pay the cost of schooling your child at an approved school." The sum of money might be $2,000, or it might be a lesser sum, say $1,500 or $1,000, in order to divide the saving between you and the other taxpayers. But whether the full amount or the lesser amount, it would remove at least a part of the financial penalty that now limits the freedom of parents to choose.

The voucher plan embodies exactly the same principle as the G.I. bills that provide for educational benefits to military veterans. The veteran gets a voucher good only for educational expense and he is completely free to choose the school at which he uses it, provided that it satisfies certain standards.[10]

The Education Voucher Institute of Framingham, Michigan, promoters of the voucher idea, have identified the reasons for the lack of a more widespread implementation of the plan, including opposition from the public school establishment. However, poor people and those who are viewed as conservative might be the prime supporters of more choices for their children in the future.[11]

Comprehensive School to Comprehensive Education Another proposal that deals with the restructuring of the public schools is *The Education of Adolescents* by the National Panel on High Schools and Adult Education. The Panel concluded that the educational needs of learners cannot be met even in an improved school system and that an educational system must be set up linking school and non-school settings. This proposal calls for a dramatic restructuring:

The goals of comprehensive education cannot all be achieved inside schools. The responsibilities for comprehensive education cannot be placed upon schools alone. If the school is to be relieved of the sense of responsibility of solving most, if not all of the social ills and problems of the country, then it must find ways of sharing the learning time of students with educative agencies and institutions.

Implied above is that in the process of creating comprehensive education we cannot default on our prudential concern for the welfare of students. We have mechanisms and even some defensible experience for oversight of high school students moving between the school and other agencies. The application of these experiences onto a much larger scale of operations is possible and desirable.

. . . The tradition of keeping the schools free from political meddling in order to protect the curriculum and the staff from the baleful effects of vested interests and patronage have unfortunately reinforced the isolation of the schools from all other educational enterprises.

. . . Concentrating education in the high school has also produced the excessive isolation of adolescents from all other age groups in our society. Insulating our youngest adults from contact with older generations has resulted in a breakdown in the transmission mechanisms of society. A disconnected youth society or subculture characterized by rapid change and generational hostilities has resulted.

. . . Despite the evidence of the earlier maturation of adolescents by two years in the last seventy, the schools have been required to continue a costly custodial responsibility for a school day twice as long as needed or actually used in formal instruction. We baby-sit, at very high cost during the day, the nation's nighttime baby-sitters: we trust our infants to their care, but impose childish and costly controls over them.

. . . Our expanding knowledge of human growth and development calls for the recognition that learning patterns, organizations for instruction, size of groups involved, the effectiveness of peer tutoring, the development of teachers and aides, the role of on-the-site learning as well as the proliferation of knowledge in traditional subjects make the conventional conception of the high school as the single container for formal learning an impossible constriction on programs, teachers, and administrators.[12]

The report goes on to state that certain shortcomings of the present school system must be addressed in the new educational system:

a. Reduce the isolation of the high school and the imposition of sole source obligations upon it.
b. Reduce the isolation of adolescents by opening learning centers for adolescents and other adults apart from the high school.
c. Reduce the isolation of adolescents by facilitating their early and increased part-time entry into the work force.
d. Provide for the great range in human differences in learning behaviors, needs, and interests through the development of new organizational forms, groups, and places for education.
e. Examine and expand the role of the media as both formal and informal transmitters of education. Sesame Street for adults is shorthand for saying that mastering the graphic, dramatic, script, and directing requirements of the several media for educational use has scarcely begun. Films, radio, and TV are currently minor and peripheral inside formal education. They are already powerful instruments with significant educational consequences outside the schools. Formal use for teaching outside the schools needs greater examination. Physics, or history, or consumer buying, or most of all for-

mal subjects can be "taught" through the use of dramatic, graphic, media techniques developed by television and radio.

f.   Recognize that establishing nonschool centers for complementary programs in education will require, as a consequence, changes in accrediting procedures. The old Carnegie unit with time and grade as the basis for high school graduation, for college admission, and for a job will need to be supplemented by recognition of the validity of experience and training outside the school and classroom. We would conclude that the agency needed for these purposes should be autonomous, not responsible to the high school alone, a counseling and educational evaluating agency for a whole community. Guidance counselors, psychometricians, and other auxiliary personnel need to become client-centered evaluators of all learning whether school administered, on-the-job learned, self taught, or learned through special participation in the adult world.[13]

As a result, this proposal goes on to advance a set of recommendations aimed at fundamentally altering the structure of public schools:

1.   That we replace the unattained practice and inadequate concept of the comprehensive high school with the more practical goal of providing comprehensive education through a variety of means including the schools.

     The first has sought to impose on a single institution all the variations in programs and services that the needs of an extraordinarily diverse population required. It has resulted in oversized institutions increasingly difficult to manage, artificially held to narrow pedagogic practices, overburdened with custodial responsibility, and isolated from the community.

2.   That we inaugurate educational programs for the joint participation of adolescents and other interested and qualified adults in the community. Thus we call for pedagogical programs which may be designated *Participatory Education* (learning, by doing what is socially useful, personally satisfying, and health-supporting for the individual and the community).

     We see three major areas of education that lend themselves to such combined participation—education in the arts, vocational education, and education in the operations of government.

     For educating in the arts, we would recommend the creation of a community arts center closely associated with the high school. Governed and sponsored by a Community Council for the Arts, the center would provide facilities and support for all the arts and crafts for which sustaining interest was forthcoming. Local amateurs and professionals, voluntary assistants and paid personnel would compete for program space for and instruction in sculpturing, dancing, photography, weaving, painting, interior design, and macrame for day and night programs. By enrolling adolescents and other more mature adults including grandparents, we envision that the re-integration of the generations should bring new vitality to learning, to the arts, and to community cohesion in activities where age is the most irrelevant of criteria for participation.

We recommend the creation of a Community Career Education Center. This agency would be the vehicle for new forms of vocational education such as reducing emphasis upon job training in the high school and increasing work experience, on-the-job training, job finding resources, and career information activities, all located and carried on in the community. We would urge the removal of those regulations except for safety and health regulations including tax and insurance penalties that handicap and limit the employment of adolescents. We would not urge the special reduction of the minimum wage laws. Using youth to displace the marginally employed, the old, and the handicapped, or as a competitive source of cheap labor, is a disservice to both the economy and to education. With half the high school age group already in the work force, our suggestions are to facilitate the growth of employment opportunities for still more as a necessary adjuct to formal education. It is in the market place that post-pubertal youth has a traditional place for learning economic responsibility, the first abc's of job-holding diplomacy, of new adult roles, beyond the models of family and school. We are not arguing the virtues of a work ethic, rather the removal of the artificial delay in education for maturity, which the segregated grouping of the high school has innocently imposed. We see the need for coordination between manpower-training programs, federally supported, and much vocational education in the schools. Given the startlingly poor results found by cost-benefit studies of conventional vocational education, we recommend that federal and state subsidies for in-school shop classes be made transferable at local option to various on-the-job training, job placement, and job subsidy programs.

The education of citizens for a republic is central to the concept of education, as much for us as it was for Plato. The Panel recommends that adolescents, in addition to the academic study of the social sciences and their methodology, should be involved in government—in all appropriate agencies within the larger community. The involvement should be diverse: voluntary, including internships to specific positions; aides; part-time employees at appropriate wage scales; and observation for short-term study assignments tied to school seminars and classes.

In addition, schools themselves must be collateral training places for such immediate participation in society. Student participation with faculty and administration in the affairs of the school that affect students should not be a governance charade under adult sufferance. New models of responsibility-taking by youth are imperative: If we manage schools by fiat, we train citizens in docility, revolt, or indifferent submission. The goal is selfhood and active citizenship, which cannot be served or reached by persons unengaged in the conduct of their lives. A self-governing republic requires much of its members. They must be willing and able to serve themselves and their commonwealth.

The schools need to be the *laboratories-for-error* in learning the roles of citizens. This means realistic participation in the operation and management of the school. It is the only fail-safe institution available for learning the consequences of neglect, venality, and the appeals of power. Studied experiments in such consequences should be part of the school's curriculum in citizenship.

Finally, every community needs a permanent group of citizen volunteers, including adolescents, whose functions should be to observe, investigate, and publicly to report on all government operations, not as tattletales but as concerned citizens. Their range of concerns would be all that local interests combined with talent could sustain. But the function of citizen inquiry into government needs reinforcement, and the leaven of older adults with adolescents' idealism should be helpful to the political health of any town (and safeguards that students do not become "Red Guards").

One cannot teach about, learn about, or experience citizenship without behaving politically. One cannot care about the consequences of public behavior, of public policy-decisions, without having developed an "engaged" political sense. Therefore, a pedagogy of citizenship is essential and should be required for all institutions of adolescent education, which would have among its outcomes civility, caring, cooperativeness, nonaversive criticism and with emphasis on a lively concern for the common good in real situations, in and out of school.

3. That in addition to these three major programs in the arts, vocational, and citizenship education, we recommend the establishment of small, flexible and short-term, part-time schools open to all those qualified and interested. For example, a writers' school open daily for afternoon and evening sessions for small seminars and tutorial sessions staffed by professional writers and teachers in such fields as journalism, poetry, drama, fiction, and political advocacy. If talents and interests warranted, mathematics, astronomy, and nature study schools could be sponsored among the many other fields of human learning.

4. That we concentrate compulsory daily attendance from an all-day session to an academic day of 2-4 hours. On the operational theory of gradualism, the Panel recommends such initial steps as reducing all-day attendance requirements for seniors, then as experience warrants, adding more. Reducing the school day without providing complementary educational activities in the community with other adults is not recommended.

    With a high school academic day of 2-4 hours, every adolescent on some days of the week could be deeply involved in one or more "schools," or programs, or work, or service as a co-equal part of his or her education. Real learning takes intensity and time. Two to four hours a day several days a week, or daily, is a necessary concentration of effort by the musician, football player, dancer, politician, or scientist. The present all-day high school is a costly intruder on this need for both time and program variety. We see these new institutions and programs as complementary rather than as competitive alternatives. Hopefully the number of non-high school options will exceed by far any individual's available time.

5. That we reemphasize the basic role of the high school as society's only universal institution for the education of the intellect.

    By casting off those activities and responsibilities which have accrued through the years, we believe the resources of the high school can be concentrated in such areas of maturing intellectual competency as learning to write in clear prose, to be proficient in the arithmetic of handling and budgeting money, to be competent in using the resources of the public library, to be able to assemble information from a variety of sources germane to an area of personal and community concern. Rationality, orderly inquiry, the patient accumulation of skills, the testing of ideas, the measuring of current experiences against the fields of literature and history, the rare and wonderful teacher who can become the right mentor and model, we are, as a Panel, cautiously in agreement, that all of these are more likely to happen in a formal school than in any other "arranged" learning environment or within the tribal occasions of "peer groups." Directing the focus of the high school's efforts on them will come only with the reduction in the global goals of secondary education. There must be a careful removal of some ancillary functions and services that are not centrally educative and supportive of the high school's mission. We must create functional descriptions of literacy and test for such performance. Charge the schools with teaching all citizens how to "read" the press, the periodicals, the radio, the cinema, television, and each other. Education through the media is at least as powerfully formative of attitudes as formal schooling and may be more decisive in setting values, tastes, public behavior standards, and the consumer habits of the economy. We are too accustomed to school courses whose outcomes are inferred though rarely assured. That is, we assume that the study of history will add to a citizen's capacity to understand current affairs; we assume that the study of a foreign language will produce some conversational competence in that tongue as well as some degree of affection for those for whom the language is native; we assume the study of mathematics beyond arithmetic computation will train the mind in logic, inference, and the difference between inductive and deductive reasoning. But the evidence is heavily to the contrary. It is our hope that the removal of non-academic "fat" will result in a needed lean and earnest devotion to the development of a maturing intellect.

6. That we establish a Community Guidance Center. Move such qualified personnel as counselors, psychologists, social workers, and technicians in the construction, administration, and analysis of test and other evaluative procedures from the high school and other agencies into a new center independent of educational agencies. The center would serve as an evaluator of educational results obtained from whatever source. With opportunities for learning available from school, work, study, the media, and community service, it is important to develop and locate the means for accrediting acquired competencies and skills in an agency whose allegiance is to the learner and not to the instructional source. Employers and colleges are under pressure from the courts and from experienced and responsible critics to recognize that Carnegie unit transcripts are less predictive than direct statements descriptive of a candidate's relevant proficiencies to the job or academic success. Establishing a new agency to serve as evaluator and ombudsman will bring greater realism to the efforts of all educational pro-

grams including those of the school. Moving youth in and out of high school on part-time, full-time, and intermittent schedules creates the need for a coordinating organization discharging the responsibility we usually subsume under the term, *in loco parentis*. This kind of organization would coordinate the movement of adolescents through time and space into relationships with the organizations in which instruction and planned learning take place. It would function to guide that movement (or arrange for such guidance). It would maintain prudential concern for where students are during their "school" hour and be concerned with the evaluation of learning. But rather than having the task of teaching, of being the educational delivery service, its function would be the arranging for delivery of service: scheduling, evaluating, registering, monitoring, and continuously communicating information on adolescent education to their students, their teachers, and the public. (National Assessment revised for local use is a beginning module for such an organization.)

7. The local educational agencies need to understand that all the preceding recommendations are to be considered as working hypotheses to be rigorously tested through small scale adaptations, careful monitoring, and ruthless evaluation.

8. That citizen and adolescent participation in planning and reviewing change in education is vital to its installation and maintenance.[14]

Such a basic reformation, in which the educative functions are shared between the school and its community, involves such serious redefinitions that they present as much of a threat to the existing school system as the voucher plan. This is why plans of this kind are not adopted—too many people are threatened, and resistance is high.

The voucher plan is often accused of dismantling the public school system to the extent of fostering its demise. The community as educator plan retains the public school system but joins other educative agents and agencies in the community to the system. Both are viewed as radical, yet elements of both survive in the school reform movement and in the concept of excellence.

We are left with a conundrum. If a direction based on improving our current school system is implementable but inadequate, and if restructuring efforts are adequate but non-implementable, then what is our choice? Decisions concerning the appropriate course of action to take in order to restore excellence to education in the United States are ultimately political in nature.

THE POLITICS OF REFORM AND CONVERSION

Bringing about holistic change in the form of restructuring is difficult. Systemic reform through restructuring affects everyone in the system. This means that there are people within the system who will oppose it for very personal reasons—what happens to me under this plan—and by people whose interests may not be furthered by the plan. In other words, all of the plans for implementation must be brought about by political process. This is true at the local level and at all other levels of government—regional, state, and federal.

The voucher plan for reformation of the schools—which would fundamentally alter the structure of the public schools by introducing choice and competition into it—has been proposed in Michigan, California, Minnesota, and Tennessee. However, in each case, it has been systematically defeated politically. Teachers' organizations and many citizens have opposed it on the grounds that it would bring about an ultimate demise to the public school system which has for so long served the common needs of society. At local levels, new ideas have found support in the hands of some and not others, resulting in a political tug-of-war.

This is why change has not always been as successful as anticipated and why many people who review proposals, whether policymakers or parents, who believe they make sense on paper and who then support them, find out later on that they were not fully implemented. It is one thing to talk about concepts and to analyze, refine, and manipulate them in the abstract. When they reach the real world, they are dramatically transformed and do not appear to be anywhere near the original idea. Consequently, all change is political and must undergo a political process—involving participation of interested parties, gaining consensus, establishing appropriate policies, and being translated into action. It is the translation into action phase that affects the people in the front lines of the school system, such as teachers, administrators, support staff, and community. Most of the people inside the system need retraining and a period of conversion from what they are presently doing to what the proposal suggests they would be doing. People do not automatically acquire the behaviors associated with the new system; they need time to move from the old to the new. This time is seldom provided for in most reform legislation. What has taken years to inbreed in people, the ways of the old system, is often assumed to be dropped with the new. These people need to work out all of the roles associated with the new system to help form a totally new social structure, that once in place, will become a primary force for shaping how the people will behave in the new system. Unless this happens, the tendency will be for people to assume the old behaviors. Many ideas, therefore, begin to falter because they have not had time to take hold and be nurtured.

Political and organizational factors need to be considered when talking about holistic change. During the period of transition, attention needs to be given to the people who have to learn new behaviors so they can work out their concerns and anxieties associated with the transformation. This anxiety, this resistance to change, is natural. Any serious effort at reform must deal with it. When people talk about "quick fix," they sometimes refer to the idea that a proposal is made and enacted by legislation. The assumption is that as soon as it is law, the proposal begins and soon effects can be assessed. But there is a developmental process that has to take place, and those who are eager for immediate results will be disappointed because what they are assessing is really the effects of the transition. The actual system—the new system—has not actually been put in place and cannot be assessed or evaluated. Too often a good idea which is being translated into action is dismissed as ineffective because the assessments were premature. The end result is that whatever is operational tends to remain operational.

If an idea for a whole new delivery of educational services is reviewed on paper with every aspect of the system worked out, then it is assumed that what was on paper will be associated with the implementation. Very seldom does theory translate into practice. For example, in New York during the late 1960s, decentralized public schools were proposed. The initial proposals on the decentralization were not the proposals finally implemented, yet the concept of decentralization remained, and those that had talked about the concept of decentralization initially were disappointed in what was finally implemented. Those who were at the implementation stage assumed that the concept of decentralization was indeed implemented and that the results were not always what the proposers of the reform had envisioned. In reality, there were two different concepts of the proposal: one that was made on paper and one that actually became operational.

While every state in our nation is now engaged in school improvement, the form and shape of these reforms differ markedly and are in large measure a function of the particular political process operating in each state. Consequently, while there is political consensus on the need for reform, there are deep political differences as to the nature and direction of that reform.

Historically, the issue becomes ironical. The need for reform becomes so acute as to call for further legislative initiatives. Yet, the political and economic realities that are always present motivate policymakers to modify these plans. The result too often does not attain the productivity expected, which further frustrates students, parents, and citizens who had assumed that the school reform passed by their elected officials was destined to solve the problem. The situation gets worse, forcing a new round of crisis-oriented activities leading to a new set of school reform proposals which in turn are subjected to the same forces.

While this process is taking place, frustrated parents may exercise the option of sending their children to private schools, the so-called middle-class exodus from urban public schools. Finally, desperate efforts, such as legal actions, court ordered rulings, and parent and student boycotts emerge.

A new vision of excellence presupposes accepting the notion that the present school system may not be able to fulfill this new mission. This does not, of course, mean scrapping the present public system of schooling. It still serves well the needs of many. Given the diversity and pluralism in the United States, it is unrealistic and unnecessary to expect an across-the-board thrust for a newer model of public education. The aim is the *conversion* from the old to the new. In the process, those who want to remain with the present model of schooling should have the right to do so. Those who seek options to the present structure should have the same right. Unlike the old standardized and uniform public school system, the newer version includes options and choice; it is not simply imposing one orthodoxy for another.

The first step is to make contact with *the system as it is.* School improvement proposals have been politically viable partly because they do not threaten the existing arrangements—there is no expectation of dramatic fundamental change. School improvement proposals are the first step of a visionary modernization plan. The politics of modernization calls for integrating school improvement with restructuring initiatives to form a new synthesis.

If the evidence suggests that excellence may not be achieved with the present school system or even an improved one, and if plans such as the free market system of education are too controversial for implementation, is there a system that can be based on the best of both the old and newer state-of-the-art trends? The present school system cannot produce the new goals to which the nation has dedicated itself and even improving the present system will not be enough. Then what? While a totally new model that delivers excellence and that can be examined, does not in practice exist, we know a great deal about the elements that may go into a new model. We also can examine many of these elements in the field because components of the new system are part of the older school system. These components reflect contemporary knowledge and, if allowed to develop, possess the capacity for contributing significantly to the remodeling of education. Much more than "innovative pieces" aimed at making the existing structure work better, they are the building blocks of a new model. Many are at crucial stages of cultivation within the older system. Needing further nurturing to continue growing, they may be overpowered by the weight of the existing structure. That is why the current debate on school reform and excellence is so important. Public policy can either enable these components to advance, or it can contribute significantly to their decline. No serious school reform package can create a completely new public system of education alongside the existing school system. All reform begins with the existing system, even those that over time are designed to create a new contemporary model. This is an evolutionary process with revolutionary impact. The best strategy is to synthesize school improvement with restructuring reform, as John Goodlad advises us. This is the process of *modernization.*

Leadership is essential for this synthesis. The involvement of business and industry with school reform makes them not only knowledgeable parties about but also powerful processors of model reform. When they speak, political officials listen. Professional and civic associations and officials from higher education are also influential participants. These voices need to be coordinated on behalf of sound educational reform.

Educational, political, and economic conditions appear to be ripe for an investment in a redesigned system of education. Fortunately, we need not scrap the old while we build the new. The old still needs to carry most of the burden despite its shortcomings. This is why school improvement is a necessary stage in the multiphased process of modernization. School improvement is not an *end* but a *means* to the ultimate restructuring and remodeling of education. If school improvement becomes an end rather than a means, a once-in-a-century opportunity for designing a new human learning paradigm will be missed. The public schools as agencies of the government must depend on new policies for their survival or they will decline.

NOTES

1. John A. Scileppi, *A Systems View of Education: A Model for Change* (Lanham, Maryland: University Press of America, 1984), 1.

2. John I. Goodlad, *A Place Called School: Prospects for the Future* (New York: McGraw-Hill Book Company, 1984), xvi.

3. Scileppi, *A Systems View of Education: A Model for Change,* 3.

4. Mario D. Fantini and Gerald Weinstein, *The Disadvantaged: Challenge to Education* (New York: Harper and Row, Publishers, 1968).

5. Emily Feistritzer, "Commentary," *National Center for Education Information Reports,* 24 June 1985, 7.

6. Harvey A. Averch, Stephen J. Carroll, Theodore S. Donaldson, Herbert J. Kiesling, and John Pincus, *How Effective Is Schooling? A Critical Review of Research* (Englewood Cliffs, New Jersey: Educational Technology Publications/The Rand Corporation, 1974), 173.

7. John Naisbitt and Patricia Aburdene, *Re-Inventing the Corporation* (New York: Warner Books, Inc., 1985), 166.

8. Svi Shapiro, "Choosing Our Educational Legacy: Disempowerment or Emancipation?" *Issues in Education,* Vol. II, No. 1, Summer 1984, 12–13.

9. *Forum,* January 1985, 28.

10. Milton and Rose Friedman, "What's Wrong With Our Schools," Chapter 6, *Free to Choose: A Personal Statement* (New York: Harcourt Brace Jovanovich, Inc., 1979), 140–151.

11. Chris Pipho, "Student Choice: The Return of the Voucher," *Phi Delta Kappan,* March 1985, 461–462.

12. Mario D. Fantini and Anita Moses (editors), *Resources for Improving Education: A Study Guide for Educational Administrators* (Fort Lauderdale: Nova University, 1976), 98–100.

13. *Ibid.,* 100.

14. *Ibid.,* 101–106.

State-of-the-Art Principles to Guide Reform Efforts 5

CURRICULUM AS LEARNING ENVIRONMENTS

Many recent studies have recommended action in the area of curriculum: reemphasizing basics and established standards, more testing, more homework, more hours in the school day, and more days in the academic year. The reports also recommend a stronger interest in mathematics, science, computer literacy, and languages as part of a greater emphasis on international cooperation and multicultural orientation. There is also an increasing educational concern with environmental, energy, and nuclear war issues. Responsibility for health and nutrition has moved to the school, with such courses as family life, sex education, and values. Career education and continuing, nonformal education (lifelong learning) are also growing in importance.[1]

Many states involved with school reform are mandating a basic curriculum, competency testing, and school-based accountability. Some states are also calling for continuous staff development and curricular updating through re-accreditation programs. Concurrent with these efforts are cutbacks in curriculum due to economics and politics, which creates debate on what constitutes a basic curriculum and what is extracurricular—useful but expendable—during periods of fiscal constraint.

In part, this conflict can be compared to the private sector's concern with efficiency and productivity. In the "taxpayers' revolt" of the 1970s and early 1980s, taxes which either held steady or were cut supplied funding and material resources for the public schools.[2] Areas not considered basic—such as music, art, physical education—were curtailed in many communities as efficiency measures. Schoolpeople have been forced to seek alternative sources of funding or to tap resources in the community. Community personnel and resources are increasingly being used in schools to fund extracurricular subjects, such as artists to provide art education, health care professionals in health education programs, business and industry personnel for technological and career education, and recreation departments for physical education and club activities.

Short-term trends contain seeds of long-run emphases in education reform: the recent emphasis on early childhood education reflects the attitude of prevention over cure in the fields of human service; the advent of user-friendly technology provides tools for learners to gain control of their own education; and the priority given to the traditional basics is a positive response to the national call for the restoration of excellence.

However, the problem with this reform agenda is not only its narrow focus but the expectation that excellence can be implemented within the traditional structure of the public schools. This dated structure perpetuates dichotomies that mediate against the attainment of excellence in modern education. Among the most critical is the separation of quality from equality—quality in the traditional structure comes at the expense of equality. The present system by nature produces dichotomies between management and labor, school and community, special education and regular education, and adults and youth in our society.

The short-term trends in school curriculum exist in the context of larger and more fundamental changes affecting the overall structure. Long-range trends involve a basic reconceptualization of curriculum, not simply as subject matter but as an *environment for learning*. While the short-term trends emphasize academic subjects, the long-term emphasis will be on competencies themselves—behaviors that are judged to represent the achievement of the standards. The present emphasis on *input*—the subject matter, the courses—will gradually give way to *output*—the actual demonstration through performance of the objectives sought.[3]

STATE-OF-THE-ART THINKING: IMPLICATIONS FOR EXCELLENCE AND REFORM

Basic to a modern system of education is the application of state-of-the-art knowledge generated by research, new theoretical formulations, and experience. The school system must assume the responsibility for reviewing and identifying procedures that appear to be more productive and applying these procedures for the benefit of the learner; schoolpeople exposed to new ideas that appear to work have a moral responsibility to assess and apply those ideas. However, employing one effective procedure in a context that itself is antiquated may diminish effectiveness. Identifying a new procedure does not, of itself, guarantee its success, since it is dependent on many factors, including the context in which the procedure is being tested or applied. The purpose of this section is to identify a set of state-of-the-art concepts which, if applied in a coordinated fashion, will significantly increase the possibility of achieving excellence.

ALL PEOPLE CAN LEARN

The first concept, the first principle of human development, is that *all people can learn under the right conditions*, and it is the responsibility of effective organizations to determine the right condition for each and every learner. Ronald Edmonds, whose research on school effectiveness has been cited earlier, indicates that "all children are eminently educable. . . . the behavior of the school is critical in determining the quality of that education."[4] Programs can be organized to fit individual learners. With the recognition of the theory of stimulus response comes the concept of programming the environment to be productive with individual learners. While each learner is unique, each also possesses the capacity to learn: there are no non-learners.

Ralph W. Tyler, the noted researcher, summarizes the conditions for effective learning:[5]

1. Motivation
2. Clear Learning Objectives
3. Appropriate Learning Tasks
4. Confidence that Supports Willingness to Attempt the Task
5. Rewards and Feedback
6. Sequential Practice
7. Transfer

Tyler observes that

Some children are called non-learners, but close observation reveals that these children are learning. They may not be learning what the school seeks to teach. They may be learning to play basketball, to gain friends, to do other things that seem important to them, and appear to be impervious to teaching in the classroom, or in the home, or in the Scout meeting. But they are learning.[6]

Psychologists such as B. F. Skinner experimented with the concept that anything that can be conceptualized can be learned, and therefore anything can be learned if the environment is prepared accordingly. Experiments with animals proved that the right environmental conditions caused desired responses. The same principle applied to the educational system means that whatever goals were being considered are made explicit and environmental programs are designed to achieve those goals. If a program does not achieve the intended goals, then it is redesigned until it does. There are no learner failures, only program failures. If one curriculum is not effective, then another one must be employed and, if necessary, another and still another until one is found. This concept has been extended to learners considered handicapped. Public Law 94–182, the so-called "Bill of Rights for Handicapped Learners," guarantees every handicapped child a "less restrictive environment," specially designed through an individual program.

CHOICE

Since all learners can learn under the right conditions and since there are no learner failures, only program failures, a second state-of-the-art concept is that people should have choices from among a number of legitimate learning environments and that there should be an attempt to match the environment to the learner. Consequently, *choice* and *alternatives* and *options* become essential to a modern system.

We have been through several decades of alternative education, including alternative schools and schools-within-schools.[7] If one learner did not respond to Program A, the learner had access to Program B and, if necessary, to Program C—all by choice. In the standard organization, not all learners were expected to learn. Indeed, if all learners learned, there would be some question about the standards used because conventional wisdom suggested that only those most capable succeed, while all the others fail. Under more democratic thinking, the schools attempted to include more learners; on the basis of equality of opportunity, schools developed procedures such as tracking in which all students were given the opportunity to remain in school but were not given access to the same quality education. John Goodlad and others have suggested that the tracking system stratifies the learning population and differentiates qualitatively among learners so that inequality is perpetuated. The principle that there are no learner failures—only program failures—is the opposite of conventional school wisdom. If learners do not learn, then the problem is with them and with their background. The only alternatives provided are "tracks." Learners unable to succeed in the fast track are placed in successively slower tracks and are not exposed to the same content as those in the more academically oriented tracks—the quality of the tracks differ.[8]

True alternative education legitimizes alternative environments that are different means to common ends. For example, an alternative education based on choice might include a traditional environment, a non-graded environment, and a Montessori environment. These three different settings offer three different concepts of education based on legitimate theoretical and pedagogical considerations. Teachers equally well prepared in each alternative could offer legitimate options as a means of achieving the common goals.

Another major proposal that emphasizes choice is the voucher plan advocated by such prominent economists as Milton Friedman. Each student or family would be entitled to a voucher for the cost of up to one year of schooling, redeemable in a school of the family's choice—public or private. Education would become a competitive, free market enterprise and would increase the purchasing power of educational consumers while also increasing the supply of options available to them. Productive schools would gain more customers and succeed, while those less productive would go out of business. Those who advocate the voucher and tuition tax credit plans view present public schools as government-supported public utilities devoid of the competitive forces that operate in the private sector. The voucher plan would introduce competition and choice into the structure of education.

MULTIPLE INTELLIGENCE OR TALENTS

A responsive education system is accountable for identifying and cultivating a learner's talents. There might be one learner who is gifted in planning, another in leadership, in humor, mathematics, or human relations. All these talents differ among individuals. The ability to be sensitive to these talents becomes very important since these talents, if recognized and fostered, become the basis for the learner's ability to formulate a positive self-concept, to develop a sense of personal power, and to obtain the recognition needed to feel inter-connected with others in society.

On the other hand, if there is a reliance on one type of talent only—such as intellectual functioning or talent in mathematics—then there are many individuals who will have a difficult time competing successfully. Those who may have an enormous talent in human relations or in humor, for example, but who may not adapt as quickly in the traditional intellectual areas, may be at a complete disadvantage in the competitive environment of the school. This may damage the learner's self-concept, creating a feeling of powerlessness. The recognition of multiple talents and different modes of intelligence provides an inclusive view that is much more cognizant of human experience.

In *Frames of Mind: The Theory of Multiple Intelligence*,[9] Howard Gardner identifies and describes seven distinct areas of human ability or intelligence: linguistic, musical, logical-mathematical, spatial, bodily-kinesthetic, and two modes of personal intelligence including both interpersonal and intrapersonal abilities. Gardner's theory of multiple intelligences challenges the traditional definitions and tests of intelligence that focus mainly, if not exclusively, on linguistic and logical-mathematical abilities. As Gardner explains:

> Most people in our society, even if they know better, talk as if individuals could be assessed in terms of one dimension, namely how smart or dumb they are. This is deeply ingrained in us. I became convinced some time ago that such a narrow assessment was wrong in scientific terms and had seriously damaging social consequences. In *Frames of Mind*, I describe seven ways of viewing the world; I believe they're equally important ways, and if they don't exhaust all possible forms of knowing, they at least give us a more comprehensive picture than we've had until now. . . .
>
> Most intelligence tests assess the individual's abilities in those two areas. But my list also includes spatial intelligence. The core ability there is being able to find your way around an environment, to form mental images and to transform them readily. Musical intelligence is concerned with the ability to perceive and create pitch patterns and rhythmic patterns. The gift of fine motor improvement, as you might see in a surgeon or a dancer, is a root component of bodily-kinesthetic intelligence. . . . Interpersonal involves understanding others—how they feel, what motivates them, how they interact with one another. Intrapersonal intelligence centers on the individual's ability to be acquainted with himself or herself, to have a developed sense of identity.[10]

Whether we are talking about multiple intelligences or multiple talents, the implications for the learner are profound. The kind of organization needed if one considers the multiplicity of intelligence or talent would differ markedly from what exists today. For example, recognition for those talented in the arts seems confined to the fringes. In the value structure of the school, those who perform well in academic subjects, especially science and math, are the ones who most fully reap the benefits of the present school culture.

FATE CONTROL

Fate control—the ability of the learner to control his or her own fate—is central to increased motivation. In his comprehensive study, *Equality of Educational Opportunity*, James Coleman[11] found fate control to be most powerful in determining success. If one is pushed to "the margins" as Robert Sinclair and Ward Ghory[12] have defined it, then the sense of assuming control over one's own development becomes severely restricted. Conversely, a sense of success in school may help learners acquire the internal sense that they have the capacity to control their own destinies. If the only criterion for success is the ability to do well on standardized tests, that factor alone may condition the learner's self-perception and sense of fate control. The idea that every learner is able to learn and create the conditions for success becomes essential to fate control.

THE PSYCHOLOGY OF INDIVIDUAL DIFFERENCES AND HUMAN DIVERSITY

The psychological concept of normal and abnormal behavior viewed in absolute terms has given way to the recognition of individual differences and human diversity. To subject masses of unique people to standardization develops a discontinuity between individuals and the environment. To be sure, many can adjust to any environment, but many more cannot. Each person must have an opportunity to reach an individual maximum level of efficiency. It is not enough that certain learners reach great levels of efficiency; under an operational definition of excellence, all achieve it. The psychology of becoming—that is, the psychology of not only who you are but what you can become—is a realization of the dynamic nature of personality.

In the traditional school structure, a person who is having problems at the fifth grade or sixth grade level may be viewed as a risk in terms of future development and success in the school environment. The older psychologies—the orientation of the normal/abnormal psychology and the psychology of adjustment—are based on classification and labeling, from standardized tests associated with the notion of group norms. These standardized tests attempt to determine those who are able to adjust and achieve under certain norms, and those who are not. Their fixed scores are intended to reveal where the learner fits into the scheme of things. Such a classification system is meant to provide ways of grouping learners for instructional purposes through a series of labels such as slow learner, under-achiever, late bloomer, disadvantaged, and deprived. These labels become an intrinsic part of the normal operation of the organization. Teachers, administrators, and counselors use these labels. However, labeling human beings is a way of limiting them. We traditionally do not expect as much from those who are classified as slow as we do those who are classified as fast.

These expectations of the learner affect the learner's own aspirations (as documented by the self-fulfilling prophecy).[13] The result is devastating to the potentialities of learners. Yet people who have been classified as slow are able to achieve significantly. Albert Einstein, considered slow, a dropout from vocational school, became one of the giants of the 20th century with his Theory of Relativity. Many people who did poorly in school have made a significant contribution to society.

It becomes dangerous to forecast the degree of an individual's success or failure. The present structure, with its reliance on systems of human classification to determine entrance to programs, schools, and universities, is based on faulty knowledge. The operational assumptions in school assert that what we ought to promote are those who are working with their minds and try to gear those who are working with their hands to other kinds of activities. This amounts to *unequal education*, which, by definition, cannot be *excellent education*.

EVERYONE HAS THE RIGHT TO BE FULLY EDUCATED

All citizens in a free and just society have a right to be well-rounded, to possess a world view, to have all the academic and analytical tools to achieve a more complete state of becoming. How each individual chooses to exercise and explore this fundamental right is a different question.

Once, during a taxi ride from the airport in New York to downtown Manhattan, I talked to a taxi driver who was insightful and extremely informative. Impressed, I asked where he had gone to school, and learned that he had completed his master's degree at a local university. Applying traditional thinking, I asked, "You have a master's degree and you are driving a taxi cab. Why?" He turned around and asked, "What's wrong with an *educated* taxi driver? What's wrong with an educated butcher?" Everyone has a fundamental right to a quality education; a limited education restricts human potential.

The recent debate over general education focuses on what each learner must possess to be prepared to become all he or she is capable of becoming. True equality in education is the ability of all people to attain quality, but the traditional structure has not been able to fulfill these goals. Efforts to achieve equality have resulted in massive remedial or compensatory public policy, trying to rehabilitate those who cannot adjust to the programs in the school because the problem is always perceived with the learner and not with the institution. The programs must be adjusted to fit for quality and equality to be achieved.

TELECOMMUNICATIONS AND THE POTENTIAL OF ELECTRONIC TEACHERS

The discovery of electronic learning tools has dramatically changed ways of processing and acquiring information. Computers, television, and other forms of electronic tools are now being used in schools and some youngsters who were not learning the basics under traditional methods are now achieving basic skills through the use of computers and electronics. Most studies of the effectiveness of computer assisted instruction (CAI) focus on how students' achievement and outcomes are affected. An analysis conducted by James Kulik and his colleagues at the University of Michigan showed that secondary school students who received CAI scored higher on objective tests than those students who received only traditional instruction. Kulik's analysis also revealed that CAI improved retention and speed at which students learn. Studies conducted by the Educational Testing Service, working in collaboration with the Los Angeles Unified School District over a four-year period, found CAI was also effective in compensatory education for students in grades 1–6.[14] Computer instruction can also have affective/motivational outcomes, enabling students to move at their own pace and avoid both peer pressure and embarrassment over mistakes.

The advent of interactive television carries with it a host of new possibilities. Television is now the major tool by which people gather information and learn the actual culture of society. The present generation is the first generation to have been weaned on television programming and its responsive style of entertaining. To stay competitive, programming has to hold the viewer's attention. The computer, to attract and hold attention, has to be user-friendly. Clearly, this is not the case with school. School is not there to entertain; the entertaining style of television and the didactic nature of school are diametrically opposed.

The other aspect of television and electronic communications is speed. Television brings the viewer anywhere in the world in a matter of seconds. Instant replay is taken for granted. Computers are capable of achieving solutions to problems in microseconds. All this has an impact on the psychoneurological structure of children. They are greatly influenced by electronic time. They like things that are fast—fast music, fast foods, fast cars—because they have been socialized to speed as a part of the electronic age.

The school's orientation to time is different. At best, activity in the classroom moves at the speed of sound. Students' lack of interest in school has to do with different modes of socialization. For some students, it can be perceived as a time warp. While it might be argued that more computers are being used in school, and therefore the schools are catching up, it must be recognized that most of the computers are being put into a traditional school structure, which limits their use and effectiveness.

THE LINKAGE OF SCHOOL AND NONSCHOOL LEARNING

The advent of telecommunications has other consequences. Through tele-communications networks, the best people and programs can be employed to promote learning for all learners. Programs such as NOVA and people like Carl Sagan can bring into each classroom and each home the ideas of people who have excelled in a variety of fields. Telecommunications transports the very best to all people; it is a way of equalizing opportunity. With computers and telecommunications, people can proceed at their own rates. In the end all learners will have attained the same mastery.

With telecommunications, the concept of where, when, and how learning takes place is altered. Cable television and home computers carry educational activity into the home by linking school and nonschool learning environments. Professional educators are not the only teachers of the young; parents, peers, television, the workplace all teach. The intent of a modern educational system is to link these learning environments so that they can have maximum impact on the development of every learner. Consequently, school and nonschool learning become part of an overall curriculum that is both formal and non-formal, in which learning takes place at any time and in multiple ways.

TESTING AND EVALUATION AS DIAGNOSTIC AND HELPING TOOLS

How can progress be assessed in the quest for excellence? The bottom line of all testing related to excellence is *learning:* how well are people learning? All of the devices and modes of delivery end up as contributions to this ultimate end. Consequently, tests should be diagnostic so that any necessary or advisable corrective measures can be taken.

Too often in our schools this is not the case. Tests are used more as determinants of who wins and who loses, to separate the able from the less able, and as an "objective" means for ascertaining who should be promoted, assigned to fast tracks, and admitted to college. This kind of testing is an obstacle course in a scholastic race that often rewards speed and memory at the expense of ingenuity and creativity. Testing may not accurately measure those traits involved in academic success that it sets out to measure. As John Gardner points out:

> Performance in later life places heavy emphasis on precisely those attributes not measured by scholastic aptitude and achievement tests. The youth who has these unmeasurable traits—e.g., zeal, judgment, staying power—to a high degree may not be identified in school as a person of high potential but may enjoy marked success in later life. Similarly, the young person extremely high on scholastic attributes which the tests can measure but lacking in other attributes required by success in life may prove to be a "morning glory."[15]

Tests have been used to label learners, rather than diagnose them. For example, standardized achievement tests such as the Test of Basic Skills compare learners with others of the same age or grade level and rank them by indicating the percentage who rated higher or lower along a single dimension. Perhaps the most telling example of the dangers with standardized testing is illustrated by John I. Goodlad on the BENET Intelligence Test given on Ellis Island in 1912 by Harvard Professor H.H. Goddard:

> His conclusions, after administering these tests: of Italians, 79% feeble-minded; of Hungarians, 80% feeble-minded; of Jews (and that's interesting—he doesn't identify Hungarian Jews, or Italian Jews, or Russian Jews, but a special category), note, 83% feeble-minded—a rather interesting figure given the academic success of Jewish people in this country; and Russians, the worst villains, 87%.[16]

The Parent Teacher Association (PTA), in collaboration with Educational Testing Service (ETS), has developed a brochure that attempts to identify several types of tests:

> *Standardized Tests*—compare students' performance;
> *Achievement Tests*—reveal what a student has learned in a particular subject;
> *Classroom Tests*—show what the student has learned and what the teacher has taught;
> *Aptitude Tests*—measure the capacity of the student to succeed in various career areas including advanced academic work;
> *Norm Reference Tests*—compare similar groups who took the same test;
> *Criterion Reference Tests*—measure what the student has learned in a particular subject.[17]

No test reveals all there is to know about any learner, and no test should be used as an exclusive measure for any student's capacity.

Howard Gardner provides a useful perspective on tests, based on his theory of multiple intelligences:

> Five hundred years ago in the West, a tester would have emphasized linguistic memory because printed books weren't readily available. Five hundred years from now, when computers are carrying out all reasoning, there may be no need for logical-mathematical thinking and again the list of desirable intelligences would shift. What I object to is this: Decisions made about 80 years ago in France by Alfred Binet, who was interested in predicting who would fail in school, and later by a few Army testers in the United States during World War I, now exercise a tyrannical hold on who is labeled as bright or not bright. These labels affect both people's conceptions of themselves and the life options available to them.[18]

Current overreliance on testing has been stimulated by the growing pressures to improve student performance. In their efforts to achieve educational reform, many states are mandating testing programs for promotion and graduation. However, tests can provide important information to *help* learners move towards their goals by noting real areas of strength and targeting areas that need attention and improvement. In this regard, tests and measurement have moved increasingly in the direction of criterion reference testing, which shows how well a learner has mastered specific objectives taught in the different school subjects. Such tests help teachers, parents, and students better direct their efforts.

This helping process needs more and better tests. Given the growing evidence that all people can learn, the posture of any new policy on assessment should acknowledge the growing criticism of test bias that has prompted the American Psychological Association to request a ten-year moratorium on the Wechsler Intelligence Scale for Children and has led consumer advocates such as Ralph Nader to be critical of the testing industry. Even popular books such as *None of the Above*[19] have been critical of some of our major tests such as the Scholastic Aptitude Test (SAT), which is viewed as a poorly constructed self-serving instrument whose scores can be increased through coaching, whose results are unrelated to intellect or potential, and whose use is too absolute.

RESEARCH AND DEVELOPMENT

The discovery of better products and processes through research and development is one of the hallmarks of excellence in the private sector. A built-in capacity to generate better modes is part of a total system that includes discovering new ideas, testing those new ideas, and carefully preparing the system to incorporate and effectively use those ideas. Scant attention has been paid to R&D in the public schools, however. A study or a book might influence the field for awhile, or some prestigious institution might seem to generate new knowledge. The work of individual professors and the results of individual studies might find their way into the literature and from there, into the schools' practice, but there is no systematic built-in capacity for improving education. New knowledge needs to be incorporated not by chance, but by design. With systematic attention to R&D and training, new ideas can be formulated, people can be trained, and new knowledge can be tested and applied. This sequence must become an integral part of the system.

Eventually R&D will evolve into stronger collaborations between the knowledge producers and the knowledge users. Universities, schools of education, and model or laboratory schools can cooperate with other agencies along with business and industry to form networks for R&D efforts. The goal of equality requires that we make the best knowledge and technology available to everybody, and there is no better way to ensure this than to build R&D into the system.

LIFELONG LEARNING IN THE EDUCATIVE COMMUNITY

We are now entering an age of education in which learning will be the most valued and important of all lifelong processes. The interrelationship of the many and varied learning environments in our society will constitute this lifelong learning system. Many professionals have long recognized the need to constructively connect the schools with their communities and have urged a linkage of school and nonschool agencies.[20] Noted historian Lawrence Cremin[21] proposed an "ecology of education" in which the community would become the basic context for education, interconnecting all of the educative agencies. More recently, John I. Goodlad[22] summarized the results of his eight-year study of the schools with the concept of the "educative community." Many voices, including the most urgent cries for educational reform, now call for a "learning society." The influential report of the National Commission on Excellence in Education envisions the contemporary learning society as follows:

> In a world of ever-accelerating competition and change in the conditions of the workplace, of ever-greater danger, and of ever-larger opportunities for those prepared to meet them, educational reform should focus on the goal of creating a Learning Society. At the heart of such a society is the commitment to a set of values and to a system of education that affords all members the opportunity to stretch their minds to full capacity, from early childhood through adulthood, learning more as the world itself changes. Such a society has as a basic foundation the idea that education is important not only because of what it contributes to one's career goals but also because of the value it adds to the general quality of one's life. Also at the heart of the Learning Society are educational opportunities extending far beyond the traditional institutions of learning, our schools and colleges. They extend into homes and workplaces; into libraries, art galleries, museums, and science centers; indeed, into every place where the individual can develop and mature in work and life. In our view, formal schooling in youth is the essential foundation for learning throughout one's life. But without life-long learning, one's skills will become rapidly dated.[23]

For all its contemporary urgency, however, the idea of linkage goes back to John Dewey, who, early in this century, recommended a connection of school and community when he observed that the school was an integral part of the community and, indeed, represented only one of the environments through which the learner progressed, along with the home, the workplace, the neighborhood, and other community settings.[24] The harnessing of all these environments and the coordination of all these curricula to contribute to the fullest growth of each and every learner—that is what education is all about. In this process, the schools assume a coordinative role. Dewey also suggested that the schools play a mediating role, assuring that all these interconnections be made in the best interests of the learner.

In the integration of different learning environments, the school and schoolpeople serve a central and essential role. More planning among the varied potential educative environments is needed to assure that the total community has a maximum positive impact on every learner. As much as is possible, the school can work toward the same goal of excellence in education, which includes quality, equality, effectiveness, efficiency, and participation—the ingredients previously defined as essential in the achievement of excellence.

TOWARD A MORE ADAPTIVE SCHOOL STRUCTURE THAT MODELS WHAT IT TEACHES

All of these trends indicate the emergence of choices in what, how, and when to learn; they also indicate a fundamental transition from a teaching to a learning system with lifelong learning taking place in school and nonschool settings in an educative community; and they combine to suggest a new and pivotal role for the teacher and for other school professionals working within this expanded educational network.

The teacher becomes the essential and central instrument of the curriculum, connecting and coordinating the school and the nonschool learning environments. Released by the "electronic teachers," human teachers can turn to the more complex and interactive areas of the learning process, attending to the identification and support of learners' varied talents and different modes of intelligence. All of these developments must look not only to the reality of where we are—the 19th century school model of the industrial era—but also to where we are moving— the learning model of the information age of the 21st century.

One summary concerning the directions that American education may take in adapting to an information society from an industrial society is offered in Table 5–1.[25]

As we can see, many of the observations made by Peters and Waterman relating to business organization also apply to public schools, as do the trends and megatrends discussed by Naisbitt. Related to the expansion of options and choice is the growth of self-help philosophies, the emphasis on prevention rather than cure, and the efforts of people to assume more direct responsibility for their lives and their learning (and their children's learning). The increasing incidence of home education—in which parents turn away from the public schools to teach their children themselves at home—is a development that is significant in revealing the trend toward more consumer choice while also indicating further the serious shortcomings with traditional schooling for increasing numbers of families.[26]

Historically, the school's most important relationship has been with the home and the parents. Now, however, there are many new partners. The historical connection between the schools and the home needs to be maintained, but new links also need to be established. Thus, we see leaders in business and industry, members of the medical profession, and a host of other community agencies drawn into partnership with the schools. David S. Seeley has proposed that in the future, education needs to be developed through partnerships between school and community.[27]

The transition from the current bureaucratic factory structure to a more flexible, adaptable structure will progress through phases. We are into the first phase of identifying weaknesses and mounting improvement efforts. It is important to watch the major reform agenda. A renewed structure is one that more nearly meets the formula for excellence we have prescribed for modern American education.

TABLE 5-1
Directions for Education

Goals of Education	In an Industrial Society	In an Information Society
Cognitive goals	Basic skills	Higher-order skills and basic skills
	Specific training	Generalizable skills
	Unicultural	Global education
	Literacy	Many literacies, more than one language
Affective goals	Large organization skills	Small-group skills
	Organization dependent (Loyalty to school, employer)	Independent, entrepreneurial
Curriculum	Learning simple discipline skills	Interdisciplinary programs
	Standardized programs	Varied program options
	Computer as a vocational skill	Computer as learning tool in all programs
Job preparation	Single-career preparation	Multiple-career preparation
	Late skill development	Early skill development
	Distinct vocational education programs	Career/vocational education as integral part of educational experience
Delivery Systems		
Changing institutional patterns	Single district system focus	More variety at level of individual school
	Central office management	School-based management
	Top-down, insulated decision-making	Bottom-up, participative decision-making
	Group instruction	Individualized instruction using technology

Source: Reprinted, by permission, from National Association of Secondary School Teachers.

This new structure will remove the dichotomies that characterize our present operation:

Quality vs. Equality	Time vs. Place
Teacher vs. Learning	Intellect vs. Emotion
School vs. Nonschool	Hidden vs. Overt
Management vs. Labor	

These dichotomies have mediated against productive learning. The emerging structure with its focus on the learner and learning will facilitate the synthesis of these present dichotomies into more holistic processes. Removal of the bureaucratic barriers that impose these artificial separations will allow a more natural and organic environment for learners. The learner, regardless of age or background, would have access to all the resources available from all the environments that make up the education system. Advisors will assist the learner and make maximum use of these resources and environments to enhance the attainment of a full and complete education. In so doing, the entire community becomes an environment for learning. People live what they learn and learn what they live. The new structure will model the very behaviors it expects of the learner in a free and just state-of-the-art system.

A host of new tools now exist that could restructure the school—to reform the entire educational system, in fact—and allow for the diversity and individuality of all learners. The new technology (computers, television, and telecommunications networks) can enable learners to choose where, when, and how they want to learn. Computer assisted educational programs can allow the learner to progress through subject matter and curriculum at his or her own pace. If user-friendly software can be developed to teach the basics and other appropriate areas, then human teachers can be freed from those tasks to do what they do best to facilitate the best possible educational environment and opportunity for each learner. There are also increasingly refined and sophisticated means of identifying teaching and learning styles, an increased concern for matching those teaching and learning styles appropriately, and new ways of identifying talents and diagnosing intelligences.

Further, the increased use of community resources and the recognition of the importance of in-school and out-of-school learning environments also expand our options for restructuring the entire educational system. As flexibility within the school structure expands, more options and choices are needed for the individual learners. These options should allow for individual differences in personality, abilities, and learning style. They should also encompass an expanded definition of learning incorporating the educative environments that exist outside the school. To provide a full range of educational services the schools must go beyond their own four walls to the resources of the community. The community may become the basic unit of learning, not the school. Linkages with community agents and agencies, collaborative ventures with business and industry, human service agencies, community organizations, and civic groups are but some of the many options available to expand the current educational system to include those learners otherwise pushed to its margins. To do so, the schools need structural transformation. The process for this reformation involves not only a recommitment to excellence but an expansion of the view of education.

NOTES

1. *Action for Excellence,* The Task Force on Education for Economic Growth (Denver, Colorado: The Education Commission of the States, 1983); Ernest L. Boyer, *A Report on Secondary Education in America,* for the Carnegie Foundation for the Advancement of Teaching (New York: Harper and Row, 1983); John Goodlad, *A Place Called School: Prospects for the Future* (New York: McGraw-Hill, 1984); *A Nation at Risk: The Imperative for Educational Reform,* a Report by the National Commission on Excellence in Education (Washington, D. C.: U. S. Government Printing Office, 1983); *Report on the 20th Century Fund Task Force on Federal Elementary and Secondary Educational Policy* (New York: The 20th Century Fund, 1983); Theodore Sizer, *The Dilemma of the American High School* (Boston: Houghton-Mifflin, 1984).

2. This "taxpayers' revolt" has been most visibly manifest in the passage of Proposition 13 in California and Proposition 2½ in Massachusetts. In addition, in the five-year period from 1977 to 1981, seventeen other states passed legislation or enacted constitional amendments limiting the growth of state spending or taxation.

3. Mario D. Fantini, "Adapting to Diversity—Future Trends in Curriculum," *NASSP Bulletin,* May 1985, 15–22.

4. Ross Zerchykov, "School Effectiveness: Public Schools Can Teach All Children," *Citizen Action in Education,* Vol. 8, No. 1, April 1981, 1.

5. Ralph W. Tyler, "Conditions for Effective Learning," *Education in School and Non-school Settings,* Eighty-Fourth Yearbook of the National Society for the Study of Education, edited by Mario D. Fantini and Robert L. Sinclair (Chicago: National Society for the Study of Education, 1985), 204–208.

6. *Ibid.,* 203.

7. Mario D. Fantini, *Public Schools of Choice: A Plan for the Reform of American Education* (New York: Simon and Schuster, Inc., 1974); Mario D. Fantini, editor, *Alternative Education: A Source Book for Parents, Teachers, Students and Administrators* (New York: Anchor Books, 1976).

8. John I. Goodlad, *A Place Called School: Prospects for the Future* (New York: McGraw-Hill Book Company, 1984), 150–66.

9. Howard Gardner, *Frames of Mind: The Theory of Multiple Intelligence* (New York: Basic Books, Inc., 1983).

10. Howard Gardner, "PT Conversation: The Seven Frames of Mind," *Psychology Today,* Vol. 18 (6), June 1984, 21–26.

11. James Coleman, et al., *Equality of Educational Opportunity* (Washington, D. C.: U. S. Department of Health, Education, and Welfare, Office of Education, 1966).

12. Robert L. Sinclair and Ward J. Ghory, "Becoming Marginal," a paper presented as part of the Symposium, "Responding to Demands for Curriculum Improvement: Starting at the Margins," American Educational Research Association Annual Meeting, Chicago: April 1985.

13. Robert Rosenthal, *Pygmalion in the Classroom* (New York: Holt, Rinehart, and Winston, 1968).

14. Gerald W. Bracey, "Computers in Education: What the Research Shows," *Electronic Learning,* November/December 1982, 51–54.

15. John W. Gardner, *Excellence* (New York: Harper and Row, 1961), 50.

16. John I Goodlad, "Conditions for School Reform Related to Marginality," A speech presented at the 1985 Annual Meeting of the American Educational Research Association (Symposium: "Responding to Demands for Curriculum Improvement: Starting at the Margins"), Chicago, Illinois, April 1985.

17. *Plain Talk About Tests*, National Parent-Teacher Association (700 N. Run Street, Chicago).

18. Howard Gardner, "PT Conversation: The Seven Frames of Mind," *Psychology Today*, Vol. 18 (6), June 1984, 21–26.

19. David Owen, *None of the Above: Behind the Myth of Scholastic Aptitude* (Boston: Houghton Mifflin Company, 1985).

20. Mario D. Fantini and Robert L. Sinclair, Editors, *Education in School and Nonschool Settings*, Eighty-Fourth Yearbook of the National Society for the Study of Education (Chicago: National Society for the Study of Education, 1985).

21. Lawrence A. Cremin, *Public Education* (New York: Basic Books, Inc., 1976).

22. John I. Goodlad, *A Place Called School: Prospects for the Future* (New York: McGraw-Hill Book Company, 1984).

23. National Commission on Excellence in Education, *A Nation at Risk: The Imperative for Educational Reform* (Washington, D. C.: U. S. Government Printing Office, 1983), 13–14.

24. John Dewey, *Democracy and Education* (New York: The MacMillan Company, 1916).

25. Marvin Cetron, *Schools of the Future: How American Business and Education Can Cooperate to Save Our Schools* (New York: McGraw-Hill Book Company, 1985), 135–36.

26. John Holt, *Teach Your Own: A Hopeful Path for Education* (New York: Delecorte Press/Seymour Lawrence, 1981); John Naisbitt, *Megatrends* (New York: Warner Books, Inc., 1982), 144.

27. David S. Seeley, *Education Through Partnership* (Washington, D. C.: American Enterprise Institute for Public Policy Research, 1985).

Modernization and Excellence 6

Modernizing the educational system involves revising goals, restructuring programs, and integrating the best of the old with the new to achieve excellence. The need for modernization is evolutionary, changing to meet the needs of society. The task is to move toward improving the schools while planting the seeds for remodeling them. Most current reform efforts sponsored by states are aimed at strengthening not modernizing public education.

In dealing with issues of educational modernization and excellence, the schools' capabilities and relationship with the community must be redefined, and resources that can be shared between the schools and the various agencies in the larger community must be identified. The present disconnection that exists between the schools and the community is evident in parents' discontent with the schools, which includes choosing to educate their children at home; in the concerns expressed by business and industry over the quality of public school graduates; in the criticism leveled at teachers and at the teaching profession; in the tax revolt manifested in Proposition 13 (in California) and Proposition 2½ (in Massachusetts); and in the educational reform efforts now underway in 46 states. The school needs to be reconnected to the community.

PERFORMANCE STANDARDS AND GOALS

Excellence will be achieved in schools when *all* students are pushing the boundaries of their potential. Since quality and equality are interdependent, the modern system will be considered productive when it delivers quality to the many, not the few. All levels of government must assume responsibility for modernization. Each state must set goals addressing the rights of all learners to a full and complete education, and local school districts must develop objectives and curriculum programs to meet these goals.[1] The states, accountable for the maintenance of excellence, must assist local schools in mounting a first-class delivery of educational services.

TRADITIONAL AND NEW BASIC LITERACIES

A modernized system will achieve maximum performance standards for every student in traditional basic skills fundamental to future learning—English, mathematics, science, and social studies. Educational technology, especially computer-assisted diagnosis and instruction and interactive telecommunications, guarantees that more concepts and skills can be taught to more people than ever before. Every learner should have an individually tailored program to promote high performance in the traditional basic skills (reading, writing and mathematics) and an understanding of the underlying principles in the humanities (social and natural sciences).

The information age and global community of the next century will create new "basic skills" and demand new competencies. "New basics" or literacies will take into account the changing nature of society and new modes of communication and transporation. These new basics will be fundamental to future learning for each person, just as the old basics now enable people to function in the world.

TECHNOLOGICAL LITERACY

Students will develop the skills needed to function in an increasingly technological society. They will understand the growing field of robotics, the ways in which engineering and technology affect their lives and, most importantly, they will develop computer skills to achieve personal, academic, and professional goals. They will be able to make informed judgments about software or develop their own. They will understand the growing economic, social, and psychological impact of computers on individuals and on society. States have already made a major commitment to increase teacher training in the uses of educational technology, especially computers.

MEDIA AND TELECOMMUNICATIONS LITERACY

Because of an increasing reliance on mass media for information and transmission of culture, students should be able to analyze media programs and their effects on audiences; understand how productions are created; and be aware of telecommunications systems—satellites, fiber optics, direct broadcast, dishes, and microcomputer/video disc systems—and how they can be used.

The state of Alaska currently has the most comprehensive system of educational telecommunications in this country. Three components make the Alaskan system a model of technology for both educational management and instruction: (1) the Administrative Communication Network transmits policy and procedural information; (2) the Alaska Knowledge Base enables teachers to draw on research relevant to their activities and share classroom ideas; and (3) Individualized Study by Telecommunications provides a centralized system of coursework, testing, and instructional software available through computer terminals in different communities and villages. Able to transmit data through print, audio, and video, this system is often used for teleconferencing.

MULTINATIONAL/MULTICULTURAL LITERACY

Changing economic factors and new technologies are making the world's countries more interdependent. From their earliest years in school, students should have the opportunity to learn foreign languages, including Chinese, Arabic, Russian, Spanish, Swahili, and Japanese. They should also have an understanding and appreciation for cultural diversity to accept themselves and others both as individuals and as members of different cultural, religious, ethnic, and gender groups, all evolving toward a global society.

Canadian leaders felt the preservation and sharing of their diverse cultural heritages were important enough to establish a Minister of Multiculturalism to oversee a network of program officers. Programs developed at the national, regional, and local levels in ethnic history, performing arts, and folklore have greatly enriched school programs.

CIVIC LITERACY

Students will understand their responsibilities as members of an organized society and their roles within this society, including those of consumers and citizens in a democracy. With the breakdown of traditional families and neighborhoods, students will need to learn new community building skills to develop group goals and to make decisions about public issues. They will need a sense of the factors that affect ethical and moral decisions. Students will develop an understanding of legal issues and of justice; they will consider the effects of racism, war, and genocide on individuals and nations. They will study how institutions work, how they affect individuals, and how individuals can affect institutions. They will consider the effects of change and possible future changes on society. Students could learn more about these areas by participating in local access cable television stations, setting up day care centers in high school, running errands for the elderly and the infirm, and working on local environmental projects.

On the global level, a recent project set up by the United Nations in designating 1985 as International Year of Youth actively involves young people in studying and finding solutions to world problems. Similar programs that seriously consider the civic perceptions and skills of youth could follow at the state and local level.

AESTHETIC LITERACY

Given the growing scientific and technological nature of society, it will become more important for individuals to balance their lives through enjoying various forms of art. Music, visual art, dance, drama, and literature all address important life issues and can provide fresh perspective on what it means to be human in a technological age. Schools need artists-in-residence programs and community-based cultural activities. The arts can also be used to enrich teaching in other curriculum areas.

In Massachusetts, the Cultural Education Collaborative coordinates forty museums, theater companies, historical societies and science centers specifically to increase arts activities for school children. Each year, thousands of students take part in school-based activities, visits with working artists, and trips to museums.

CAREER LITERACY

Students will understand which fields are more likely to hold employment opportunities for the future: electronics, robotics, leisure and recreation industries, international relations, health care, geriatrics, and work-at-home cottage industries. They will be aware of their own talents and how they might fit into various available fields. Career awareness courses will bring successful community people into schools to describe their jobs and will take students into workplaces.

PROBLEM SOLVING AND CREATIVE AND CRITICAL THINKING

In order to function in an environment of rapidly increasing knowledge, students must know how to find, organize, and use information, including the ability to analyze critically and synthesize. They must learn to practice creative, intuitive thinking, and problem solving.

Edward deBono has developed the concept of "lateral thinking" as opposed to "vertical thinking."[2] The latter is the more traditional, sequential, logical pursuit of a problem. Lateral thinking moves in an unconventional, haphazard fashion, leaping for alternative solutions.

Whenever possible, all of these skills will be introduced into the curriculum through interdisciplinary methods. For each of these curriculum goals, students should not only have knowledge of an area, but should also be able to *apply* that knowledge to productive personal and societal development.

SECONDARY PERFORMANCE GOALS

As society has changed, it has added responsiblities to the schools' charge. Industrialization called for vocational education. An automotive society needed driver education. Courses in homemaking, nutrition, sex and drug education, and legal education all became the responsibility of the public schools. Some critics have indicated that assimilation of these activities has diluted the ability of schools to meet their primary goals. During the recent period of economic restraint, many communities abandoned these activities, and some have also eliminated art, music, and athletics. The modern education system must acknowledge the importance of these areas and recognize that other educative agencies in the community may be in a better position to deliver such services in cooperation with schools. In a conference entitled "Building a Learning Society," noted historian Henry Steele Commager warned that "the schools can't do it all" and need the help of other community agencies.[3]

DELIVERY

Modernization goals can be achieved through a comprehensive system of interdependent delivery components:

- ☐ Competition and choice
- ☐ Increased utilization of educational technology
- ☐ Varied strategies for teaching basic skills
- ☐ Ongoing training for educational personnel
- ☐ Partnerships between schools and communities
- ☐ An individualized, personalized approach to learning
- ☐ Continuous updating of curriculum
- ☐ Research and development
- ☐ Urban strategy
- ☐ Addressing special problem areas

COMPETITION AND CHOICE

A modern public system of education includes both competition and choice. To better respond to the diversity of the learner population, a variety of options can be developed through citizen and professional participation. In fact, the modern public system can borrow a page out of the private school experience by offering a range of education options to parents, students, and teachers. These can be modeled after particular philosophical plans such as Montessori, Paideia, Classical, Multicultural, and British integrated day, or they can emphasize *talent-based* plans such as sciences, arts, communications, health, and technology. These options can take the form of separate schools or "schools-within-schools."

Schools of choice are based on the assumption that teachers and students have different styles of teaching and learning and that more compatible models are desirable and can be achieved if alternatives and choice are operating in the public schools. This would establish a type of "voucher" system inside the public schools and perhaps between public and private schools.[4]

INCREASED UTILIZATION OF EDUCATIONAL TECHNOLOGY

Although some educators claim that computer-assisted instruction offers only one use of new technology, they cannot deny that the machines have revitalized many students' interest in learning. As Frank Riessman has pointed out, students enjoy the computer, and it "fits the style of young people across class and racial lines."[5] Nearly all studies of computer-assisted instruction indicate that students who used the machines had better achievement test scores than those in control classes. The few studies that have compared speed of learning determined that computers could save students as much as 39–88% of the time necessary to learn certain skills. These results suggest that computer-assisted instruction should be available.

Seymour Papert, of the Massachusetts Institute of Technology, and others claim that computers are most useful because they change the way students think.[6]

Generations of students have been told they had either correct or incorrect answers; students who learn to program computers are more flexible. Kathleen Lyman, Chairperson of the Education Department at Simmons College, has worked to establish computer programming in Boston area schools and is convinced that it can teach problem solving and thinking skills in ways never before possible for *all* students. "Because the computer can make very abstract concepts concrete," Lyman says, "it has the potential to move children quickly through stages of cognitive development."[7] At a more advanced level, Conrad Wogrin, head of the University of Massachusetts Computing Center, claims that recent incoming college students who have used computers for years can think in more advanced ways than any preceding group of students.[8]

VARIED STRATEGIES FOR TEACHING BASIC SKILLS

A massive infusion of educational technology supported by individualized tutoring is needed to improve the teaching of basic skills. Hardware and software systems can now aid in teaching, record keeping, and diagnosing learning problems. Those who teach the traditional basic skills best should be given more responsibility for teaching the basics and helping to train other teachers, especially beginning teachers. Superb teachers could be more influential through teaching "Master Classes" at the state or regional level as part of an ongoing system of teacher training and renewal. Schools should arrange more individualized approaches to teaching the basics, instituting tutoring by peers and other volunteers, especially retired teachers. Universities could provide direct support through a program called "Project Basic," assigning their students to tutor in public schools.

The successful application of technology will redefine the role of educators. Teachers will be able to spend more time teaching students how to apply the traditional basics and integrating the new basics into the core framework of curriculum. The role of principal and teacher in this process is to utilize the resources of school and community fully and to meet the goals for which the schools are accountable.

ONGOING TRAINING FOR EDUCATIONAL PERSONNEL

Instead of attempting to deliver all services directly, teachers in a modernized system will fulfill a coordinating role to create a new and more responsive, comprehensive system of education. Administrators will ultimately be accountable for achieving modernization goals and must demonstrate leadership in resource management. In one such management model, local businesses in Springfield, Massachusetts, allowed their employees to work with individual public school students. The manager of a large bank reported with pride that a formerly failing student tutored by his employee now has a "B" average. Similarly, Raleigh, North Carolina, has 433 "partners" to their school system, including among them Governor James Hunt, who work with students needing extra attention in certain areas.

Teachers and administrators already in the field will have training and opportunities to prepare for the demands of modernization through individual plans for renewal and development, degree programs, inservice workshops developed at district level, and school-based programs. Whenever possible, these activities will take place in the actual school settings.

Training for modernization will include skills in the pedagogy of individualization and community collaboration, use of technology and modern instructional techniques, updating in areas of academic expertise, work with parents, the identification of student talents, and strategies for responding to cultural and linguistic differences. States might create centers to offer year-round inservice training to teachers and schools. Resources that offer training according to teachers' requests should be well publicized, and districts should be encouraged to develop programs.

PARTNERSHIPS BETWEEN SCHOOLS AND COMMUNITIES

Goals for modernization are broad and comprehensive. The schools cannot take complete responsibility for meeting these goals, but schools and communities together can share resources that will promote and improve learning. In a modern system, the school is an integral part of the community. It is the primary learning environment, but not the only one. Families, parents, television, the media, religious institutions, businesses, libraries, and museums all play a role as teachers or educative agents. For such an interdependent system to be functional, the schools must play a linking and coordinating role.

One of the major areas for school/community collaboration involves the secondary goals that schools have inherited and the delegation of these goals to appropriate educative agents and agencies in the community. For example, insurance companies or state police can teach driver education; universities can assist in needs assessment and new teaching methodologies; business and industry can help keep schools current in science, math, and computer technology; medical complexes can assist with health education; the arts community can assist in aesthetic literacy; and interdenominational religious groups could collaborate to provide ethical and moral education (adhering, of course, to school law and educational policies).

School-based foundations can play two important roles in partnerships between communities and schools. First, many school-based foundations have formed over the past ten years specifically to raise money for public school programs. Some provide general funds to schools for use at the administrator's discretion, and others determine their own funding priorities. The San Francisco Education Foundation, founded by a group of civic leaders and educators after California's Proposition 13 cut the amount of school revenue, supports outstanding programs ranging from efforts to improve basic skills to cultural programs, including creation of murals and an all-city orchestra.

Second, foundations can foster school-community collaboration. The San Francisco Foundation recently established the Daniel E. Koshland Awards Program to recognize both private citizens and professional educators who forge links between school and community. The 1985 awards to individuals in San Francisco's Western Addition neighborhood included $1,000 to each person and $5,000 to a non-profit youth organization nominated by the awardees. The Foundation used the awardees' knowledge of the community to disperse funds responsibly. The awardees further formed a task force to have an even greater effect on education in their area of the city.

AN INDIVIDUALIZED, PERSONALIZED APPROACH TO LEARNING

The increased use of educational technology frees teachers to spend more time analyzing student needs and designing individualized programs to meet those needs. The best modern system of education would include an individualized curriculum plan carefully tailored for each student, with accountability shared by parents and school officials. For example, a student could start school earlier and leave earlier for advanced college placement or arrange to study partially in school and partially at home.

An important part of this personalized program should be the opportunity for each student to cultivate a talent—whether it be writing, speaking, leadership, athletic, or artistic talent. Every attempt should then be made to coordinate each student's talents with career goals and training.

CONTINUOUS UPDATING OF CURRICULUM

Curriculum developers at the local, regional, and state levels should continuously research information and encourage participation from academic centers and the research and development departments of business and industry. Whenever possible, researchers from academia, professional associations, and the corporate world should give presentations to students and teachers, perhaps coordinated by regional officers of the state department.

RESEARCH AND DEVELOPMENT (R&D)—MODEL SCHOOLS AND MODEL SCHOOL DISTRICTS

Research and development should become a primary mechanism for modernization. Each state should set up a network of model schools and model school districts as demonstration centers of exemplary curriculum to stimulate research, development, training, and evaluation. Regional and national schools and universities should collaborate to improve learning.

Individual regional model schools would focus both on advanced methods of dealing with basic literacies and on the cultivation of specific content areas. Each school could have a theme, such as

☐ Math/Science/Technology
☐ International Affairs (to include foreign languages, international understanding, and the study of peace)
☐ Arts (including media, communications, and entertainment)
☐ Medical Arts and Health
☐ Classical Studies
☐ Environmental Studies
☐ Financial/Legal Affairs

To avoid the elitism that sometimes develops at theme schools, full-time students could be chosen from an application process, and students and teachers from other schools could attend week-long special sessions. Other teachers and administrators could attend training sessions at theme schools and transfer program ideas to their local districts. When possible and appropriate, universities and private industries might co-sponsor individual model school coalitions of cooperating schools. Similarly, model school districts would demonstrate system-wide approaches to modernization.

Research and development efforts in the area of educational technology need to be given priority. Partnerships among schools, colleges, and corporations can create the sorts of products and materials needed for a contemporary system of education.

Research and development goals can also encourage school-based foundations, inservice training, and annual conferences sponsored by state legislators in cooperation with professional organizations, businesses, and industries to feature successful educational practices.

Some students have already expanded their possible career options through the use of computerized guidance programs. The System for Interactive Guidance Information (SIGI) allows students to work at their own speed in comparing their set of personal and work values against those in various fields of employment. This interactive program allows the user to identify values and make choices. Such systems can also provide lists of training opportunities in given fields.

AN URBAN STRATEGY

A special urban strategy based on what we have learned from a series of recent studies to determine factors in school effectiveness, will assist those schools that serve the largest numbers of students. It will include the following components:

City-Wide Partnerships   The recently established Boston Compact links business, industry, and higher education to plan programs for school improvement and job placement. Realizing that many urban youth drop out of school because they have no employment prospects, the Compact convinced 200 area companies to provide a total of 1,100 summer jobs and to hire 400 students immediately upon graduation. In a corresponding move, 27 local colleges and universities have agreed to increase the number of students accepted from the Boston area.

Magnet Schools   Related to competition and choice, a portion of a city's schools will be transformed into programmatically distinctive learning environments that are so appealing in quality that they attract diverse students. Based on family choice and student interest, magnet schools would provide both quality and equality. The quality of the program would serve as the magnet for achieving a more natural integration than the socioeconomic nature of the neighborhood in which a school is located.

In the merged city-county of Raleigh, North Carolina, a system of 55,000 students, half the parents are now choosing from among magnet schools for their children. Their options include Classical Studies, a traditional environment with strict dress and discipline codes; International Studies, to emphasize different languages and cultures; Gifted/Talented Schools, which attempt to develop the gifts and talents found in *all* students; and Extended Day Schools, open from 6:30 A.M. to 7:00 P.M. These settings can be located in medical schools, colleges and universities, museums, concert halls—literally anywhere in the community.

Mobilization of Community Resources   Some of our richest educational resources—universities, medical complexes, the arts community, and volunteers— are located in cities and could be tapped for urban schools. A community service corps based on student volunteers from colleges and universities who could earn credit for tutoring in schools could be established.

Introduction of Computers and Telecommunications into Schools   All students in urban schools have access to computers. Greater use of telecommunication networks could consolidate resources and bring institutions together.

School-Based Management and Staff Development   School effectiveness studies have identified the importance of school-based management for improving student performance. Continuing staff development for teachers already in the field should be made available to schools so that teachers and administrators can work for change as a team. Greater use should be made of leadership academies, teachers' centers, and summer institutes focusing on such subjects as math, science, and computers.

Parent-Community Advisory Council   Each school should have a community council to promote more effective communication between parents and teachers and to coordinate resources.

ADDRESSING SPECIAL PROBLEM AREAS

Although the primary target of modernization is elementary and secondary education, a responsive system of education cannot ignore the critical problems of unemployment and adult illiteracy. Once the educational resources in a community are harnessed, the new schools will be able to deal with such problems.

Unemployment among the handicapped and minority youth will require special attention at the local level to discover individuals' educational problems and to continue to assist them once they have jobs. Career ladders of continuous opportunity will need to be created through the cooperation of employers who are willing to work with educators and students. State departments of education and employment could assist localities to coordinate resources.

Especially useful would be the linking of regional technical high schools of the Job Training Partnership Act (JTPA) at community colleges. The process of retraining for new careers is critical to ending the chronic unemployment of youth under 25 in general and minorities in particular. The grassroots delivery inherent in these community-based agencies can begin a constructive process of relearning to open new opportunities for adults now trapped in a cycle of despair.

ROLE OF THE STATES

The role of the states will be enabling, facilitative, and coordinative. They will work through established organizations, collaboratives, and local initiatives to address modernization goals. Each community will develop a plan of objectives and curriculum to meet state goals. Regional offices of state departments of education, in cooperation with educational collaboratives, roundtables, professional associations, and universities, might set up resource teams that localities can call on to help develop their plans. As an example of a good beginning, the Massachusetts Department of Education is currently establishing a computerized resource bank for different curriculum areas and has set up a Math/Science Clearinghouse to assist teachers and school districts in planning.

EVALUATION

Qualitative and quantitative evaluation in schools ought to be ongoing, revealing factors needing improvement in the delivery system and for individual learners. Systematic assessment can provide information for self-correction of both the parts and the whole system. Each school should carry on regular internal evaluation to facilitate planning and decision-making. States should make technical resources and assistance available to localities to design their evaluation systems. Any evaluation should utilize up-to-date assessment procedures, including criterion-referenced tests and anthropological methods, such as participant observation.

Testing of individual students should be designed to help students reach higher levels of proficiency and schools reach higher levels of productivity. Criterion-referenced tests contribute more to student assessment and progress than norm-referenced tests. For research and evaluation purposes at the state level, test results from stratified random samples of a crosss-section of students thoughout any given state would provide an opportunity to gauge how a new educational delivery system is working without penalizing individual students. If teachers want comparative information from norm-referenced tests, they could be given a full report, with only a random sample going to the state department of education. Testing should be used for self-correction and diagnosis, not as a tool to discredit a district, school, teacher, learner, or family.

FINANCING

Schools do not now have the mechanisms to modernize. Every attempt must be made to identify and use existing resources more productively. New money will be needed to modernize the system and to facilitate better use of old money. Conversion capital should be used for the following activities:

- ☐ Articulating overarching goals that will encourage participatory process through the state;
- ☐ Mass infusion of new educational technology into schools;
- ☐ Establishing model schools/model districts;
- ☐ Staff development programs;
- ☐ Incentives for involving the private sector in donating equipment and employees' time to schools;
- ☐ Better salaries and benefits for teachers;
- ☐ Programs for areas of special consideration; e.g., job training, adult literacy;
- ☐ A state-guaranteed minimum school expenditure per pupil.

Since it is grossly unfair for any citizen to be denied equality by virtue of place of residence, state school finance formulas must be continuously reexamined to ensure equity. In many states, for example, there are communities in which the annual per student expenditure is under $2,000, while others exceed $3,000 or $4,000. However, it is also unfair to limit the capacity of communities to support their schools. Some communities might be designated as special socioeconomic zones for incentive grants. Further, state officials can play an important role in setting federal educational policy, making the federal government an ongoing partner in school reform. Federal support, especially for equality and for R & D, should be close to 8–10% of the overall cost of public education.

TRANSITION TO A MODERN SYSTEM

Because local school systems do not have the means to transform their schools into a modern system, each state should develop a transition strategy. The state legislature and/or governor could create a task force to design this strategy by addressing the following:

1. Coordinate a state-wide dialogue and review of performance standards and goals to include input from professional organizations, school districts, and parents.
2. Recommend specific and detailed modernization legislation, including a phasing-in process.
3. Develop guidelines with the state department of education for localities to design modernization plans with full community participation.
4. Involve academia in the definition of content and performance standards in curriculum.
5. Establish a planning process for model schools and model school districts.
6. Institute procedure for a massive program to retrain educational personnel.

Only with attention and support from policymakers can dialogue on the major issues involved in updating schools be stimulated. These are the first important steps toward restructuring schools for the new technological age.

TOWARD A LEARNING ECOLOGY

The involvement of the community in school reform is essential in two distinct and fundamental ways: first, in participating as citizens in governing the schools; second, in participating as an integral part of the larger human learning system formed by the entire community. The community, family, church, workplace, social and cultural agencies, and government own the public schools and thus have a reason to participate in their policies. They also contribute directly to the educational process. Since schools exist as an integral part of the community, to serve the community's needs, the community has a right to use the resources and facilities of the school. In many communities, the school buildings are open to the community in the evenings, on weekends, and during summer for community agencies and organizations such as Scouts, 4-H Clubs, and other youth groups. In Flint, Michigan, for example, in the 1970s, the Charles Stewart Mott Foundation helped the local schools become exemplary community schools engaged actively in community education.

In *Community Education: From Program to Process to Practice*, Jack D. Minzey and Clyde E. LeTarte gave the following definition of community education.

> Community Education is a philosophical concept which serves the entire community by providing for all of the educational needs of all of its community members. It uses the local school to serve as the catalyst for bringing community resources to bear on community problems in an effort to develop a positive sense of community, improve community living, and develop the community process toward the end of self-actualization.[9]

Such a concept of the school as integrally aligned with the needs and activities of the community is not new. It is, in fact, a part of the historical basis and tradition of the school. What changes is not the fact that this dynamic school-community relationship exists, but how it plays itself out in different eras and in different localities. All of the agencies and institutions in the community are still necessarily interrelated, although the days of the same homogeneous community based on the agrarian model are long gone, replaced by the complex interwoven fabric of the post-industrial era. Policymakers must recognize that efforts to link school and community agencies are not new or unprecedented. Prophetically, in 1916, Dewey described the central role of the school in an education system that includes not only the formal classroom but all the educative environments of the community:

> I believe that the school must represent present life—life as real and vital to the child as that which he carries on in the home, in the neighborhood, or on the playground.[10]

Dewey also suggested that the schools play a mediating role to ensure that each of these interconnections is made in the best interests of the individual learner.

Dewey's ideas on school and community have been played out in a variety of directions in different communities and in a number of different eras, during which the boundaries between school and community and the balance of responsibilities among the two have varied considerably.[11] A theoretical exploration of the potential of community education, especially relevant to our school reform efforts today, is summarized in "The Random Falls Idea," a major proposal by Archibald Shaw and a team of educators in the 1950s.[12] "This is a proposal for redesigning our program of secondary education," wrote the authors of "The Random Falls Idea." "The components are not radically new. The total concept may seem to be." Those involved in today's school improvement efforts may well be impressed by the contemporary appeal of some of these components:

> This proposal rests squarely on what is known about youths, communities, and about today's and tomorrow's social and economic change. It is designed to foster American ideals, to further Americans' aspirations, and to give every youth the chance to develop into a richly endowed adult who is altogether worthy of citizenship in our democracy.
>
> It is a program of apprenticeship, partnership, and achievement in citizenship—of youth development through meaningful partnership in civic and community living—of community improvement through that same partnership and focus—and of national strength through the development of the nation's human, institutional, and physical resources by the maximum achievement of the potential of each individual within the framework of a healthy democratic society.[13]

The proposal sought to integrate the secondary school program with the community by vocational and service contracts, a solid curriculum of basics and special learning areas, teachers serving as advisors, community service for students, an extended school day and year, and the concept of the school utilizing the entire community in its educative efforts.

These various elements can be seen in recent developments translating theory into practice. The alternative education movement of the 1960s and 1970s expanded the idea of the school setting and the utilization of the community's resources. For example, in Philadelphia, the "Parkway Program" defined the entire city and its resources as "the school" and thus developed the "school-without-walls" model,[14] which many other cities then adapted to their own needs. Another popular and successful alternative model was the magnet school, which drew students from all over a given district on the basis of specialized curriculum rather than geographic location. Specialized schools were often developed in connection with communities' needs and resources. Dallas, for instance, developed a number of magnet schools based on its urban resources: a Transportation Institute located in the central business district; a Creative Arts Academy near the city's theater and museums; a Health Professions Center located in a medical center. The magnet schools of Milwaukee are compared to college campuses, with participating high schools specializing in career-oriented curricula.[15] Since magnet schools have proven successful in attracting students from all over a district, they have been effective in integrating urban school districts, another important aspect of educational reform efforts. Noted historian Lawrence Cremin has proposed an "ecology of education"[16] in which the community serves as the overall context for education, interlocking all educative agencies within and outside the school, and John I. Goodlad, in an eight-year study of the public schools, concludes that the community should be the major educator.[17]

Public policymakers need to understand the effects of the growing disconnection between schools and communities. The schools have become isolated institutions caught in the midst of bitter school-community struggles. The parental protests, school boycotts, picket lines, and riots that occurred in the New York City School System in the 1960s were indications of the community's severe dissatisfaction with the schools. They were also expressions of the public's need to reclaim control of the schools and to achieve school reform at the same time. Subsequent school reform proposals sought to link the schools with their localities.[18] Connections between the school and educative settings in the community must be supported by public policies aimed at educational improvement.[19]

Responsive public policy is necessary before school and nonschool educative environments can be linked. Community education exists as a philosophy and a program that many state departments of education, many local school districts, and many people working at the federal level are currently willing to address. The Community Schools and Comprehensive Community Education Act of 1978 provides, at the national level, a framework for community schools. Under its statement of findings and policy, Congress declared that

- ☐ the delivery is an integral part of the local human service delivery system;
- ☐ the school is a primary institution for the delivery of services, and may be the best instrument for the coordination of frequently fragmented services, including parental involvement in the delivery of such services.

Congress also indicated that schools should

- ☐ provide educational, recreational, cultural, and other related community and human services in accordance with the needs, interests, and concerns of the community agencies through the expansion of community education programs;
- ☐ coordinate the delivery of social services to meet the needs and preferences of the residents of the community served by the school, and to provide for a research and development emphasis in community education that can contribute to the improved formulation of federal, state, and local policy.[20]

LINKING SCHOOL AND NONSCHOOL LEARNING RESOURCES

Community involvement in schools also means economic and political involvement. While the demands and responsibilities imposed by society on the schools have increased dramatically, the economic resources allocated to meet those increased responsibilities at best remain stable and in many cases decline. The 1960s decade of federal aid to education has led to the popular notion that excellence cannot be achieved by simply throwing money at the problem. The public is now wary of reforms that cost money. School reform efforts have also shown that there are no answers to be found in simple band-aid approaches. It is clear that school reform—offering the public the excellence it demands in education—must be achieved at reasonable financial costs.

The involvement of the community in school reform also means that senior citizens, business, industry, higher education, civic, religious, cultural, and scientific agents and agencies become political partners with parents. It is one thing for parents and educators to collaborate on public school issues; it is quite another for the power of business and industry to join in the effort. When the different elements of the community speak in unison, elected officials listen.

Not only has the economic climate of the country changed, but the social situation is also undergoing a series of major transformations. The realignment of church, neighborhood, family, and workplace within our society affect the socialization and education of youth. All learning does not and indeed should not take place within the four walls of the school; the school is just one component in a series of educative environments in the community. Substantive restructur-

The School Structure

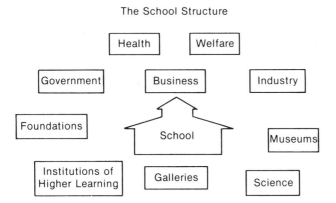

FIGURE 6.1
The School Structure
Source: Mario D. Fantini, Elizabeth L. Loughran, and Horace B. Reed, "Community Education: Towards a Definition," unpublished paper, 13.

ing requires functional connections between school and nonschool learning environments. Community participation in school reform is essential so that the schools reflect and serve the needs of their surrounding communities.

The schools can draw on the experience and expertise of community agencies, such as medical centers, libraries, museums and galleries, business agencies, local industries, and civic institutions. Figure 6.1 shows how the school can function as the central, comprehensive institution, with the community serving as an educational resource.[21]

We can, however, expand this to consider the community itself as a series of potential educational environments. As indicated by the second diagram (Figure 6.2),[22] this redefinition of the educational system includes all the resources of the community.

Under such a matrix, the schools can draw on the experience and expertise of members of various community agencies such as medical centers, libraries, museums, businesses, and civic institutions. The following list [23] indicates how some of these agencies may assist the school in its central comprehensive role as educational resource for the community:

EDUCATIONAL SERVICE	COMMUNITY AGENT
Sex and drug education; nutrition	Medical agencies
Legal literacy	Legal agencies
Moral education	Interdenominational religious committees
Arts and crafts education	Recreational facilities, arts associations

EDUCATIONAL SERVICE	COMMUNITY AGENT
Career counseling	State employment offices
Career education	Business and industry
Computer literacy	Colleges, universities and high technology industries
Science/Math	High technology
Economics	Chamber of Commerce
Civics	League of Women Voters
Driver education	Insurance and automobile agencies; state police
Basic skills	Tutors (students) from higher education as community service

There are many different ways in which the community can participate in the schools, and it is important to emphasize that there is no one model, no one best way. Rather, there is a sort of continuum involving different kinds of participation, all of which get played out in current school reform efforts.

The essential political realignment of the school with its community is made necessary by the declining numbers of school-age children since the baby-boom years of the 1960s. Parents, once the public schools' major political partner, are

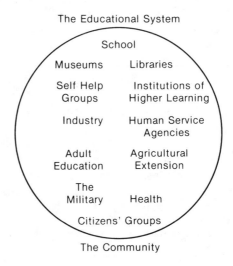

FIGURE 6.2
The Educational System
Source: Mario D. Fantini, Elizabeth L. Loughran, and Horace B. Reed, "Community Education: Towards a Definition," unpublished paper, 14.

in the minority, and other constituencies must be mobilized to support the public schools. New organizations, such as the Public Education Fund in Pittsburgh, have come into being with the primary aim of reducing the isolation of the public schools from the general community. The opportunity presently exists to build productive partnerships with other interested parties in the general community, including senior citizens, business, industry, the arts, cultural and civic agents, human service agencies, and higher educational institutions. These groups represent political as well as economic resources and add dimensions to the learning environment of a modern system of education.

As indicated, community participation now includes not only parents but all the educative agents and agencies in the larger community. While parents are undeniably important, and while there has been a historical connection between the schools and the family, there are many more potential educators and possible educative resources out in the community. These potential resources need to be actively involved in education if we are to achieve school improvement under current conditions. We need to enlarge the framework of community participation in the entire process of learning. The school, as one essential educator among many, cannot do its job successfully unless the other agents and agencies in the community do theirs.

The community must share in the costs of this comprehensive education system, although these costs need not mean more money for the schools. Currently, the schools sometimes duplicate or attempt to duplicate the services and facilities that already exist elsewhere in the larger community. More must be done with the resources that are already available. The question becomes how to do this in a careful, comprehensive, and systematic way.

NOTES

1. Much of the material on pages 1–25 is adapted from "Towards a Modernization Policy for American Public Education: Regaining Excellence" (co-authored with Lynn J. Cadwallader), which appeared in *Scholar and Educator*, a journal published by the Society of Educators and Scholars, Vol. 9, No. 2, Fall 1985, 3–19.

2. Ralph Fletcher, "Thoughts on Thinking," *USAIR*, 1984, 51–56.

3. Henry Steele Commager, "The Schools Can't Do It All," *Community School Journal*, Vol. XII, No. 3, April 1985, 8–10.

4. Mario D. Fantini, *Public Schools of Choice: A Plan for the Reform of American Education* (New York: Simon and Schuster, Inc., 1974);
   Mario D. Fantini, editor, *Alternative Education: A Source Book for Parents, Teachers, Students and Administrators* (New York: Anchor Books, 1976).

5. Frank Riessman, "Can the Computer Reduce Inequality in Education" (Editorial), *Social Policy*, Vol. XIII, Winter 1983.

6. Seymour Papert, *Mindstorms* (New York: Basic Books, 1980).

7. Interview with Kathleen Lyman, Chairperson of the Education Department at Simmons College, conducted by Lynn Cadwallader, November 1983.

8. Interview with Conrad Wogrin, Director of Computer Services at the University of Massachusetts, conducted by Lynn Cadwallader, November 1983.

9. Jack D. Minzey and Clyde E. LeTarte, *Community Education: From Program to Process to Practice* (Midland, Mich.: Pendell Publishing Company, 1969), 26–27.

10. Reginald D. Archambault (ed.), John Dewey on Education (New York: Random House, 1964), p. 430.

11. Mario D. Fantini, "John Dewey's Influence on Community and Nonformal Education," *Comunity Education Journal*, Vol. XI, Number 4, July 1984, 4–10.

12. Archibald B. Shaw and John Lyon Reid, "The Random Falls Idea: An Educational Program and Plant for Youth and Community Growth," *The School Executive*, March 1956, 47–86.

13. *Ibid.*, 48–49.

14. John Bremer and Michael Von Moschzisker, *The School Without Walls: Philadelphia's Parkway Program* (New York: Holt, Rinehart and Winston, Inc., 1971).

15. Sally Reed, "What Ever Happened to Alternative Schools?" *The New York Times Fall Survey of Education*, 15 November 1981, 2.

16. Lawrence A. Cremin, *Public Education* (New York: Basic Books, Inc., 1976).

17. John I. Goodlad, *A Place Called School: Prospects for the Future* (New York: McGraw-Hill Book Company, 1984).

18. Mayor's Advisory Panel on Decentralization of the New York City Schools, McGeorge Bundy, Chairman, *Reconnection for Learning: A Community School System for New York City* (New York: Frederick A. Praeger, Publishers, 1969).

19. Douglas E. Mitchell and Dennis J. Encarnation, "Alternative State Policy Mechanisms for Influencing School Performance," *Educational Researcher*, Vol. 13, No. 5, May 1984.

20. Sections 801–815 of Title VIII—*Community Schools* (PL 95–561), "Community Schools and Comprehensive Community Education Act, 1978."

21. From "Community Education: Towards a Definition" by Mario D. Fantini, Elizabeth L. Loughran, and Horace B. Reed, Unpublished paper, 13.

22. *Ibid.*, 14.

23. Mario D. Fantini, "School/Community Partnerships: Modernizing the Educational System," Unpublished paper prepared for the 1983 Educational Leadership Institute, College Park, Md., 1983, 13.

While modernization cannot be achieved in one great across-the-board swoop, progress is being made throughout the United States. Since modernization represents a combination of traditional school improvement efforts with a major restructuring of the school system itself, most reform efforts start where the schools are. The first phase of modernization appears to strengthen existing patterns rather than demonstrate serious departures from current operational practice. In the second phase, a combination of old and new patterns emerges. Finally, in the third phase, the new structure is dominant. Then this "new" becomes institutionalized and commonplace, and is in turn challenged by a newer generation of ideas. So goes the progression. This cycle is essential for keeping current and responsive to changing conditions and necessities.

Currently, there are many important and exemplary school reform efforts in the nation as educators and legislators tackle modernization of the public schools. This section will highlight a number of such efforts containing the elements that have been identified as being central to a modern system of education.

STATE LEVEL INITIATIVES

School reform has been a high priority in virtually every state in the nation. The federal government may have helped trigger the national dialogue through its sponsorship of the Commission on Excellence in Education report, *A Nation at Risk*, but the states have picked up the theme. Ultimately, local governments within the states must assume the bulk of the fiscal responsibilities aimed at school improvement as Figure 7–1 makes clear.[1]

Examples of modernization are taking place throughout the United States. The Education Commission of the States, in its monograph *Action in the States*, provides a useful map indicating the states that are seriously engaged in plans for improving K–12 education (Figure 7–2).[2]

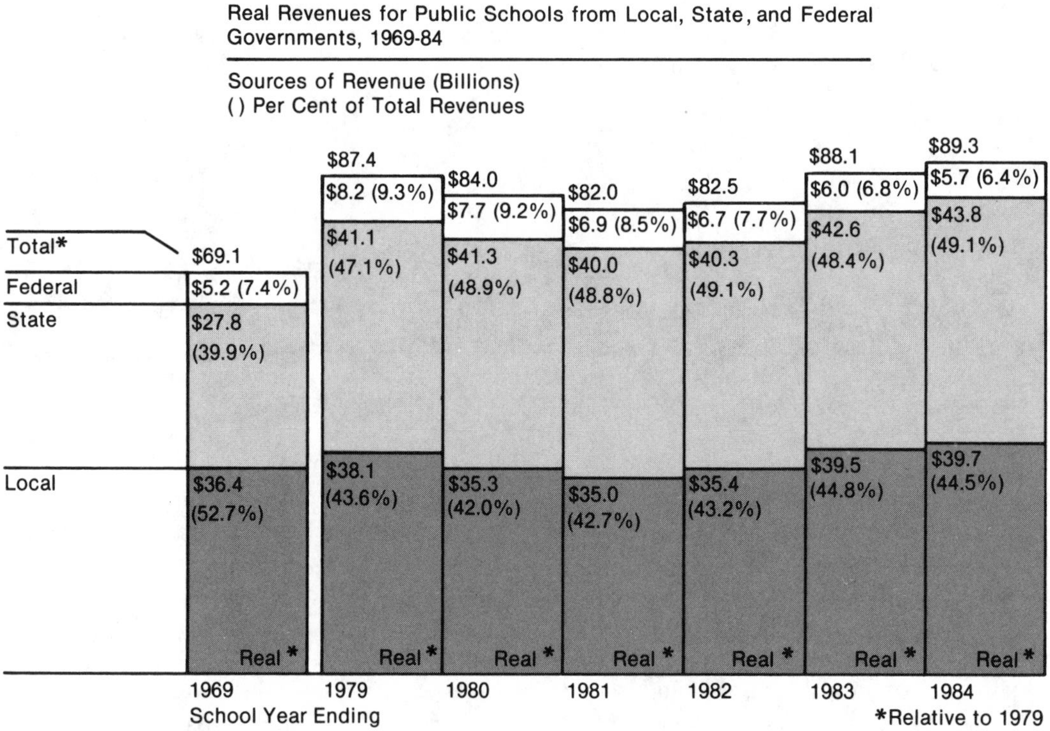

Real Revenues for Public Schools from Local, State, and Federal
Governments, 1969-84

Sources of Revenue (Billions)
( ) Per Cent of Total Revenues

FIGURE 7-1:
Sources are Education Finance in the States: 1984 (ECS) and the National Education Associa-
tion, Estimates of School Statistics, 1983–84.
*Numbers may not total exactly because of rounding error.

The Education Commission of the States offers the following overview of
state-initiated school reform:

> If the progress of educational renewal in our country could be judged solely
> by the number of states that have either implemented or are developing state
> plans to improve the public schools, one would have to say renewal is well
> under way. Forty-six states are working on comprehensive state action plans—
> usually collaboratively developed by governors, legislatures, state and local
> boards, business leaders, and educators—to reform education in public elemen-
> tary and secondary schools. Many of the states (27) initiated their plans in the
> last 14 months and are now carrying them out, while 14 more states are still
> refining their plans. Another five states, ahead of the national reform move-
> ment, had initiated statewide plans in the early 1980s.
> 　　State reform plans have emerged from a broad public consensus on the
> centrality of education to an economically healthy and vigorous society. State

Comprehensive State Plans for Improving K-12 Education

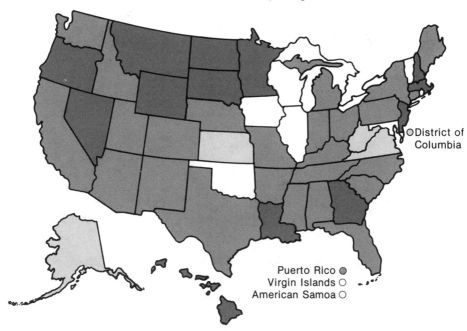

○District of Columbia

Puerto Rico ●
Virgin Islands ○
American Samoa ○

◻ Initiatives legislatively enacted or endorsed by state board of education in last 14 months
◻ Initiatives legislatively enacted or endorsed by state board of education 14 months to 3 years ago
◼ Currently awaiting legislative or state board action

FIGURE 7–2:
Source: Chiefs, governors' education policy staff and state legislators. Data current as of 6/15/84.

leaders have reached out to diverse groups through public hearings or special forums and brought citizens from all walks of life together to work toward a common goal. While it is too early to judge the impact of state plans, the planning process itself has proven to be a useful new way of communicating about education.

Because each state must measure education need by its internal barometer, state plans are diverse in content and establish many different processes for change. Nevertheless, states share a number of concerns: improving the teaching profession, integrating technology into instruction, upgrading the school curriculum, strengthening graduation standards, raising teacher certification requirements, promoting business involvement in education, and working on ways to finance excellence. More than 250 individual task forces are examining these issues and others to provide state leaders with recommendations that can be used to lay a solid foundation for education reform.[3]

Specific state level efforts highlighted by the Comission are outlined below:

Alabama's state board of education adopted virtually every recommendation in "A Plan for Excellence: Alabama's Public Schools." The board has appointed about 30 task forces to phase in more than 50 improvement measures ranging from tougher graduation standards, mandatory kindergarten, revisions in teacher certification requirements, and improved professional development to the appointment of special panels to study issues such as school finance and teacher compensation.

Alaska conducts a basic-skills testing program for grades 4 and 8. Several rural schools have shown remarkable student improvement as a result of local school board and district education reform initiatives. Accordingly, the department of education has been directed to develop model curricula, initiate school achievement profiles, develop goals for elected school board members, and identify resources to improve teaching and learning.

The *Arizona* State Board of Education has identified specific skills to be attained in all required subjects for promotion from 8th grade and graduation from 12th grade. The board is considering a grade 3 "checkpoint."

The *Connecticut* General Assembly approved a bill proposed by the state board of education that will expand the state's basic skills assessment program ·to 4th, 6th, and 8th grade students. The new testing system will respond to several priorities: raising standards, identifying students with remedial needs, focusing attention at earlier grade levels (the current statewide test system is administered in 9th grade), and providing a better tool to assess student achievement statewide.

Georgia's educational review commission, a blue-ribbon panel appointed by the governor, has tentatively approved a statewide basic curriculum content plan. The plan lists essential skills and provides a curriculum framework for all subjects. It also defines basic academic skills students will be expected to have for each subject at every grade level.

The *Illinois* state superintendent has submitted statements for student learning to the state board of education, to replace current program-related, time-allotment mandates. These outcome statements broadly define the least students should learn and be able to do as a result of their schooling. Each school district is required to develop board-approved objectives consistent with the outcome statements and to monitor and assess student achievement. Schools are required to report student progress to the public and to develop remediation plans for low-achievement areas.

The *Kansas* State Board of Education and the state legislature have approved an initiative requiring a pre-certification test for all teacher candidates who have successfully completed a teacher preparation program and are seeking initial certification. During 1984 and 1985, a test will be selected and validated. The test requirement becomes effective May 1, 1986.

Kentucky's "academic bankruptcy" bill provides state department technical assistance to districts failing to meet state standards. Districts refusing to cooperate are subject to state intervention and possible removal of local school officials. Districts are required to publish annual performance reports and develop improvement plans to correct deficiencies or noncompliances.

Maine's 1984 teacher certification law establishes a clear-cut policy that upgrades and strengthens state requirements for teaching. The ultimate goal of the legislation is to enhance the quality of teaching, and in turn, produce better-educated students.

The *Michigan* State Board of Education developed "Better Education for Michigan Citizens: A Blueprint for Action." Recommendations focus on: (1) improving learning by strengthening graduation requirements and college preparation, establishing written student performance standards and lengthening the school day and year; (2) creating a better learning environment through a comprehensive school-planning process; (3) strengthening the education profession with more emphasis on professional development, certification, and salaries; and (4) improving the delivery of educational services through jointly-sponsored district programs.

Missouri's state board of education and members of the department of elementary and secondary education developed a comprehensive package for school reform out of recommendations from "Reaching for Excellence: An Action Plan for Educational Reform in Missouri." The recommendations included higher graduation standards, improved elementary curriculum in science and mathematics, and identification of academically gifted students at all levels.

The *"Montana* Educational Challenge Project," funded by a Mellon Grant from the Council of Chief State School Officers, will improve the state's onsite accreditation process. New review procedures will involve representatives of higher education, K–12 teachers, administrators, and staff members of the office of public instruction.

Nebraska's comprehensive education bill of 1984 makes sweeping changes in the current teacher certification process. Prior to entry into teacher training, individuals will have to pass a basic skills competency test; prior to certification, teacher candidates must pass subject-matter competency tests. The bill creates a four-tiered career ladder (apprentice, initial, standard, and professional). All new teachers will receive a nonrenewable apprentice certificate and will be required to take part in an entry-year assistance program.

New Jersey's revised teacher preparation and certification program allows people who have not completed a college teacher preparation program to qualify for certification if they have a bachelor's degree, have passed a subject-matter test, and have successfully completed a state approved one-year internship administered by local districts. Candidates for internships are screened through local interviews designed to evaluate their academic background (which must include 30-credit hours or equivalent work experience in the subject to be taught) and personal and ethical characteristics.

New Mexico's staff accountability program, effective July 1, 1984, requires (1) a basic skills test, to be administered to all teacher candidates, (2) passage of the NTE core battery by candidates for initial certification, and (3) a performance evaluation plan to be coordinated with the recertification process. The state board of education has defined teacher competencies to be included in the evaluation plan, and the state department is identifying skills for effective administrators.

In *New York*, the Regents Action Plan has three major coordinated aspects to improve education. The plan increases course requirements for graduation, expands statewide testing to monitor both student achievement and the quality of increased courses, and requires a comprehensive assessment report. Every public school will report student achievement results to the community, and the state will monitor achievement, providing help and motivation to low-achieving schools.

North Dakota's 1985 legislature will consider a cohesive set of educational reform recommendations, being developed by a coalition of educational organizations, which will consider national report recommendations as well as feedback from two state governor's conferences. The group will emphasize increasing the capacity of local educators to assess needs and develop and carry out improvement plans.

The *Oklahoma* legislature, in a major reform of the teacher education and certification process, has passed new legislation increasing minimum requirements for entrance into teacher education programs, extending the amount of required field experience and requiring students to demonstrate subject-matter competence. The legislation also funds teacher-consultant, entry-year assistance and staff-development programs.

The *Oregon* Action Plan for Excellence, which accelerates the state's pursuit of performance-based schooling, is organized around four themes: (1) assuring student success in mastering essential learning skills, (2) enhancing the self-renewing capacities of schools for achieving greater effectiveness and productivity, (3) providing support systems for schools as they establish good policy and practice, and (4) assuring educational quality at a reasonable cost. The state board and the legislature will work out specific initiatives based on the recommendations of eight citizen/educator task forces.

Pennsylvania's governor developed public commitment to a clearly defined agenda for education reform. "Turning the Tide: An Agenda for Excellence in Pennsylvania Public Schools" proposed comprehensive programs to address concerns about the state's public schools. To support reforms, the governor has asked that 68% of the state's new general fund revenues be spent on education. This is the largest single-year increase in state support for education since the 1960s.

In response to a directive from the governor of *Puerto Rico*, the department of education developed a "Plan for Excellence in Education." The plan outlines the philosophy, goals, objectives, and long- and short-range activities for the department. A statewide education conference, attended by 750 participants, reviewed and approved the plan, and the governor has appointed a cabinet-level committee to prepare and submit legislation for funding the new initiatives.

In February 1984, the *South Dakota* State Board of Education began requiring local school districts to prepare plans that describe the content of every required course. The plan must include course objectives, an outline of the course content, evaluation procedures, and standards for passing. The board expects these plans to upgrade the quality of instruction, improve local district curriculum planning, facilitate the state department's dissemination of successful programs and practices, and help identify curriculum needs.

The *Texas* State Board of Education will implement recent legislation prescribing a core curriculum for all students, designed to guarantee every student a specific sequence of essential elements. Minimum time allotments within the school day will ensure that adequate instruction is provided. High school graduation requirements have been increased.

The *Vermont* State Board of Education's revised standards for approving public schools provide a curriculum framework for elementary and secondary schools, define student performance requirements, and require schools to assess performance and report the results to the public. Volunteer schools will implement the standards beginning September 1984.

Virginia's model high school, the Governor's Center for Educational Innovation and Technology, to open in September 1984, will serve as a showcase and laboratory training/demonstration center for exemplary educational practices. Attention will be focused on defining successful conditions for secondary student learning.

Wyoming's state superintendent appointed a blue-ribbon committee on quality education to determine how the state can preserve equity while achieving excellence. The committee is studying student achievement, classrooms, and educators, and will submit a final report in September 1984.[4]

In Massachusetts, the governor referred to the school reform package passed in his state in 1985, "Improving the Public Schools of the Commonwealth," as the most important legislation in his lifetime.[5] Among the elements central to this piece of legislation are equal educational grants, school improvement funds, statewide testing, minimum starting salaries for teachers, and early childhood education. This act will insure educational excellence and equity for all students in elementary and secondary schools of cities and towns, regional school districts, and independent vocational schools of the Commonwealth.

The courts have played a central role in education over the years, and their influence extends to setting quality standards. In what has been referred to as an historic case in West Virginia, Judge Arthur M. Recht (Ohio County Circuit) "ruled that the West Virginia school system, and the method of financing that system, violated the state constitution."

The judge's monumental 244-page opinion, in which he measured the schools against an elaborate—some say utopian—set of standards, included a scathing indictment of those responsible for running and providing for West Virginia's public schools, and called on the state legislature to do "no less than . . . completely reconstruct the entire system of education" in the state.[6]

The judge ruled that the criteria of excellence developed by the West Virginia State Department of Education should be used as standard for the state. He stated:

It is the legislature that must adopt standards of a high-quality system of education and provide the resources to guarantee that those standards are implemented.[7]

Even a brief overview such as this quickly demonstrates both the variety of school improvement approaches and the seriousness of the movement. While all states are not engaged in structural reform, all are aimed at school improvement, Phase I of a multiphased effort to update schools so they can respond more fully to current realities. All present reform measures can be the starting point for modernization. However, if all of the present energy expended in school reform adds up to little more than improving the present schools, the necessary transformation for renewal of the public education system will not be achieved nor will the quest for excellence be realized.

In a few states and localities, dramatic changes have been effected that will alter the total structure of public education in those localities. Using data from the Education Commission of the States, the efforts in North Carolina, Arkansas, and Tennessee to achieve school improvement will be outlined. Then a detailed profile of Atlanta, Georgia will illustrate sweeping changes in educational structures.

Profile: North Carolina

North Carolina Governor James B. Hunt, 1983 chairman of the Education Commission of the States' Task Force on Education for Economic Growth, carried out Task Force Recommendation 1 by setting up the broadly representative North Carolina Commission of Education for Economic Growth in Raleigh in October 1983. The commission developed comprehensive recommendations focused on those educational improvements needed to ensure strong economic growth and prosperity.

In April 1984, Hunt and the commission released the report and recommendations, which covered six broad areas: partnerships for improving education, the curriculum of North Carolina's schools, teachers and teaching, the learning environment, leadership and management of schools, and serving special groups and meeting special needs of the schools.

The report, "An Action Plan for North Carolina," recommended increases in the base pay of educators, a career growth program for teachers and administrators, a center for the advancement of teaching, a student information management system to reduce unnecessary paperwork, and increased funding for professional development programs.

For students, the commission recommended a competency-based curriculum with clear expectations for learning and a testing program to measure performance at grades 3, 6, and 9. Student promotion will be based on mastery of skills, and free summer remediation will be offered to students who need help.

Another recommendation will limit K–6 class sizes to 26 students. School boards were asked to tighten policies on homework, discipline and classroom interruptions, and to promote positive values.

The commission recommended strengthening the role of the principal and called for a principals' management program at the University of North Carolina.

Finally, the commission called for initiatives to meet special needs, such as "centers for excellence"—outstanding model schools—as well as additional appropriations for purchasing textbooks, supplies and equipment, and for furnishing computer labs for all schools.

Since the recommendations were released:

☐ The North Carolina General Assembly has passed a $300 million expansion budget for education.

☐ The state board of education and local boards of education are moving to carry out the recommendations.

☐ Local task forces on education for economic growth are forming.

☐ The business community is actively engaged, through the Business Committee on Education, in building partnerships with public schools.[8]

Profile: Arkansas

In a special session called by Governor Bill Clinton in late 1983, the Arkansas legislature approved the most comprehensive education program in the state's history. The program, much of it developed out of recommendations from a legislatively established and highly visible task force, the Education Standards Committee, was strongly supported by both education stakeholders and the general public. Hillary Rodham Clinton, the state's first lady, spearheaded the committee's effort, and, with an intense public awareness campaign, garnered support for funding an improved education system for the state.

Funds for the new education program will come, in large part, from an increase in the sales tax from 3% to 4% that is estimated to raise an additional $154 million in revenue. School districts will be required to raise their property tax rates to the statewide average to pay for their share of education improvements and will have to allocate up to 70% of their revenue to bring teacher salaries closer to regional averages. In March 1984, voters in 84 Arkansas school districts approved millage increases to finance measures enabling them to meet the new standards for state accreditation.

Among the improvements for which new funds will be used are:

☐ Smaller classes: no more than 25 students per class in grades 1 through 3, and no more than 28 students per class in grades 4 through 6.

☐ More principals and counselors per district.

☐ More course offerings in high schools, including language arts, science, mathematics, foreign languages, fine arts, computer science, social studies, physical education and health, and practical arts.

☐ Educational services for more secondary students, who will remain in school two years longer because the top age limit for compulsory attendance was raised from 15 to 17.

☐ Functional academic skills tests for practicing certified personnel, with prescribed remedial programs and subject-area tests.

☐ Testing programs for students in grades 3, 6, and 8 with requirements for individual attention for students who do not meet passing standards.

Besides overall funding and a new funding formula, the special legislative session approved programs for teacher, school, and student recognition; effective schools; parent involvement; leadership training; additional funding for technology; and testing for teacher certification. The session also created several committees, including

☐ The Arkansas Teacher Education/Certification/Evaluation Committee, charged with developing statewide standards for in-class evaluation and certification and recertification requirements (to report to the governor by November 1984).
☐ The School District Reorganization Study Commission, charged with developing a master plan for school district reorganization (to report to the governor by December 1984).
☐ The Commission to Study the Feasibility of Establishing a School Facility Bonding Authority, charged with making specific recommendations on the possibility of creating, developing and funding such an Authority (to report to the governor by November 1984).[9]

Profile: Tennessee

Tennessee's comprehensive reform act of 1984, signed by Governor Lamar Alexander in March 1984, established a five-step career ladder with annual salary incentives from $500 to $7,000 for Tennessee's 46,000 teachers. A one-cent sales tax hike and an amusement tax will fund this program. The five steps of the career ladder are

☐ Probationary teachers, who, after a positive evaluation, will be recommended for certification by their school board after their first year.
☐ Apprentice teachers, who serve three years and receive annual $500 supplements, must receive tenure at the end of their third year and move to the next level or lose their jobs.
☐ Career-level one teachers, who are certified for five more years and receive annual supplements of $1,000, supervise interns and probationary teachers in addition to teaching.
☐ Career-level two teachers, who are certified for another five years and are eligible for $2,000 and $4,000 annual salary supplements with 10- and 11-month contracts respectively, work with remedial and gifted students, and supervise apprentice teachers in addition to normal duties.
☐ Career-level three teachers, again certified for five years, are eligible for $3,000 annual supplements for 10-month contracts, $5,000 for 11 months and $7,000 for 12 months. They may evaluate other career-level teachers in addition to career-level two duties.

Evaluations by the school board of the state mark each year in the career ladder sequence and are keys to teacher progress up the ladder. School boards evaluate probationary and apprentice teachers, as well as those at career-level one. But the state may spot-check career-level one evaluations, or conduct its own at this stage. Disagreements will be settled by regional certification boards and may be appealed.

In a state mechanism, career-level three teachers, not in the same district, will evaluate career-level two and three teachers. The state began testing its evaluation criteria in February.

No quotas have been placed on the number of teachers who can reach the advanced ranks. However, it is possible for teachers to go down the ladder if they refuse to take additional responsibilities or fail to meet other requirements.

Under a "fast-track" provision in the legislation, about 32,000 teachers could qualify during the next year for career-level one. Practicing teachers can qualify for the ladder by passing the National Teachers Examination and receiving their school board's recommendation, or by successfully completing a local staff-development program that meets minimum state standards.[10]

LOCAL REFORM INITIATIVES

ATLANTA, GEORGIA: URBAN SCHOOL REFORM

Atlanta, Georgia, has an urban school system that has turned itself around, reversing the spiral of decline that has characterized many big city school districts.

Years before the states were busy with school reform legislation, the Atlanta Public School System under Alonzo Crim, new superintendent of schools in the 1970s, proposed a basic strategy:

Two jobs await us. *First, we must close the skills gap between our schools and our future.* I propose:

☐ to develop new and better curricula for teaching science, math, language skills, and computer literacy;
☐ to improve the quality of teaching by upgrading the skills of today's teachers, helping to attract highly qualified new people to teaching, reducing paperwork, and in other ways bolstering teaching as a profession and improving teachers' working conditions; and
☐ to help local school systems assess their own needs and follow their own paths toward higher standards through a new national Fund for Excellence.

Second, we must close the ambition gap between American higher education and American higher achievement. I propose:

☐ to expand student and institutional aid so that low- and middle-income students can again go as far as their talent and hard work will take them, and so that American voctional schools, community colleges, colleges and universities will be assured of a stable financial base;

□ to adopt a new national policy to foster graduate education and research through merit-based fellowships to faculty and students in areas of critical national need; and

□ to launch a five-year program to refurbish laboratories and libraries, so that the tools for our academic scientists, engineers, and their students are state-of-the-art.

Some will reject this strategy outright, on the ground articulated by President Reagan, that federal efforts in the field of education are at the root of our current problems. Granted, not every federal program has succeeded. In a era of budgetary stringency, it is vital to build on the experience of the past two decades by redeploying resources to initiatives with demonstrated records of success. But the point is that there are many such efforts—for example, Project Headstart and Chapter I (formerly Title I), both of which have helped raise achievements among disadvantaged students.

We have also learned that states and localities can successfully address many problems if they are allowed the necessary flexibility, and that cooperation between the public and private sectors can be extremely fruitful. Federal commitments are no substitute for all-out efforts by every other level of government and sector of society. But wisely designed and prudently administered, federal initiatives can catalyze and focus the burgeoning nationwide dedication to improving education for all. It is in this spirit that I offer an agenda for excellence.[11]

The Atlanta Public Schools have an enrollment that is 90 percent Black, second only to Washington D.C. in minority enrollment. There are 117 schools in this district; all but two qualify for federal assistance based on poverty. When Dr. Crim took over the schools in early 1973, most of the students were performing well below the national norms in academic achievement, and the community had come to believe that little could be done to improve the situation. The public had lost confidence in their schools. With the appointment of Crim, a series of town hall meetings were conducted, attended by over 10,000 citizens who established four priorities:

1. Improve significantly the reading, writing, speaking, listening, and computational skills of students.
2. Assist students in handling their futures—job placement.
3. Allocate the system's resources to students equitably.
4. Improve communications between school staff and the public, between school staff and students, and among school staff members.[12]

The community was prepared to help in the achievement of these priorities.

Out of a town meeting for 200 business, industrial, political, and educational leaders in which the governor of the state also participated came a partnership of higher education, the Atlanta Chamber of Commerce, and the Atlanta Public Schools. This Atlanta Partnership initiated four programs:

Adopt-A-School, which allows business firms or religious congregations to "adopt" a school or program within the school system. In 1982–83, 70 schools and/or programs were adopted by 122 organizations.

Affirmative Action Job Placement, which aims at motivating and funding jobs for the bottom quarter of the senior class.

The Advisement Program, which has a twofold goal: member organizations provide expertise in many subject areas to the schools, and each of the district magnet schools has an advisory group to assist in relating programs to development in industry. One of the magnet schools—the Harper Magnet School for Financial Services—for instance, has an advisory committee representing eight banks and the Federal Reserve.

The higher education community is also collaborating with the schools through faculty exchanges of principals and professors, joint venturing for grants, a university's taking over substitute teaching in one region, and joint sponsorship of a metropolitan summer school for gifted students.

Forty interdenominational congregations involving Christian, Jewish, and Moslem faiths have worked in tutorial and youth advocacy programs. During the 1982–83 year, more than 5,000 volunteers were working in the Atlanta schools with 1,000 directly participating as tutors.

Parent-Teacher Associations (PTA) have played active roles in the Atlanta Public Schools. Now exceeding 18,000 members, the new PTA is anything but the "cookie sale" variety. Most of their initiatives focus on such tough problems as low achievement, politics, poor health, teenage pregnancies, and venereal disease. One newly formed parent organization in a predominantly white neighborhood—the Northside Parent Association—took on the issue of "white flight."

All of this community involvement contributed to an overall strategic plan which focused on student success. Dr. Crim suggests:

> . . . first, that there be some success, and second that success be visible, under-stood, acknowledged, and rewarded. This may seem obvious, but in fact it is a form of "chicken and egg" dilemma. It has stymied school administrators, teachers, parents, and children in troubled school systems for years. If perfor-mance is poor but rewards such as promotion are given, low achievement is reinforced. On the other hand, if poor performance is continually surrounded by the stigma of failure, there is little motivation to change.[13]

To break out of this cycle, a *Systematic Objective Plan* was established involving a careful planning and management process aimed at achieving the goal of increased student achievement in the basics—reading and mathematics. Each individual school, led by administrators, faculty and staff, collaborated on setting school ob-jectives, assessing needs, mapping out approaches to meeting these needs, and developing appropriate staff development efforts. School teams evaluated these improvement efforts as a basis for further planning.

This process helped teachers talk to one another on the crucial matter of student progress while promoting better coordination among the different grade levels. The overall impact made teachers more knowledgeable about school goals and how these goals were being met.

A *Pupil Progress Policy*, also part of the overall strategy for improving academic performance, involved a personalized procedure for assessing and guiding the progress of individual learners to give added assurance that each student will be assisted to reach school goals. Individual programs are monitored by computers that provide quarterly profiles of each learner's progress to tutors, parents, and administrators.

Coupled with this individual profile is an *Analysis of Pupil Retainees.* These students who are not progressing toward the goals are identified and research assistants assume the task of providing the reasons for this non-progress. The overall intent is to develop better approaches to help these students progress.

The Instructive Division of the school district has been given the responsibility for establishment of *Systemwide Standards* that are used to guide curriculum areas, especially those in reading and mathematics.

A *Celebration of Learning* initiatives has also been established in which those students who perform at or above the national norm in the *California Achievement Tests* are rewarded with a certificate of excellence, while those who perform below the norm but have made progress receive a certificate of improvement. The superintendent of schools explains how this process works:

> The occasion of celebration of learning occurs during the first week of September. Parents are invited, and free transportation is provided. This year (1983), certificates were given to 31,181 for having attained the national norm and to 11,516 for making significant progress—a total of 42,697, or three-fourths of the pupils in grades K–11.[14]

A key component in the Atlanta Public Schools' effort to regain excellence was the students' participation. Dr. Crim explains:

> In our efforts to build a community of believers, we also turned to students themselves for contributions to creating this condition. We assumed that neither the 1985 goal relating to national norms nor the annual 20 percent targets would be reached if students themselves did not expect to reach them.[15]

To generate student enthusiasm for the 1985 goal of the school reaching national norms in academic achievement, a town hall meeting was held in 1980 for student leaders in the secondary schools (middle and high schools). Pledges were made by school officials to parents, business and industrial representatives, and to the students on the goal of reaching national norms. The student leaders also pledged to go back to their respective schools to work on support for the goal.

Student town hall meetings are now an annual event, an important occasion for interacting with school personnel and communities on common concerns.

Most standard curriculum efforts do not succeed with all children—many who come from very low income homes are not well served by the traditional offerings. Consequently, a number of initiatives were made available for such students, including comprehensive early assessment programs for all primary students, compensatory education in which supplementary instructional assistance is provided, English as a Second Language (ESL) programs, and full day kindergarten programs. Many such programs would not be delivered without the contributions of federally-funded programs.

Because teachers are identified as the critical element in the Atlanta Public Schools, keeping teachers involved and updated becomes a central priority. Staff development has become the mechanism for improving teacher performance. Through ongoing staff development, teachers have been encouraged to try new approaches to assess the effectiveness of their methods. Support systems including the following have been provided:

Reading/Math Center in which K–12 teachers spend from three days to a week in specialized inservice sessions;
School Reports in which research assistants publish summaries of individual school program efforts;
Staff Evaluation in which staff become involved in the formulation of appropriate evaluation instruments for teachers and other school personnel.

School administrators are also given central roles in the Atlanta Public Schools' quest for excellence. Three principles have been used to help school administrators, especially principals, better achieve systemwide goals: (1) working from the bottom up, (2) focusing on the most effective research, and (3) encouraging open dialogue and participation. Again, as with teachers, staff development is essential. In this capacity, a systemwide program—the Administrators University—provides principals with training in management, supervision, and leadership behavior.

One of the unique dimensions to the Atlanta Public School story involves the Community Service Requirement. Effective in the 1984–85 school year, the Atlanta Board of Education approved a required course, "Duties to the Community," for all students entering ninth grade. A brochure informs the student of expectations under this policy:

This Community Service Requirement will provide you with the opportunity to give productive service, which will mutually benefit the community and you as a student volunteer.

As a volunteer, you will not receive pay for your service; however, you will receive one half (1/2) unit or 7½ hours of credit, and the opportunity to know and relate to the needs of the community in which you live.

Student volunteers are required to

☐ Contribute 75 hours of Community Service, beginning in the ninth grade and completed by the end of the 11th grade.
☐ Write an acceptable essay or composition to be evaluated by your advisor or counselor.
☐ Help to identify the agency or organization where you would like to serve.
☐ Keep daily records of hours served.
☐ Report to your Advisor or Counselor about your experiences on a weekly basis.
☐ Keep a positive attitude.[16]

What have all these ingredients been able to achieve in Atlanta? Dr. Crim wanted to create a community of believers. His results speak for themselves:

> We have exceeded the national norm in another important respect as well. Students enrolled in *elementary* schools are now scoring *well above the national norm* in both reading and mathematics: Fifty-three percent of the students scored at or above the national norm in reading, and 61 percent scored at or above the national norm in mathematics. The combination of grades K–8 has reached the national norm as well. In reading, 50 percent of the students in that group scored at or above the national norm while 57 percent scored at or above the national norm in mathematics.
>
> We have indeed gone beyond expectations regarding the annual improvement required to reach the national norm at all grade levels by 1985.
>
> Another index of progress is performance at the tenth grade level on the *Basic Skills Tests*—a test designed and required by the state for graduation from high school. Implementation of the requirement began in the fall of 1982. The results show that 82 percent of our students mastered the objectives in the reading test and 67 percent in the mathematics test. Even though these percentages of mastery were below the statewide averages, they were significantly higher than our schools' performance in the field test administered to the 1981 tenth grade. The scores in 1982 were eight percentage points higher in reading and 19 percentage points higher in mathematics than those of 1981. It is anticipated that the results of the fall testing program in 1983 will exceed those of 1982.
>
> *Analysis of the rates of progress and of achievement suggest that the school system has made significant gains by identifying and using the programs, strategies, and resources necessary for the overall improvement of academic achievement.*[17]

Finally, Dr. Crim reveals some of the implications of the Atlanta Public Schools' success to other school sysetms:

1. *Challenge staff and pupils to improve their own performance.* Seek quality performance. Clearly enunciate objectives and expected accomplishments in measurable and/or observable terms. Recognize and reinforce improve-

ment and excellent performance. Develop performance profiles—performance of students and of staff. Seek to derive data for these profiles as a normal outgrowth of the processes used in pursuing the objectives.

2. *Stress the significance of involving in the decision process persons who will be affected by the decision.* Have a climate of open communication and of visible activities and results. Place decision-making responsibilities at the level nearest to the point of action that is practical and reasonable. Seek the contributions which can be made by members of the larger community including parents, volunteers, and representatives of business, civic, cultural, religious, higher education, and other groups. Form an active partnership between the school system and the various community groups, one characterized by mutual service and open communication. Periodically provide opportunities for pupils, staff, and the public to express their opinions and concerns.

Finally, developing a community of believers from within the school system as well as from the larger community is a complex effort. It needs to be tailored to the local environment and adjusted to accommodate new events. A community of believers is essential in attaining the priority and support of the high quality schooling our young people deserve.[18]

The Atlanta case study is being repeated in other cities such as Houston, and Washington, D.C., where superintendents have reported similar results. In these cities, the leadership has been long and steady, allowing the nurturing of community support and fundamental improvements to take hold. In Denver, the school board and superintendent have agreed to make their school district a 21st century model. Local initiatives are increasing rapidly as state reform legislation is implemented throughout the nation.

PERFORMANCE STANDARDS AND ACCOUNTABILITY

A central component of modernization is the emphasis on performance outcomes, which the public has agreed the school system must deliver to the learners. These standards may be stated in behavioral or competence terms—what the learner is expected to do as a result of attending school, or they may be stated in terms of "indicators"—high school graduation rates or dropout rates.

States such as Maryland have spent considerable time planning and developing statewide behavioral or competence objectives. For example, a student graduating from high school must be able to write a critical essay on a topic such as individual liberty that is free of grammatical errors, or a student entering high school must be able to read and comprehend *A Tale of Two Cities* or some other literary classic. The advantage of depicting standards in behavioral terms is specificity; its disadvantage is complexity.

Another approach to student performance involves such indicators as the percentage of high school students accepted into colleges and universities, and student alternative roles. Illinois has passed legislation requiring localities to submit a report card to the parents and taxpayers of the district, the governor, and the general assembly:

> . . . The report card must describe the performance of the district's students *by attendance center* as well as by district and describe the district's use of its financial resources. The report card must be completed and disseminated prior to October 31 of each school year, beginning with the 1986–87 school year.
>
> In general, the report must contain information on each school attendance center, the school district, and the state, which indicates the present performance of the school, the state norms and the following year's targets for the particular school and school district. In addition, the report card must include the following indicators of school attendance center, district, and statewide student performance:
>
> (a) percentage of students who placed in the top and bottom quartiles of nationally normed achievement tests;
>
> (b) composite and subtest means for college-bound students;
>
> (c) student attendance rates;
>
> (d) percentage of students not promoted to next grade;
>
> (e) graduation rate; and
>
> (f) percentage of student transfers out and transfers in.
>
> The report card must also include the following indicators of district and statewide school performance:
>
> (a) average class size;
>
> (b) percentage of students enrolled in courses in high school mathematics, science, English, and social sciences;
>
> (c) amount of time per day devoted to mathematics, science, English, and social science at primary, middle, and junior high school levels;
>
> (d) percentage of students enrolled in college preparatory, general education, and vocational education programs;
>
> (e) pupil-teacher ratio;
>
> (f) pupil-administrator ratio;
>
> (g) operating expenditure per pupil;
>
> (h) per capita tuition charge;
>
> (i) a graphic display of district expenditures by fund;
>
> (j) average administrator salary; and
>
> (k) average teacher salary.[19]

While the indicators of performance approach is less complex than competence-based outcomes, its weakness is a lack of specificity about the individual learner. The indicators usually reveal group norms.

A third and the most popular approach to performance standards is the required subjects approach. Students graduating from high school must pass a minimal number of courses in certain fields such as four years of English, three years of mathematics, and four years of a language.

While this approach is simplest in form and easiest to administer, its weakness is that it does not guarantee either mastery or competence by the student.

A combination or integration of the above approaches is making sense to localities. For example, the Amherst (Massachusetts) School System requires not only a minimum set of core requirements but states them publicly in competency-based language. For instance, in junior high school "introduction to fiction,"

The student should be able to
(1) Demonstrate an understanding of such literary terms as
    a. setting and mood
    b. character development
    c. conflict (human vs. others, vs. nature, vs. themselves)
    d. suspense
    e. elements of plot
    by identifying examples in assigned readings, applying these concepts to personal experiences through writing, and role-playing or dramatizing these concepts.
(2) Develop skills in recognizing and using logic and sequence by
    a. analyzing the plots of stories
    b. completing open-ended stories
    c. writing alternative endings to stories
    d. using a given body of knowledge to draw conclusions and make predictions
    e. discussing the motivations for actions of characters in assigned stories.
(3) Cite examples of universal human themes in fiction such as
    a. adaptation and survival
    b. growth and maturation of the individual
    c. affinity with nature
    d. means of attaining justice.[20]

In high school "journalism," the objectives may appear as follows:

The student should be able to
1. List and discuss the forces which regulate the press.
2. Recognize appeals to emotions.
3. Recognize the major local, state, and national news stories being covered by the press in any given week and keep aware of the important issues being discussed in the media during the course of the semester.
4. Examine the development of freedom of the press in the United States.
5. Identify the elements inherent in the news.
6. Recognize editorializing in news stories and state opinion in news stories properly.[21]

Statewide performance standards serve to unify reforms carried out at the local levels. This balance between centralized and decentralized responsibilities provides a constructive dynamic between two crucial accountability levels of the system. The degree of tilt in favor of centralized or decentralized authority may differ with the needs of each state, but the two sectors are necessary parts of the whole. Unity with diversity appears to be a reasonable synthesis for advancing the excellence agenda while maintaining the values of public accountability and local responsibility.

COMPETITION AND CHOICE—DIVERSE MEANS TO COMMON PERFORMANCE STANDARDS

Competition and choice are strategic components of both the short- and long-range restructuring and modernization of the public school system. They provide legitimate means for a community to decide on its educational program. The decision process usually involves parents, students, and teachers choosing from among a range of legitimate educational options. Those who prefer more established, traditional programs, of course, are free to choose them, as are those who seek something different.

Providing opportunities for competition and choice within the public schools allows people to make initial contact with the schools, which, in turn, stimulates the community to respond, perhaps in a pluralistic way, to their public school program. Without competition and choice, an educational program is imposed on the learners as clients, who have little to say about their own preferences.

One example of such pluralism would be matching individual learners to programs and teachers. Teachers and students each have their own styles; matching styles of teaching with styles of learning could provide a new way of individualizing school programming while maintaining support from the community.

Incorporating choice in public schools embraces most of the principles identified in preceding chapters: they employ the consumer idea of freedom of choice in the public schools; and these alternatives have been developed through the joint participation of parents, teachers, schools, and community. The creativity and entrepreneurial energies of these agents have been encouraged to modify the previously uniform styles of teaching, and the learner gains a sense of empowerment through making an important decision about the kind of education that is most compatible with his or her goals. Of course, since such programs do not exist in a leadership vacuum, leadership has been exercised by educators and public officials to maximize local initiatives through greater decentralization of decision making. The result fosters use of diverse means to common organizational ends.

MAGNET SCHOOLS

Public schools of choice now appear in districts throughout the United States. One form, the magnet school, has been established in nearly every big city to provide distinctive programs and in part to encourage desegregation.[22] Magnet schools, emphasizing one particular curriculum area such as art, science, languages, or commerce, are usually located in different geographical regions of a city, allowing integration to take place through a process of student choice. Students are naturally attracted to magnet schools by the substantive drawing power of their programs.

New Haven Magnet Schools of Choice.   The New Haven (Connecticut) Public Schools, one of the early pioneers, illustrates some of the qualities of the magnet schools that can be found in many public school systems:

> In the early 1970s, New Haven began exploring the idea of "magnets," or schools of choice—schools which would draw their students from all over the city because of their particular curriculum or design. Because of their success in diversifying the city's educational opportunities, the number of magnets has grown in 1984 to six. The magnet alternative is now available to students at all levels, from kindergarten through 12th grade. These schools have certain elements in common: Admission to each is open to all New Haven students and is based on a lottery designed to ensure a racial, social, and academic balance in each student body. Many magnet school students participate in the city-wide Talented and Gifted program, in varsity sports at the comprehensive high schools, and in such regional opportunities as the *Educational Center for the Arts.*[23]

Some additional excerpts from their brochure illustrate the variety of programs possible in a magnet school structure:

West Hills School (Grades K-5):

The WEST HILLS curriculum is based on the developmental approach as formulated at the Bank Street School of Education in New York City. It integrates all learning experiences and processes, to help children make sense of their world. Teachers are respectful of and sensitive to the individual differences and unique learning styles of children. In regular consultation with Bank Street specialists, teachers respond to these differences by planning curriculum and devising teaching strategies appropriate to the developmental level, strengths, and weaknesses of each child. The success that the children experience develops a sense of achievement, sustains enthusiasm, and leads to further mastery.

  The core curriculum focuses on the environment. Chosen science and social studies themes are pursued for extended periods and in depth, providing experiences in the community beyond the classroom, and opportunities for children to learn basic research skills and to pursue their own interests. On all developmental levels, children help to make major curriculum decisions. The emphasis on individual development, and constant participation in decision-making, enables each child to learn how to attack problems—to learn how to learn.

Conte Arts Magnet School (Grades 5-8):

At the CONTE ARTS MAGNET SCHOOL, children are taught to see, think, and move in ways they never considered before. Alongside the full spectrum of academic disciplines, students study the four major arts disciplines, experiment wtih different materials and equipment, and acquire skills they can develop and enjoy throughout their lives. Any student in New Haven with an interest in the arts is welcome to apply; *no audition* or particular academic rating is . required for admission. Based on principles and practices developed by the Center for Theatre Techniques in Education, the Conte philosophy is founded on the idea that the skills of the artist—a creative approach to problem-solving, an ability to express one's self—are the same skills required in all academic disciplines, from history to English to science. It is the school's goal to help students make the connections, to understand how one art form builds on another, how all disciplines relate to one another, and to help students draw on their arts experiences to develop a new approach to learning. Clearly it is working: Conte Arts Magnet has been singled out by the U.S. Department of Education as one of the country's finest secondary schools.

High School in the Community (Grades 9–12):

Housed in New Haven's oldest operating school building, the HIGH SCHOOL IN THE COMMUNITY was also New Haven's earliest venture into non-traditional alternatives in high school education. Established in 1970, it has been designated an "exemplary educational institution" by the U.S. Department of Education.

HSC offers a full academic program and strong college-preparation. The curriculum emphasizes the traditional major subject areas (English, math, science, social studies, foreign languages). The organization of the school day and year, however, is far from traditional. The focus of the student's day is a four-period "block class," which meets five days a week, for one nine-week quarter. Block classes are often team-taught and inter-disciplinary (an introduction to psychology, for example, might be taught by an historian and an English teacher, while a course on "technology" might be given by a science teacher and an English teacher). The block configuration allows students to concentrate their attention and gives teachers more flexibility in planning lectures, projects, and special activities. In addition, each student takes two one-hour courses, which meet daily and extend over a period of a quarter, a semester, or a year. The extensive course list includes more than 80 choices for study.

The Sound School (Grades 9–12):

THE SOUND SCHOOL offers an educational opportunity unique in New Haven and unique in the United States: It is the only complete public American high school with a marine orientation. The school will soon be housed in a new facility directly on the New Haven waterfront on Long Island Sound, where its "floating classroom," the 66-foot schooner *J. N. Carter* is docked. Its 200 students will have the opportunity to acquire all the basic academic skills required for a high school diploma while exploring their rich marine environment and its history. For some 95% of Sound School students, the school is their first experience on the water; it provides an extraordinary chance for urban youth to explore a whole new world.

The Cooperative High School (Grades 9–12):

THE COOPERATIVE HIGH SCHOOL offers its students a rigorous academic program in an intimate, supportive environment. With a strong emphasis on the humanities, the school provides students with individualized academic programs, small classes, and instruction using a variety of teaching methods. Enrollment is limited to 240 New Haven students, in grades 9–12. Each of the school's 18 teachers, coordinated by a full-time guidance counselor, takes responsibility for counseling (both guidance and curriculum) the 15–18 students in his/her homeroom group. All teaching and administrative staff members participate in every aspect of school life, from curriculum planning to team teaching and counseling, thus encouraging an atmosphere of commitment to every individual student. The school makes an effort to draw atention to individual students' points of excellence (athletic, academic, artistic) to help build confidence and identity.

The High School for Business and Computers and The High School for Health Professions (Grades 9–12):

THE HIGH SCHOOL FOR BUSINESS AND COMPUTERS and THE HIGH SCHOOL FOR HEALTH PROFESSIONS each admitted their first group of 100 freshmen during the 1983–84 school year. This innovative new approach to high school education will give motivated youngsters the chance to explore a career field which excites them while completing a rigorous basic four-year high school curriculum. Each program will accept 100 freshmen each year, with an ultimate projected enrollment of 325–350 per program.

    The school's curriculum is geared to offer its graduating seniors three options: direct entry into the work force, admission to a two-year college or training program, or admission to a four-year college or university. This is not a trade school however. Neither program is equipped to *train* for a career; both are equipped to *prepare* students to pursue higher level professional training in their chosen areas. Heavy emphasis is placed, especially during the first two years, on a high-standard, basic education, which will give students a general program comparable to that at a comprehensive high school.[24]

    The fact that such examples can be and are being repeated in most of the big city schools serves as testimony to their growing importance to the community.

COMMUNITY SCHOOL DISTRICT 4 IN NEW YORK CITY

Other school districts that have provided models of competition and choice have had a profound effect on the revitalization of the schools. Community School District 4 in New York City provides another good example of how the principles of competition and choice can work.

    For over a decade, a predominantly Hispanic population has been pioneering alternative education in New York. From mini-schools to separate schools emphasizing different careers and talents, this urban school system has given educational consumers—parents and students—a right to decide which public school best fits their needs and aspirations. The purposes, goals, and assumptions guiding District 4's alternative schools program are described as follows:

Purposes:

To provide opportunities for children and their parents to select an alternative school environment that better meets the individual needs and abilities of the children.

To facilitate the goals and objectives of all schools in the district by introducing new, smaller autonomous educational units and redistributing the school population. The result for alternative and regular schools alike is the potential for greater personal attention and more continuity from year to year, better planning for individual attention, and family/school interaction.

To encourage professional staff members to develop innovative programs and to give them the opportunity to participate in the decision-making process necessary for the establishment and success of the program.

To encourage greater parent participation and involvement in the educational programs of their children.

Goals:

To develop the intellectual, social, emotional, physical, and creative potentialities of all children in Community District #4.

To raise the achievement levels in the basic curriculum areas with a special emphasis on improving reading, writing, and mathematics.

To instill a sense of pride and confidence in the children's own accomplishments and in the cultural heritage that is their birthright.

To develop and encourage a greater understanding and awareness of those qualities which are essential to individual dignity and that lead to effective citizenship in a democratic society.

Basic Assumptions:

When teachers are given the opportunity to develop an educational program, with clearly defined objectives, emphasizing a special interest, education, or individualized, departmentalized instruction—a meaningful, successful learning environment can be achieved. Inherent is the belief that when professional staff agrees on a common approach, philosophy, and set of objectives, the opportunities for success are greatly enhanced.

When children and parents are given a choice in selecting their own school out of several alternatives, the children's interest and motivation for learning are significantly increased and the school is able to better develop interests and raise achievement.

Smaller schools are better able to deal with the multiplicity of challenges that children face on a day-to-day basis. The staff and children are able to establish a close positive relationship; they simply get to to know each other better and that is most important in establishing an educational environment that is conducive to learning and development.[25]

The different options offered include:

- ☐ Harbor Junior High for Performing Arts
- ☐ Isaac Newton School for Math and Science
- ☐ The Key School (individualization based on learning styles)
- ☐ The Academy of Environmental Science
- ☐ East Harlem Career Academy
- ☐ Creative Learning Community Prep School
- ☐ College for Human Services Junior High School

Alternative programs are identified at all levels in the district. In addition to a senior high school center for science and mathematics, there are twenty-two special programs available at the elementary and secondary junior high school levels. These optional programs are described in both English and Spanish, making sure that information about the programs reaches a diverse population of prospective students and parents. The world of options opened up by District 4 has had a measurable revitalizing effect on students, parents, and teachers. For example, one of the alternatives—College for Human Services Junior High School—emphasizes service and caring through internships in day care centers, health care, and community agencies. Extensive newspaper coverage in the city shows that general public interest can be aroused by an educational approach that is based on competition and choice.

STATE SUPPORTED OPTIONS AND CHOICE

The implementation of competition and choice programs is also illustrated by the passage of important new educational legislation. Several states—notably Florida, Tennessee, and Minnesota—have considered competition and choice related legislation. The Florida legislature passed bills initiating alternative educational programs over a decade ago. Although the Florida legislation initially responded to those learners perceived to require special programming, more recent attempted efforts are broader in scope, referring to the concept of a school of choice. The idea of alternative programs has been adapted so that any learner for whom the present school program is not working may be eligible to participate in special programming.

A statewide task force in Florida that studied the issues presented the following recommendations to the legislature:

The Task Force Recommends That:

1. The legislature authorize yearly incentive grants to districts for the planning and development of programs and schools of choice.
2. Student eligibility for alternative education be modified to include students who demonstrate special talents, interests, or readiness for a unique alter-

native program or school of choice based upon specific eligibility criteria approved by the district school board.

3. Programs and schools of choice offer basic subject areas required for high school graduation or pupil progression, but shall be granted flexibility in course title, design, content, delivery, and assessment. The DOE shall develop policies and rules that permit such flexibility and that facilitate credit transfer to other educational programs or districts.[26]

Tennessee and Minnesota have attempted to introduce voucher-like proposals for their states. Their competition and choice plans involve private as well as public schools.

The Access to Excellence Bill introduced in Minnesota proposed a plan that would provide parents and students with choice beyond local district boundaries. The following sections of the bill illustrate its intentions:

Access to Excellence

Section 1. (PURPOSE.)
The purpose of the access to excellence program is to give parents and students increased opportunity to find excellence in education while giving local school officials increased opportunity to offer excellence in instruction to students.
Section 2. (ACCOUNTABILITY.)
The program is based on accountability.
(a) The state will be accountable for developing clear statements of expected learner outcomes and appropriate tests.
(b) Local districts will have more responsibility in designing programs to educate students.[27]

While this bill has not passed the Minnesota Legislature, it does show the continued interest of citizens and government in competition and choice as a legitimate means of reform in education.

EDUCATIONAL TECHNOLOGY

A revolution in the use of electronic technology is taking place in the schools today. In just a single year, for example, the use of microcomputers has tripled.[28] In 1985, more than 85 percent of the schools were using them. As important as this trend is, it represents the tip of the iceberg in advancing technology. Soon voice responsive interactive computers that will be simple to use and able to perform many functions now only imagined in science fiction will be available. Robotics will find its way into education as it has in manufacturing. Cable television and computers will be linked to deliver information and knowledge. Teletext is now available in the home for continuous updated "newspaper" coverage. Such systems also have the potential to deliver much of the present subject matter curriculum. Already cable television is making our foremost scholars available to learners who would not otherwise have access to them. An interactive educational network could provide two-way communication between teacher and learner.

Plans for the use of these new electronic tools are well underway. One of the most ambitious is Allied Project Athena at the Massachusetts Institute of Technology (M.I.T.). One of the major goals of Athena is to promote a new educative environment that opens new ways of learning.

> . . . Our present educational environment does not differ greatly from that of twenty or even one hundred years ago, despite the appearance of new media technologies that seem to harbor great potential for positive changes in the educational process.
>
> Students learn by listening to teachers presenting new concepts, by reading books and journals, by working problems and receiving some form of corrective feedback, and by observation and trial and error in the laboratory.
>
> Athena is based on the hypothesis that the imaginative use of an interlinked network of computer workstations can greatly enhance the quality and effectiveness of our educational program. Given the opportunity and the means, we believe that M.I.T. faculty, working with students and with the help of support staff, can develop software tools that will significantly improve the ways in which students learn concepts, develop intuition, and expand their creative abilities.
>
> . . . We hope that Athena will create throughout the Institute a dynamic environment conducive to exploring, inventing, and evaluating new ways of tackling both old and new problems.
>
> Eventually at least 3,000 workstations equipped with computational and graphic capabilities will be installed and linked together through a campuswide network. This hardware, together with software and support services, will be available to all M.I.T. faculty and students to help them rethink and redesign methods of learning in the classroom and the laboratory.
>
> . . . We believe that computers can be used beyond mere calculation to create environments that enhance exploration, experimentation, and therefore learning. We foresee, for example, the development of interactive modes of instruction based around a teaching facility with workstations available to each student and to the instructor. Such a system could be used in a number of ways:
>
> - Students follow at their workstations what is being done at the instructor's workstation. If they wish, they can capture the material presented by the instructor in their files for further review, reference, and development. An instructor might use this mode, for example, to compare DNA sequences spanning an eon of evolution or to illustrate the perturbations of crystalline structures under a variety of conditions.
> - After observing an instructor's work, students use that work, perhaps with modifications and extensions, to deal with new situations. An instructor might create a model bridge design, for example, and students would then modify the design to test the effect of different traffic load conditions.
> - Students work on their own at computer-based exercises, with instructors

and teaching assistants available for tutorial assistance. After performing a chemistry experiment, for example, students might use the computer to simulate a wide range of related experiments or to compile and analyze the results of their own and other students' experiments.

- Instructors employ programs designed to simulate the behavior of complex organizations and systems to illustrate real-world economic and political situations. This allows the introduction of models more complex than those normally used in the classroom and in problem sets to exemplify concepts. After suitable orientation, students might use such a system to follow out and compare the consequences of difficult policy alternatives.

. . . Outside the classroom, students might try experiments of their own or pose "what if" questions to check and refine their understanding of basic concepts. The educational significance of providing carefully selected environments in which students can explore in this way is supported by a substantial body of theory and experience.

. . . Finally, looking well ahead and extrapolating from current computer science research, it may eventually be possible to create systems that tutor students directly and assist them in solving problems. As the student develops a step-by-step solution to a problem, the computer constructs a network relating the steps to each other. In addition, it has been taught to recognize the most common errors students make in such problems. Given this knowledge and the ability to perform mathematical manipulations, the computer prompts the student whenever he or she makes a mistake in either formulating the problem or carrying out the associated mathematics.

These are only a few examples of "new ways to learn." If Athena is a success, we shall discover along the way many more innovative ways to employ computers effectively in the educational process, even as we improve our understanding of how computers affect the learning environment. These innovations will spring from the creative talents of our faculty and students.[29]

The signal sent by Project Athena throughout the educative world is strong and clear. The new technology can help transform the delivery of education, making equality available to more people than ever before.

Another proposal for the use of new media technology is satellite education, in which academic and career oriented services can be transmitted across the world. Based on an open university concept pioneered in Greenland, the satellite school or college can use cable television to reach interested learners even in remote areas. The idea is to bring quality educational programming to more people in the comforts of their own homes through television. Couple television with computers and telephones, and one assembles the most powerful retrieval tool ever devised. This technology has the capacity to link people with the expertise they need. It can also help to build educational clusters that provide human support and a sense of community among farflung learners. These combined technologies can thus create enhanced learning for more people in more places.

COMPUTERS IN THE SCHOOLS

The potential of computer technology in education at the local level must be developed as an integral part of school improvement efforts. Some results from the use of computers in schools are already beginning to surface. The Calvert County School District in Maryland has pioneered the use of instructional computers by using a Computer-Assisted Instruction (CAI) system developed by Computer Curriculum Cooperation, which offers over 25 curricula in basic skills and other academic areas throughout the elementary and secondary levels. The computer courses available to the Calvert County schools are

Elementary Courseware:

> Mathematics Strands 1–6
> Mathematics Strands 1–6 in Spanish
> Problem Solving
> Audio Reading
> Basic Reading
> Reading for Comprehension
> Remedial Reading
> Critical Reading Skills
> Language Arts Strands
> Language Arts Topics

Secondary Courseware:

> Mathematics Strands 7 & 8
> Enrichment Modules 7 & 8
> Introduction to Algebra
> Critical Reading Skills
> Fundamentals of English
> Survival Skills
> Exploring Careers

Adult Courseware:

> Adult Arithmetic Skills
> Adult Reading Skills
> Adult Language Skills 1
> Adult Language Skills 2
> High School Equivalency

Special Interest Courseware:

> English as a Second Language
> Introduction to Programming
> Basic Programming [30]

The following *Baltimore Sun* account reveals how the Calvert County schools use this computer program and the superintendent's assessment of its impact:

> Every elementary school student in Calvert County had a daily session with a computer last year.
>
> For 10 minutes every day, every student went through a personalized mathematics lesson on a computer terminal. For an additional 10 minutes, fourth and fifth graders, and some third graders, took a reading lesson as well.
>
> Test scores—which, admittedly, are not an entirely faithful indicator—are up significantly. Visitors are coming in from out of state to see how it works. Staff morale—especially Mr. Karol's morale—is high. Money is being spent to expand the program into the middle schools.
>
> "We're no longer at a waltz tempo," Mr. Karol says. "We've got a Philip Sousa march. We're really starting to click."
>
> . . . Mr. Karol happily shows off graphs charting his schools' results on the California Achievement Test as proof that something is happening. CAT scores everywhere are going up—as teachers get better and better at preparing their students for the test. . . .
>
> Mr. Karol credits the CCC computer program for much of what is happening on the test, as reflected in last fall's results.
>
> The standard "bell curve"—with a few students doing poorly on the left, a big bulge doing average work in the middle, and a few top students on the right—has been shoved to the right. Calvert has virtually no fourth or fifth graders in the poor area on the left, and more students all the way over on the right than a year before.[31]

The superintendent also reported more formally on the improved performance of students. Here are the results in grade 5 reading:

> Before CAI, approximately 18% of the students scored in the bottom 3 stanines (below the 23rd percentile). After one year of treatment, less than 3% of these students scored in the bottom three stanines.
>
> Before CAI, approximately 48% of the students scored in stanines 6 through 9 (above the 60th percentile). After one year of treatment, approximately 73% of these students scored in this above-average range.
>
> After CAI implementation, approximately 13% of the students scored in stanine 9 (96th percentile and above). This is more than 3 times the national average.[32]

In grade 4 Mathematics, the results were reported as follows:

> Before CAI implementation, approximately 12% of the students scored in the bottom three stanines. After one year of treatment, less than 3% of these students scored in this range.
>
> Before CAI implementation, approximately 53% of the students scored in the above-average range (stanines 6 through 9, above the 60th percentile).

After one year of CAI treatment, approximately 67% of these students scored in this range (stanines 6 through 9).

Before CAI implementation, approximately 6% of the students scored in stanine 9. After one year of CAI treatment, approximately 14% of these students scored in stanine 9. This is more than 100% improvement in this range and is more than three times the national average.[33]

The next step for this school district is to team with the Maryland State Department of Education, Computer Curriculum Corporation/California, and University of Maryland, Baltimore County to produce a more comprehensive assessment of the schools. The CAI program is being expanded into middle grades and vocational and special education areas and should produce equally impressive results there.

To reach excellence, both quality and equality must be achieved—a feat that has remained beyond grasp until now. Having the finest talents available to everyone as "teachers" through telecommunications, each learner can have access to the very best. Imagine if Einstein had been made available as a world class teacher through satellite technology to all who would have liked to participate in his classes. With telecommunications, there are no teacher shortages, no quality teacher shortages, no math or science teacher shortages. The few who are considered the top in their fields will be available to the many in all schools and colleges.

Recently, the Denver Public Schools superintendent announced that one-third of the teaching staff would retire in the next five years and envisioned a major teacher shortage. How would the Denver school district be able to attract what every major national study had been proposing—the high quality teacher? This critical problem of attracting the future teachers is now becoming a national issue. Instead of immersing prospective teachers into crash programs in teacher preparation, why not identify the best teachers and make them available to all students via telecommunications?

This new educational technology is not an enemy but a familiar tool. Learning through television is no more than what most of us do when we turn on our television sets at night to view our favorite programs. Millions are exposed to the nightly news, to special programs and events. Why not tune in for education?

LINKING SCHOOL AND NONSCHOOL AGENTS AND AGENCIES—PARTICIPATION, COLLABORATION, AND PARTNERSHIPS

A modernized system of education will connect the school and school people with the other educators in the community. These networks are being developed through increased attention to community participation and involvement in the process of learning and education.

SCHOOL-BASED COUNCILS

One model for increasing school-community ties is through the school-based councils. In Massachusetts, legislation passed in 1985, "Improving the Public Schools of the Commonwealth," required school-based councils for each school in the state. The council consists of

> ". . . the school principal who shall serve as chairman; three teachers elected annually by the teachers of the building; two parents of children attending said school building chosen in elections held annually by the local parent-teacher organization under the direction of the principal of such school or, if none exists, chosen by the school committee, and one person who is not a parent of a child attending said school building, appointed by the school committee."[34]

These councils determine the expenditures of a School Improvement Fund for each school "to establish innovative academic programs, expanded services to students, purchase of instructional equipment, alternative education programs, cultural education programs, community or parental involvement programs, business and education partnership programs, staff training, or for any other purposes consistent with the intent of this section."[35]

The Illinois Education Reform Legislation of 1985 required Parent-Teacher Advisory Committees:

> Each school board must establish and maintain a parent-teacher advisory committee to develop, with the school board, policy guidelines on pupil discipline. The school board must inform its pupils of the contents of the policy and provide the parents or legal guardians of each pupil a copy of the policy (within 15 days after the beginning of the school year or within 15 days after transferring into the school district).[36]

Moving decision making to the local school level and involving agents closest to the learner is part of the decentralization trend. This "bottom-up" approach to improved productivity has the advantage of reaching the very persons upon whom a new system depends and whose investment is essential. These efforts provide opportunities for extended participation in the process of reform. The result is not only more ownership by more people, but by involving the community, the environments for human learning and development can be significantly increased.

SCHOOL-BUSINESS PARTNERSHIPS

The private sector is closely connected to school improvement efforts. There is mutual self-interest that brings these agents together: schools develop the talents that the private sector needs to carry out its business. When the human capital needs of the private sector are in jeopardy, solutions can be found in the schools. Examples of mutual self-interest involving California and Colorado may help make the point:

Profile: California

A group of concerned engineering, mathematics, and science professors at the University of California, Berkeley, looking for a way to respond to the lack of qualified minority engineering students to fill companies' Equal Employment Opportunity quotas, developed the Mathematics, Engineering, Science Achievement (MESA) program. An intensive enrichment program designed to prepare minority students for college mathematics and science courses and careers in high-technology fields, MESA has expanded from one high school to many more, not only in California, but in Arizona, Colorado, New Mexico, New York, and Washington as well. Each MESA program is directed by a board of advisors and supported by volunteers from secondary schools, universities, industry, professional, and minority organizations and community groups.

The program began at Oakland Technical High School with 25 students. Today, MESA serves over 4,000 California students in 138 high schools, with 16 MESA centers and one satellite center. Originally, the California MESA operated exclusively on contributions from private foundations and corporations, but today the state underwrites the effort with funds that must be matched by nonstate money. In 1982–83, 70 companies contributed $1.1 million to match a state allocation of $1.35 million. These companies also supply MESA students with tutoring, field trips to their companies and role models working in mathematics-based fields.[37]

Profile: Colorado

The Colorado Department of Education, in cooperation with the Colorado Business Education Steering Committee, is piloting a new project designed to provide *all* high school students with basic employability skills prior to their graduation or exit from school. This Employability Skills Project (ESP) evolved from a department concern about employer complaints that many high school graduates lacked the basic skills they needed in order to be employable. A statewide survey of employers gathered first-hand information on the skills essential for entry-level employment. First-year employees were asked how important employability skills and their own school activities were in helping them make the transition from school to work. Twelve basic categories of employability skills were identified: job seeking/career development, mathematics, computers, reading, writing, communications, interpersonal, business economics, personal economics, manual/perceptual, job retention and problem solving/reasoning.

ESP is now bringing together teams of business, education, and community leaders in 15 school districts to determine whether specific entry-level skills are taught in selected high schools. To help them with this effort, the department of education has listed 120 competencies considered essential by both employers and entry-level employees, and developed a process for examining the curriculum. In addition, the department is helping schools develop evaluation systems that assess employability skills. Where school instruction programs do not address specific employability skills, local and state partnership teams will help locate and/or develop appropriate programs.

Individual community plans may vary, but it is anticipated that all students entering the 9th grade will be evaluated for employability skills. This information will be entered in "student portfolios," which may include other items, such as current resumes, letters of application and examples of student work. The portfolio will provide non-confidential information that can be used by the student and an advisory team (e.g., a parent, business person, and a counselor or teacher) to monitor progress toward employability skills and guide course choices and job decisions. A second portfolio, suitable for presentation to a prospective employer, may be prepared.[38]

The Boston Compact   In the greater Boston, Massachusetts area, a major new school-business partnership initiative has been undertaken by the school department, the city government, and the business community in an attempt to improve the schools. The Boston Compact represents an agreement between schools and local businesses in which both sides commit themselves to identified and measurable goals. This broad-based compact includes an array of community organizations that have agreed on a specific plan of action in concert with the school department. The success of the Boston Compact can be measured by the following explicit goals of the agreement:

(1) A five percent increase per year in the number of students who graduate as compared with the number who entered ninth grade.
(2) By 1986, all graduates will demonstrate the reading and math skills necessary for employment through the achievement of minimum competency standards established by the school committee.
(3) A five percent increase per year in the number of graduates who are placed in jobs or in further education.[39]

Under this five year agreement, formalized in 1983, the school department pledged to improve student attendance and performance while more than two hundred businesses and forty cultural institutions in the Greater Boston area promised to provide permanent jobs for high school graduates.

The school department, through the superintendent, agreed to carry out the following steps:

☐ Issue a policy statement with the school committee which embraces the Compact's goals and commits the department to fulfilling them.
☐ Require that all high schools promulgate annual reports which state publicly how the school is performing vis-a-vis attendance, retention, achievement, and placement.
☐ Assign school department staff and allocate resources to continue planning in the eleven topic areas described in the Operational Plan: counseling, alternative education, job development, basic skills, arts, athletics, curriculum development, career education, computer literacy, research and evaluation, and school-based management.

☐ Continue to implement and expand existing innovations which support the goals of the Compact, such as school-based management, the Job Collaborative, and new curricula for the high schools.

☐ Assess individual high schools and the Headmasters' performance on the basis of progress toward the Compact's goals and their involvement with external agencies.

☐ Seek agreement with the Teachers Union on contract modifications which reflect the reality of the school system, provide stability for teachers, and focus on direct educational benefits.

☐ Work with the city and the business community to implement graduated career preparation throughout the high schools and to expand the Job Collaborative to all high schools by 1985.

☐ Allocate school department resources towards activities which support the Boston Compact.[40]

While the Boston Compact does not cure all the ills of a large urban school system, it indicates clear progress and strong support for the schools in their improvement efforts. One of the first year goals set for the business community by the Compact agreements, to have more than 200 individual businesses involved in the Compact's agreements with the schools, had, at the end of the first year of operation, 273 individual businesses pledging to give the Boston public school graduates a priority in hiring. Another first year goal was to hire at least 400 graduates of the Boston public schools in permanent jobs. In all, 407 graduates were hired under this program and nearly 75 percent were minority students.[41] The success of the Boston Compact after the first year provided further incentive to strengthen and expand the agreements. More than twenty colleges and universities in the Boston area renewed their commitment to the city's schools, including pledging their help in improving the schools' core curriculum, developing and supporting programs to reduce the dropout rate in the schools, and aggressively recruiting Boston public school students. The Boston Compact has been nationally recognized as a model agreement between business and education and as a major educational initiative.

School-business partnerships are increasingly receiving attention and documentation. Phi Delta Kappa's Center on Evaluation, Development, and Research has issued an Exemplary Practice Series dedicated to school and business partnerships.[42]

COMPREHENSIVE SCHOOL-COMMUNITY PARTNERSHIP

In modernization, a "learning ecology" is the general direction of education in the future. This learning ecology would not only link school and nonschool settings but would gradually expand to make the community the ultimate educator. The increased community involvement in school reform is the early phase of this trend.

The older patterns of school-community relations involving parents have now evolved to also include business and industry. Some localities have attempted to involve as many members of the community as possible in a "comprehensive" partnership for excellence.

The (Springfield) Partnership for Excellence In Springfield, Massachusetts, a broad-based community effort called the "Partnership for Excellence" provides the basis for linking school and nonschool learning resources throughout the city. The Partnership for Excellence developed a formal statement of its mission:

> . . . to provide a permanent partnership of the public, private, and academic sectors to assist the Springfield Public Schools. Its purpose is to increase standards of excellence, to develop new resources, and to provide opportunities to help students achieve their standards in order to prepare them for employment, higher education, and social responsibility.[43]

The Partnership for Excellence Plan represents the culmination of a collaborative process that began a symposium at which representatives of the Springfield Public Schools, area universities, and businesses all presented their views on the rationale for cooperation. A proposal was then presented to the Springfield School Committee requesting permission to develop the partnership and inviting approximately twenty people to participate in the planning efforts. The school committee approved the request, and the mayor of Springfield added his support to the effort. The Research Department of the Springfield Public Schools conducted a needs assessment to determine ways in which community resources could be used in the schools, and a proposal was prepared and presented to business community leaders. Members of the business community, higher education, regional offices of the State Department of Education, parents, administrators, teachers, the school committee, and various community groups were recruited to form the Partnership Task Force, which formally accepted the partnership structure. Finally, the Partnership for Excellence Plan, accepted in 1983, included a mission statement, a list of objectives and identifiable key issues to be addressed, and a directive to form study teams intended to develop action plans for ten major areas. The Task Force initially concentrated its efforts on the secondary schools to provide opportunities for students at all levels of competence for professional development. A set of objectives formulated for the partnership focused on measurable achievements in basic skills with dropouts, providing employment opportunities and access to higher education, and utilizing educational personnel.

As a result of the involvement of higher education institutions, an "Academy for Excellence" was established with the University of Massachusetts' School of Education. The academy, working closely with the partnership, responded to the expressed needs of school personnel with staff development activities delivered in Springfield using the facilities of cooperating businesses. The issues addressed included student absenteeism and school-based management. This academy could develop into a new staff development vehicle for the school district using the resources of higher education and business and industry to enrich the professional growth of school personnel and community groups.

The Lowell Model for Educational Excellence   Lowell, Massachusetts, once a prominent industrial center, fell victim to the forces of a changing economy. The smoke stacks stopped and urban decay took over. Then, elected officials and the business community began a renaissance. After this successful process of economic development, former Senator Paul Tsongas realized that without excellence in the public school system, the economic growth and the improved quality of life in Lowell would be seriously curtailed. Tsongas became personally involved with the need to create a model for excellence plan for his community. With the help of the business community and city officials, he triggered a process of review of the public school programs. He named a three-person panel and provided this panel with a $150,000 budget which enabled it to hire a staff that worked closely with interested parties in the community and started a participatory process that involved the entire community in the design of a model program.

The Lowell Public School System, on the heels of severe cutbacks caused by Proposition 2½, was at a critical juncture in 1983 when Senator Tsongas initiated the call to excellence in education. The Lowell teachers, long considered the key to restoring quality in the schools, were particularly alienated by a growing sense of loss of public confidence. And without a signed collective bargaining agreement to begin the year, they were in no mood to begin the journey toward educational excellence. Yet slowly a reform process did emerge in which the major interested parties (teachers, parents, students, school officials, business and industry representatives, members of religious, cultural, and scientific community agencies) were brought together into a broad-based community task force. This task force, in collaboration with a three-person consultant team and staff, laid the foundation for a comprehensive model for excellence.

The planning for this educational excellence was *action* oriented. The community call was and remains "give us action, not high sounding phrases." Action planning necessitated a phased implementation of a first-class school system for the community. Consequently, the Lowell Model for Educational Excellence is not merely an abstract vision, but a model that is being designed for, by, and with the community through its representatives. Priority was and is given to *implementation*. What good would come from a model plan developed by a group of outside experts and then deposited on an economically depressed community, particularly if that community had not been involved sufficiently in developing the plan to assure follow through and implementation? The results of previous, more traditional planning methods usually meant that *nothing* would really happen. There might be a written report, some media attention and then—nothing. The report would be politely filed and quietly disappear from the action scene, reappearing perhaps on the shelves of professional libraries.

The Model for Educational Excellence in Lowell committed itself to action and change. Participants in this plan were skeptical that any action would really follow this effort because of past experiences, yet they remained hopeful. Their participation and attendance at meetings despite the abuses of New England weather is testimony to the community's commitment to reestablishing excellence in the schools.

. The action planning process based on school and nonschool collaboration is continuing. Building an action model for educational excellence is not something that can be accomplished with one quantum leap. Lowell did not want some esoteric view of excellence. Their vision of excellence had a reality base that emphasized implementation.

The Lowell Model for Educational Excellence, designed as a multiphased plan of action intended to modernize the public schools of Lowell, is defined as follows:

What is the Lowell Model for Educational Excellence?

The Lowell Model for Educational Excellence is an *action* plan designed to ensure excellence in Lowell's public schools. Initiated by U.S. Senator Paul Tsongas as part of his efforts to assist in the revitalization of Lowell, this plan affirms that the Lowell school system is a crucial link to the economy and vitality of the city and the region. An excellent school system, as depicted by the model, must apply available fiscal and human resources in a sound, equitable, and creative manner to prepare students to be intelligent, productive and responsible citizens now and in the future.

The model is designed for, by, and with the Lowell community. Coordinated by a 23-member task force, staff, and study commission, the model represents the participation of over 1,700 people in a thoughtful look at what is and what could be. Through collaboration of school people, the community, and education experts, short term and long range recommendations have been formulated that can serve as a blueprint for improving the Lowell schools and for ensuring excellence of educational opportunity to all people of Lowell.

The significance of the model is a demonstration that the Lowell schools, community leaders, concerned citizens, and independent parties can be brought together to create lasting educational improvements that benefit children and the entire economic and human welfare of the community. Since education is currently commanding priority attention across the state and nation, if the Lowell Model is carried out, it will have widespread implications for improving education.[44]

The major goals of this action plan are enumerated in the same report:

- ☐ Increase communication throughout the school system and with the public.
- ☐ Improve the school's business management practices and organizational efficiency.
- ☐ Develop new partnerships and resources for learning.
- ☐ Improve the conditions for teaching and learning.
- ☐ Conduct systematic program and staff development.

☐ Increase participation in the governance of the school system.
☐ Promote equal educational opportunities throughout the Lowell school system.
☐ Support specific implementation and monitoring plans.[45]

These recommendations are to be implemented by the Lowell School Department, the City of Lowell, and the task force. In addition, a new Institute for Field Services was formed at the University of Lowell specifically for the purpose of assisting the Lowell public schools. Parents, business leaders, other citizens in the community, and community agencies are all expected to take active roles in the process of implementation of the plan. In fact, increased, positive citizen involvement is a central concern of the plan's recommendations for school improvement. For the students, this should result in new opportunities for scholarships and job training, and in a few years should result in significant gains in student performance and achievement. Teachers will have increased opportunities for higher salaries, in-service training, cooperative problem solving, alleviation of non-teaching duties, and greater access to the best instructional materials. In this partnership, parents will also take a more active and participatory role in their children's education, recognizing and seeking to maximize the learning opportunities of the home and the family. Through job commitments for qualified students and scholarships from an education foundation, the business community enters into a partnership with the schools which should eventually produce better educated and prepared public school graduates, thus reducing training costs for local employers. The Lowell Model recognizes that improved educational services and school reform are essential to the economic development and the quality of life of the area. The following is a ten-year phased plan for modernization of the Lowell Schools:

Phase I: February to June 1984:

The Lowell Model is a phased action plan, designed to build on accomplishments over time. The recommendations for immediate attention are the foundation upon which subsequent improvement can be built.

While the ultimate focus and test of efforts to improve the Lowell schools must be at the individual student and teacher level, unless one first deals with "the system," it is unlikely that efforts toward improvements will be more than shadow boxing with the real problems.

Thus, priorities in Phase I are business management and communications. Recommendations for action on the other goals are initiatives that should begin in Phase I and continue as ongoing mechanisms. However, the success of these actions and mechanisms in bringing about long-term change rests on immediate establishment of stability in the underpinnings of the system.[46]

Phase II: July 1984 to June 1985:

The initiatives of Phase I set the stage for a shift in emphasis in Phase II to the student, teacher, and individual school.

In an atmosphere of open communication and stabilized management systems (which are further strengthened in Phase II), people in the schools—principals, teachers, and students—will begin to feel that they are more in control of their educational destinies. With a clear sense of goals, opportunities and priorities, advances at the individual school level can begin to take place.[47]

Phase III: July 1985 to June 1989:

Students can learn and change only if administrators, teachers, and parents are continuing to learn and change. The focus of education in the future must shift from teaching, in the sense of conveying information and knowledge to be memorized and retrieved, to learning, in the sense of facilitating thinking, developing intelligence, understanding and respecting the viewpoints and values of other people, acting rationally, appreciating beauty, and solving problems that transcend the knowledge base of any single individual. Revolutionary advances in technology, including excellent, inexpensive computer software, telecommunications networks, and videotexts that replace textbooks, will create revolutionary opportunities for learning. The schools must be prepared to help students of all ages capitalize on these new opportunities.

The challenge for schools of the future is to anticipate changes in the needs of learners, to adapt to learning in an expanded environment, and to assist and encourage teachers to find creative ways to redirect their skills and acquire new ones. This is the mission of Phase III.[48]

Phase IV: July 1989–1994

The notions of excellence in Phase IV are presented as a general description because the nature of the Model is essentially evolutionary. As new initiatives are undertaken and evaluated, new directions will be found that cannot be projected from this point in time. However, based on current knowledge, it is possible to project attributes for Lowell's schools in an Information Age of the future. With the burgeoning of computer technology, the world's information base now doubles every four or five years; the base is projected to double every 20 months before 1990! Educators need to consider the incredible opportunities for students and rethink their own roles in an era of such rapid change.

Planning for the Information Age. The current, industrial-age model of education was well suited to employers' needs in the 1800s, but it does not fit well into an age of information.

Schools must not continue to equate intelligence with rote memorization. In the past there have been minimal expectations for literacy: reading, writing, and knowledge of math facts. However, in the age of information, being able to think logically and to retrieve and process information will become necessary parts of literacy. Since *information* will be the leading industry, supplanting goods as the basis of the economy, people who can access information and who then know what to do with that information will have advantages. Basic skills in reading comprehension and oral and written expression will still be essential, but logical thinking and creative problem-solving will take on much greater importance than in the past.

Computers, telecommunications, and videotext technologies will alter the role of the teacher as dispenser of information. Students will take more active responsibility for and be enthusiastically involved in their learning. Students may spend a portion of each day at a relatively inexpensive, by today's standards, computer/telecommunications console, reading and viewing whatever topic or information is pertinent to learning that day. For instance, in studying about the earth, the student will be able to see how the earth looks from the vantage point of different space stations. The latest encyclopedic information will be instantly available without waiting for the school system to buy new books. A profile of up to date competencies will be available at the "student profile" terminal in the school office; this will show the student's individual learning goals, as agreed upon by the student, parents, and teacher, as well as daily progress toward the goals. No longer will students have to wait until the next day or next week to obtain the results of testing. Parents who are concerned about their child's progress can review mastery gains and consider alternative strategies without waiting for report cards and failure notices. Parents will participate in meetings and teacher conferences without being physically present.

As students complete various assignments, they will meet with their teachers and other mentors who might include older students, university faculty, retired people, professionals or tradespeople. For more information, mentors and students will consult pertinent videodisc presentations by Nobel Prize winners or other eminent authorities. Teachers will concentrate on the "so what" portion of learning, helping students to question, evaluate, and apply the information for problem-solving and decision-making skills. In effect, all teachers will spend more time working directly with individual students, helping them to think and respond thoughtfully to information and materials. For the teacher, this scenario will bring freedom to spend more time doing what teachers do best, working directly with students. The hours of grading time and disciplining will be drastically reduced. Students who need extra help, encouragement, or stimulation will be a primary focus of the teacher's day, helping every student think, reason, and learn.

As students are encouraged to accelerate and learn at their individual rates, traditional grade-level designations will no longer make sense. Not all students will need to meet with each subject-area teacher each day; some will need and have more than 50 minutes on a given day. With the flexibility that can come with these new teaching tools, not all students will need the same number of years in school, nor should all students be in school the same months of the year or the same days of the week. On some occasions, students will spend long hours in the school building deeply involved in a project or experiment. On other days they will be learning at home, in hospitals, or at community agencies, utilizing telecommunications and cable television. In all cases, students will be accountable for continually demonstrating mastery of new skills. Working parents who need after school child care will be able to arrange cooperatives in the school buildings. On-site internships for tourism, robotics, health care, law, teaching, hotel management, etc. will replace vocational education options. This will reduce the need and costs for maintaining so many school buildings.

Adults and very young children will be conspicuously present in the schools, taking full advantage of the life-long learning opportunities. Most children will enter kindergarten already reading, and illiteracy will be negligible. The reputation and promise of Lowell's national park, ethnic diversity, and urban revitalization will continue to advance in synchrony with the transformed school system.

The Age of Information offers many promises. It also presents many dilemmas. To deliver the promises and to overcome the dilemmas, the citizens of Lowell must be prepared to take a close look—see where the schools have been and where they are now. Then, looking to the future with openness for new ideas and a willingness to grow and to collaborate, the citizens of Lowell can meet the educational challenges and opportunities of a very new tomorrow.[49]

UTILIZING AVAILABLE RESOURCES IN SCHOOL AND COMMUNITY MORE FULLY

One of the major components of modernization is resource management. Serious problems face major school reform efforts that only "throw more money" at improved education. This does not mean that no new money is needed to bring about the excellence agenda, rather, it means that new money becomes more strategic—a lever for converting a 20th century school system into a 21st century educational system and a way of using the old money—available resources—differently, more wisely.

MANAGING RESOURCES INSIDE THE SCHOOLS

There are effective and efficient ways of utilizing the existing in-school resources of students, teachers, and time.

Teachers cannot be expected to solve the problem of improving the basic skills—the "3 Rs"—alone. Students, themselves a major resource, are being used in many schools as peer tutors. High school students are teaching elementary school children. Some school districts have established tutorial communities inside each school. Since children can learn through teaching, their own academic skills are reinforced. And many children learn better from their peers. There would be little need for extra money. The rewards are intrinsic—each child has something to teach another as part of the caring ethic. Teachers are released to "train" the tutors to develop new approaches.

Schools are finding that it is both effective and efficient to have each teacher identify a "teaching style." In some schools, teams of teachers with similar styles create a "mini-school" within the larger school or a series of schools-within-schools. Students and parents then select the style they prefer, matching teacher style or program style with learner style. Again, these do not cost more money but result in a major educational advance.[50]

Time is another in-school resource that schools are utilizing more effectively and efficiently. If the problem of improving the basics is so vast, then more schools are using school time primarily for this issue—through *time on this task* programs in which basic skills development is given priority. At the secondary level, schools promoting the idea that every teacher is a reading teacher means that the time spent on the problem of reading is often quadrupled.

Before school time, after school time, and home time are all being programmed to tackle the goal of improved performance in the basics. Students also have preferred time for learning certain subjects as reported in a study on the effects of student time preferences.

> Fifty eighth-grade math students from rural and inner city schools were compared to determine when optimum learning occurred during their time in school. Although no statistically significant differences were evidenced *between the groups*, it was revealed that many of the students preferred to function in their learning environments in the afternoon, rather than in the morning.
>
> Two extremely interesting findings were that (1) students in the inner city school whose learning preferences matched the time when they were assigned to their math classes were *less of a discipline problem* than those who were mismatched, and (2) twelve of the students that were matched with their time preferences solely by chance also achieved academically with fewer motivational influences from their teacher.[51]

UTILIZING COMMUNITY RESOURCES

The rich educative resources of the community hold the best promise of converting an old and rather isolated schoolhouse model to an interdependent network of learning environments.

Parents, a primary resource, are teachers at home. Part of the school teachers' range of learning resources, parents are only a small part of a virtual array of volunteers who could help in the schools. The Executive Director of the National School Volunteer Program estimates that there are now over 4 million volunteers working inside our schools.[52] These volunteers include retired persons who have valuable talents to share with the young which would decrease the age isolation of the young as well as the old. School volunteers assist in creating intergenerational learning environments in schools.

The most important development in school-community relations is the "Partnership Movement" between the school and an array of community agencies that has resulted in an unprecedented increase in the resource base of education. Many public-private partnerships set up education foundations. The West Virginia Education Fund is "the first statewide non-profit, independent organization that raises funds for schools. A representative body from business, industry, and labor guides the fund, which provides mini-grants to teachers to carry out innovative projects."[53]

The San Francisco Education Fund, established in 1979, one of the oldest foundations raising money for schools, allocated over $500,000 to the San Francisco School District in 1981. The Allegheny Conference Education Fund in Pittsburgh provided the schools with over $1 million during its first three years. The Fund for Public Schools in New York City received contributions from television stations, the Zoological Society, and museums.[54] The Bridgeport Education Fund is among the first in New England.[55]

Other partnerships with business and industry take different forms. In Chicago, an Adopt-A-School Program ties 103 companies to 114 public schools:

> . . . Employees of participating businesses are required to be in the schools at least once a week.
>
> For example, engineers from Commonwealth Edison, the power company in Chicago, have taught science and mathematics at the Michele Clark Elementary School through a project in which students had to plan for a hypothetical power system in the school's neighborhood.[56]

In Dallas, over 1,000 businesses have adopted virtually all of Dallas' more than 200 public schools. The Dallas Chamber of Commerce recruits businesses, monitors the partnership, and publicizes the companies' efforts. Sponsoring businesses provide volunteer tutors and donate funds, equipment, and materials to their adopted schools.[57]

Other school-business partnerships that have brought additional resources to public education include the following:

> *The American Council of Life Insurance*, in cooperation with the St. Louis public schools, has developed a "how-to" kit on business-school collaboration for its 600 member companies. The kit includes a manual for developing successful projects and information on national programs that encourage partnerships between businesses and schools.
>
> *AT&T Information Systems* has provided high-level New Jersey educators and public officials with an opportunity to experience learning by computer at a one-day workshop, Using the Computer as an Educational Tool. This workshop was co-sponsored by Governor Thomas H. Kean's New Jersey State Advisory Council on Vocational Education (SACVE). The workshop presented material on how to select and develop courses for computer-based education (CBE), and offered demonstrations on various automated learning technology, including an interactive audio system, videodisc, and color-screen and touch-screen terminals. AT&T Information Systems has demonstrated that CBE can cut course delivery times in half and can secure nationwide training consistency. Electronic course materials can be easily updated (unlike printed materials). In addition, CBE permits simulation of sophisticated technical equipment—such as a network controller. With CBE, students can learn to operate equipment in the classroom without using the actual hardware; the computer and touch screen are used instead. Workshop attendees have requested that AT&T

Information Systems continue to share its understanding and use of technology with New Jersey educators.

The Dow Chemical Company sponsors SERV (Service Effort for Retiree Volunteers), which encourages Dow retirees to be resource persons to Midland, Michigan high schools or college classrooms. Retirees help by discussing practical applications in school subject areas or by designing new curricula. A directory of retirees' experience and degree backgrounds, ranging from mathematics, computers, and science to marketing and communications, is available to teachers and professors.

One of *Ford Motor Company*'s programs provides high schools with new automotive engines, transmissions and other parts, tools, and training manuals to help train prospective auto mechanics, machinists, and tool and dye apprentices.

IBM donated 2,000 personal computers to 130 public elementary and secondary schools as part of a $12 million program to train teachers and students to use computers. Each of the 26 large, urban school districts selected by IBM will choose up to five schools to receive IBM computers for computer literacy courses. The Bank Street College of Education and the University of South Florida will train staff development teams to conduct four-week training sessions in each district for teachers of grades 4–12. The program, to begin in the fall of 1984, is similar to a model developed last year by IBM and currently in operation in California, Florida, and New York.

Under *Texas Instruments'* project SEED, employees work in 4th- and 5th–grade classrooms one hour per day helping mathematics students discover how exciting mathematics can be and why tough mathematics courses are stepping stones to achievement.[58]

School-business partnerships have become so pervasive that "The American Council of Life Insurance, in cooperation with the St. Louis public schools, has developed a 'how-to' kit on business-school collaboration for its 600 member companies. The kit includes a manual for developing successful projects and information on national programs that encourage partnerships between businesses and schools."[59]

Several school functions could be transferred to appropriate educative agents and agencies in the community: sex and drug education could be taken over by medical or health agencies or the clergy; driver education could be transferred to the state police; and vocational education to business and industry.

All these and other extensions of the educational resource base are part of the growing realization that learning and education take place in a community setting. The community is the classroom of the future.

RESEARCH AND DEVELOPMENT (R&D)

Few organizations can keep current in meeting their goals without a research and development (R&D) capability. The private sector, operating for profit, invests in R&D as a necessary condition of success. Companies either have their own built-in capacity to generate new ideas, or they depend on external sources such as research universities. The purposes of R&D are to generate new knowledge and to develop new products. Most advances in science and technology have their roots in R&D. In the private sector, it is difficult for any company to maintain a competitive edge without extensive R&D.

In the non-profit public sector in general, and in the public schools in particular, R&D is more complicated. It is not a built-in component of most school systems. Prior to the massive entry of the federal government into education in the latter half of this century, the public schools depended on certain dominant philosophers and colleges of education for new ideas. In this century, John Dewey's theories dominated education. The Teachers College, Columbia University, and the University of Chicago provided much of the knowledge base (through the literature) for new developments in schooling.

More recently, school and university partnerships have emerged to fill the R&D gap. Harvard Graduate School of Education established SUPRAD (School and University Partnership for Research and Development) to link researchers to the practitioners in the schools.

The federal government has expanded its role in public education by establishing a national network of R&D Centers and Laboratories affiliated with higher education. Each center has a particular issue, such as vocational education or education of the handicapped, as a focus for its research. The laboratories are new, non-profit corporations that establish a regional network of cooperating agencies including higher education and public schools. Their mission is to conduct research and to help implement the knowledge gained in the schools. By 1970, there were fifteen Regional Laboratories and nine university-sponsored R&D Centers. (See Figure 7–1.)[60]

While presently R&D Centers and Regional Laboratories are funded from federal sources, states are also promoting more partnerships involving higher education, business and industry, and the schools.[61]

This potential for R&D involvement in education at the state level is promising since each state has its own academic resources that could be better mobilized to assist the schools. For instance, every state has a system of higher education that includes community colleges and research universities, many have schools of education with laboratory schools, and most state departments of education have regional offices. Networking these state-supported agencies into a comprehensive R&D complex could be accomplished. The needed resources already exist, and the states already support them.

COALITIONS

All R&D agencies do not have to be government based. A coalition of cooperating schools and colleges could support R&D efforts. John I. Goodlad, a pioneer for such collaboration, is currently preparing to establish a national network encom-

FIGURE 7-1
Regional Laboratories and R&D Centers Currently in Operation.[60]

Key

⊓ Regional Laboratories

★ R & D Centers

Educational Development Center (Newton, Mass.)

Eastern Regional Institute for Education (Syracuse)

Center for Urban Education (New York City)

Research for Better Schools (Philadelphia)

Johns Hopkins U.

U. of Pittsburgh

Appalachia (Charleston, W. Va.)

Laboratory for the Carolinas and Virginia (Durham)

U. of Georgia

Southeastern (Atlanta)

Upper Midwest (Minneapolis)

U. of Wisconsin

Central Midwest (St. Louis)

Mid-Continent (Kansas City)

U. of Texas

Southwest Development (Austin)

Southwestern Cooperative (Albuquerque)

Northwest (Portland)

U. of Oregon

Far West (Berkeley)

UC (Berkeley)

Stanford U.

Southwest Regional (Los Angeles)

UCLA

187

passing regional coalitions. The intent is to stimulate further inquiry on a key set of research issues that could lead to more informed practice in the schools.

At the School of Education, University of Massachusetts/Amherst, a coalition of cooperating schools is already in operation. The mission of this pioneering program is described as follows:

> The Coalition for School Improvement is a partnership between public elementary and secondary schools and the School of Education at the University of Massachusetts/Amherst. The Center for Curriculum Studies in the School of Education serves as the coordinating agency for the coalition. Representatives from these groups started the initial planning in the fall of 1983. This partnership is being formed to carefully develop and monitor solutions to persistent problems that now hinder school effectiveness. There are no simple, universal solutions to the problems which must be solved in order for schools to provide quality education for all learners. The coalition is designed to facilitate thoughtful planning and decision making at the local level, and to sustain energetic action to improve the curriculum, teaching, and learning in each school. The coalition will tap existing human resources in participating institutions as a means for making public schools a more powerful medium for learning.
>
> Specifically, the purposes that will guide the actions of the coalition are:
> ☐ to increase the effectiveness of schools by improving curriculum, instruction, and administrative leadership;
> ☐ to develop conditions in school and nonschool settings that increase learning for all students, particularly those who do not have a history of past academic success;
> ☐ to generate useful information about research findings, forward-looking policies, and promising practices that will assist schools to improve;
> ☐ to develop public awareness and understanding of education problems and issues.
>
> Single schools in member districts are responsible for improving conditions for learning so that all students are more likely to realize their academic potential. The coalition is organized to assist in this effort by connecting improving schools with technical services provided through the School of Education, cooperation extended by other participating schools, assistance given by various study teams, and support resulting from staff development activities.
>
> The strength of the coalition, then, lies in the combined efforts of educators at different public schools and at the university who bring creative energy to the planning and action for better schools. The coalition makes possible continuing communication among members, critical review of suggestions for improvement, and division of labor in trying ways to increase learning for all students. The coalition will assist teachers and other personnel to successfully implement the programs they desire for their schools.[62]

This growth of collaboration is certainly one of the keys to school improvement in the next decade.

The elements for a modern system of education are in process. The sustaining of this process requires the commitment of many people. The current reform ferment is responsible for much of the energy now being expended throughout the land.

A major factor in the quest for excellence in education is the teaching profession. However, it is also in a state of transition. The next chapter will review the status of the teaching profession and will determine its role in gaining excellence in education.

NOTES

1. Education Commission of the States, *Action in the States: Progress Toward Educational Renewal*, A Report of the Task Force on Education for Economic Growth, July 1984, 19.

2. *Ibid.*, 4.

3. *Ibid.*, 5.

4. *Ibid.*, 304–306.

5. Remarks made by Massachusetts Governor Michael Dukakis at a meeting held at Westfield State College to discuss educational issues related to the passage of the Massachusetts Public School Improvement Law/Chapter 188, 20 August 1985.

6. "West Virginia: Epic Mandate, Historic Conflict Over Funds, Control," *Education Week*, Vol. IV, No. 39, 19 June 1985, 18.

7. *Ibid.*, 19.

8. Education Commission of the States, *Action in the States: Progress Toward Educational Renewal*, A Report of the Task Force on Education for Economic Growth, July 1984, pp. 8–9.

9. *Ibid.*, 17–18.

10. *Ibid.*, 24–25.

11. Walter F. Mondale, Alonzo A. Crim, and Denis P. Doyle, *Educating Our Citizens: The Search for Excellence*, Alternatives for the 1980's—No. 9 (Washington, D. C.: Center for National Policy, 1983), 10.

12. *Ibid.*, 17.

13. *Ibid.*, 19.

14. *Ibid.*, 20.

15. *Ibid.*, 20.

16. Brochure, Atlanta Public Schools, Planning and Expanding Services, "Duties to the Community—Community Service Requirement (Course Number 959050)."

17. Walter F. Mondale, Alonzo A. Crim, and Denis P. Doyle, *Educating Our Citizens: The Search for Excellence*, Alternatives for the 1980's—No. 9 (Washington, D. C.: Center for National Policy, 1983), 16.

18. *Ibid.*, 23–24.

19. Illinois Education Reform Legislation, P.A. 84–126, "School District Report Cards," 18 July 1985.

20. Amherst-Pelham (Massachusetts) Regional Schools/Grades 7–12, *Language Arts Program Analysis Document*, Compiled by English and Reading Departments/Edited by Bruce M. Penniman, Department Head 1981, 17.

21. *Ibid.*, 79.

22. Nolan Estes and Donald R. Waldrip, *Magnet Schools: Legal and Practical Implications* (New Jersey: New Century Education Corporation, 1978).

23. Brochure, New Haven (Connecticut) Public Schools, "Choices in the New Haven Public Schools."

24. *Ibid.*

25. 1983 Alternative Concept Schools, Community School District 4, Board of Education, City of New York.

26. The Florida Task Force on Alternative Education, *Alternative Education: Excellence Through Choice*, A Report to the Legislature, March 1985, xii.

27. State of Minnesota "Access to Excellence Bill," February 1985.

28. Market Data Retrieval, *Microcomputers in Schools*, 1984–85.

29. Project Athena Executive Committee, *Project Athena*, Massachusetts Institute of Technology, October 1983, 10–16.

30. Dr. Eugene Karol, Superintendent of Schools, Calvert County (Maryland) Public Schools, "Computers in Education—What We Are Learning From Research," a paper presented at the Fourth Annual Computers in Education in Maryland Conference entitled "Clearinghouse for Computers in Education," 21 June 1985, 2.

31. Will Englund, "Owings Schools Take to Computers," *The Baltimore Sun*, 22 July 1985.

32. Dr. Eugene Karol, Superintendent of Schools, Calvert County (Maryland) Public Schools, "Computers in Education—What We Are Learning From Research," a paper presented at the Fourth Annual Computers in Education in Maryland Conference entitled "Clearinghouse for Computers in Education," 21 June 1985, 5.

33. *Ibid.*, 9.

34. The Commonwealth of Massachusetts Education Reform Bill, "Improving the Public Schools in the Commonwealth," H 5959/Chapter 188, July 1985, 6.

35. *Ibid.*, 6.

36. Illinois Education Reform Legislation, P.A. 84–126, "Parent-Teacher Advisory Committees," 18 July 1985, 8.

37. Education Commission of the States, *Action in the States: Progress Toward Educational Renewal*, A Report of the Task Force on Education for Economic Growth, July 1984, 44–45.

38. *Ibid.*, 13.

39. *The Boston Compact Executive Summary*, 1983, 1.

40. *Ibid.*, 1–2.

41. "The Compact Grows Stronger," Editorial in *The Boston Globe*, 31 October 1983, 14.

42. Phi Delta Kappa, Center on Evaluation, Development and Research, *School-Business Partnerships*, Exemplary Practice Series 1985/86, Fall 1985.

43. *The Public Schools of Springfield (Massachusetts) Partnership for Excellence Plan*, 24 January 1984.

44. *The Lowell Model for Educational Excellence Executive Summary Report*, January 1984, 3.

45. *Ibid.*, 4.

46. *Ibid.*, 8.

47. *Ibid.*, 17.

48. *Ibid.*, 26.

49. *Ibid.*, 32.

50. *Learning Styles Network Newsletter*, Co-sponsored by the National Association of Secondary School Principals and St. John's University (New York), Vol. 1, No. 2, Spring 1980.

51. *Ibid.*, 1.

52. Daniel Merenda, Executive Director of the National School Volunteer Program, "Implementing School/Community Partnership: A Process for Community Analysis," Presentation at the First Annual Visiting Scholars Program entitled "Pursuit of Excellence in Education," sponsored by Tennessee State University Center of Excellence/Basic Skills for the Disadvantaged, Nashville, Tennessee, 15 March 1985.

53. Education Commission of the States, *Action in the States: Progress Toward Education Renewal*, A Report of the Task Force on Education for Economic Growth, July 1984, 11.

54. Gene Maeroff, "Financially Pressed School Districts Are Trying to Obtain Private Funds," *The New York Times*, 9 November 1982.

55. *The Volunteer in Education*, A Monthly Publication of the National School Volunteer Program, Vol. IX, No. 8, April 1985, 1.

56. Gene Maeroff, "Financially Pressed School Districts Are Trying to Obtain Private Funds," *The New York Times*, 9 November 1982.

57. Education Commission of the States, *Action in the States: Progress Toward Education Renewal*, A Report of the Task Force on Education for Economic Growth, July 1984, 12.

58. *Ibid.*, 11–12.

59. *Ibid.*, 11.

60. Francis S. Chase, "R&D in the Remodeling of Education," *Phi Delta Kappan*, Vol. LI, No. 6, February 1970, 301.

61. Education Commission of the States, *Action in the States: Progress Toward Educational Renewal*, A Report to the Task Force on Education for Economic Growth, July 1984, 10–12.

62. The Coalition for School Improvement, School of Education, University of Massachusetts, Amherst, Massachusetts, 1985.

PART III
Excellence and the Profession

Modernization and the Profession *8*

As the public school system has experienced change, there have been major consequences for educators. In their attempts to respond to larger changes in society, school people have been forced into an increasingly defensive posture. Unable to keep pace with change, educators are blamed for problems created by outside forces. Struggles among teachers, as well as between management and labor, school and community, public schools and government, have proliferated. These internal divisions have caused tension between former partners and have been a drain on the professional psyche. Educators are dedicated to positive human development in a free and just society, in short, *excellence.* But they see their influence as minimal.

TEACHERS AND TEACHING

Teachers, the most important agents in the school, have been caught in a spiral of professional decline. In the early years of the United States, teaching was one of the few professions open to women. Although salaries were low, the potential for public service was great. As more men entered the profession, the traditionally low salaries of teachers became unacceptable. Teachers began to unionize, gaining strength through work actions and strikes. Organized teachers demonstrated their national potency in presidential elections and influenced national education policy (for example, the creation of a Secretary of Education in 1978 may be a direct result of growing teacher power).

Over the last sixty or seventy years, the teacher workforce has changed from a primarily middle-class female population dedicated to service to a more diverse group that has some economic power. The thread that holds these people together is an unswerving commitment to the learner and learning, although it may appear to the public that this commitment takes a back seat to economic issues. Because teaching has been one of the careers open to women, the lower salaries for teachers are tied also to the historical inequality faced by women.

Because teachers' salaries have always been low, it is often difficult to attract and retain qualified teachers. Teachers' salaries simply are not competitive in our free market system. Table 8–1,[1] based on U.S. Department of Labor information, shows the differences between the average teacher's starting salary and that of comparable college graduates working in private industry.

Many states are presently involved in legislation aimed at improving teacher salaries, recognizing that low salaries have contributed to the lowered prestige of teachers. Underpaid teachers command less professional respect in a society that values capital as an index of worth, and they are often forced to pursue other careers. Governor Mario Cuomo of New York, in a speech to teachers, speaks to this point:

> If we really value education, if it's really as important to our future as everybody says it is, then we have to make teaching a more attractive career, enabling teachers to support themselves and their families, to live decently; frankly, to secure the respect which—right or wrong—our society attaches to how much a person earns.[2]

The rising criticism of schools and the teachers' need to struggle for decent wages and working conditions contribute to the negative cycle in which teachers

TABLE 8–1

Average starting salaries of public school teachers compared with salaries in private industry[1]

1974	Profession	1984
$ 8,223	Teacher	$14,500
8,685	Laboratory technician	17,761
8,892	Librarian	19,344
9,672	Economist	20,484
11,040	Accountant	20,176
10,088	Sanitation worker	20,280
10,176	Statistician	22,416
11,284	Radio broadcaster	20,800
11,925	Bus driver (metro)	22,906
11,546	Computer analyst	24,864
11,556	Engineer	26,844
13,485	Construction worker	23,126
14,820	Plumber	24,180
16,801	Social worker	23,907
18,666	Purchasing director	37,374
19,634	Personnel director	42,978

are caught. As Boyer observed: "We are of the deep conviction that the teaching profession is in crisis in this country."[3] Teachers themselves are fully aware of their situation. In *High School: A Report on Secondary Education in America*, Boyer reports:

> Surveys reveal that teachers are deeply troubled, not only about salaries, but also about their loss of status, the bureaucratic pressures, a negative public image, the lack of recognition and rewards. To talk about recruiting better students into teaching without first examining the current circumstances that discourage teachers is simply a diversion. The push for excellence in education must begin by confronting those conditions that drive good teachers from the classroom in the first place.[4]

Being a professional educator—a teacher—means being dedicated to the noblest aspiration of civilization. Teachers, counselors, and administrators are the guardians of our most precious resources—youth. This professional family protects the best interests of the public and the young. Yet, this professional ethos has withered under our outmoded school structure. Hidden pressures have built up inside a system already overheated by pressure from external forces. The new emphasis on accountability at all levels of public education has only intensified these pressures.

During the period of accelerating public concern about accountability of educators and quality of education, unresolved grievances increasingly find their way to the courts. James Leary, in *Educators on Trial*,[5] points out that malpractice lawsuits against schools and schoolpeople are on the rise. The idea of educational malpractice is rather new. Yet, as Leary notes, "One can get a glimpse of the enormity of the problem by merely reading these recent headlines."

- ☐ Suit Seeks $25,000 for Boy Expelled from Junior High
- ☐ Irate Student Sues College
- ☐ $5.8 Million Suit Filed Against School District
- ☐ Parents Sue to Keep Girl in School
- ☐ Suits Against Educators Seen As Growing Problem
- ☐ Keeping Malpractice Out of the Classroom
- ☐ Malpractice Insurance Plan Sought by School Board
- ☐ School System Is Sued for Alleged Overcrowding
- ☐ High School Grad to Bring $5 Million "Malpractice" Suit
- ☐ Malpractice Crisis Shifts to Colleges
- ☐ California Court Case Challenges I.Q. Tests
- ☐ Ex-Principal Spent $25,000 Fighting Student Damage Suit[6]

Leary describes some of the high visibility and pressure being brought to bear on the public schools and the people who work in them:

TABLE 8-2

Education majors' average SAT scores

	All	Education
Alabama	964	828
Alaska	923	850
Arizona	981	889
Arkansas	999	865
California	899	823
Colorado	983	893
Connecticut	896	803
Delaware	897	796
District of Columbia	821	715
Florida	889	808
Georgia	823	759
Hawaii	857	783
Idaho	995	876
Illinois	977	878
Indiana	860	805
Iowa	1,088	951
Kansas	1,045	926
Kentucky	985	894
Louisiana	975	878
Maine	890	806
Maryland	889	809
Massachusetts	888	795
Michigan	973	874
Minnesota	1,028	918
Mississippi	988	810
Missouri	975	879

Source: College board

Average combined verbal and mathematics scores on 1982 Schoastic Aptitude Tests of all high-school seniors bound for college, compared with those of seniors planning to major in education. n.a.—Data not available

There is no doubt about the reality of current public pressures facing educators. With the exception of key administrators, some coaches, and music instructors, very few school employees had been subjected previously to direct public exposure or had their practices questioned. But now the impact of school-related issues featured in newspapers, magazines, and on television has affected virtually every classroom teacher and administrator in America. This is not to say that school employees at all educational levels have not provided much of the controversy. Indeed they have.

	All	Education
Montana	1,033	907
Nebraska	945	933
Nevada	917	818
New Hampshire	925	832
New Jersey	869	789
New Mexico	997	884
New York	896	838
North Carolina	827	758
North Dakota	1,068	n.a.
Ohio	958	877
Oklahoma	1,001	890
Oregon	908	821
Pennsylvania	885	820
Rhode Island	877	808
South Carolina	790	740
South Dakota	1.075	1,021
Tennessee	999	921
Texas	868	791
Utah	1,022	893
Vermont	904	829
Virginia	888	796
Washington	982	885
West Virginia	968	808
Wisconsin	1,011	901
Wyoming	1,017	855

As school people find their actions being more carefully scrutinized by parents, the business community, social agencies, lawmakers, and each other, members of the educational profession are often heard making the remark, "We are working in a fishbowl."[7]

This deteriorating professional image has affected the ability to attract promising prospective teachers. Michael Dukakis, governor of Massachusetts, who publicly confessed that his toughest job was that of teacher, expressed dismay at the dearth of high school students indicating an interest in pursuing teaching careers.[8]

The Carnegie Forum on Education and the Economy has established the Task Force on Teaching as a Profession to study this issue:

The Task Force is being created in recognition of the central role teachers play in the quality of education. It comes at a critical juncture with respect to the future of our public schools. During the 80's, the nation will need to double the rate at which new teachers are appointed, in large part because of accelerated rates of teacher retirement.[9]

But while our need for excellent teachers is growing, it is evident that the teaching profession is not attracting the most promising college students. While the shortcomings of paper and pencil tests are being documented, the public as well as other observers continue to use such tests as indicators of quality. It is not surprising, therefore, for studies to continue based on the results of the SAT. For example, in a study done by the College Entrance Examination Board, high school students planning to go into teaching had average SAT scores that were approximately 100 points lower than the average for all college bound seniors in most of the fifty states. This startling statistic is illustrated in Table 8–2[10] on the previous page.

C. Emily Feistritzer, who prepared a disturbing 1983 report on the teaching profession for the Carnegie Foundation, recognizes that increasing salaries, while desirable, will not solve the problem of quality. She believes that standards for entry and continued status in the teaching profession are too low:

> It has been very easy to become a classroom teacher. Anyone can get a degree in education because the entrance requirements are so low. Once in, hardly anyone gets fired. If we make teacher education entry requirements more rigorous, and introduce more rigor into the curriculum, we will raise the status of the professional.[11]

While it may not be surprising that the teaching profession should have trouble attracting the best and the brightest, Boyer's analysis in the same article includes this sobering warning, "Fewer students are electing to go into teaching, and those who do are at the bottom of the barrel. Preparation programs are poor, and credentialing is a mess.[12]

This sense of decline in the qualifications and preparation of teachers has become a crucial part of our national dialogue on teacher excellence. Studies conducted by Feistritzer for the National Center for Education Information indicate that "the selection, training, and certification of teachers vary widely within states and from state to state—and are in great need of reform." Specifically, Feistritzer found these problem areas in certification requirements:

☐ All but two states issue some type of substandard teaching credential to people who don't meet full certification requirements.
☐ 23 states issue substandard credentials to people who don't even have a bachelor's degree; all but four of those states renew such certificates.
☐ Only 18 states require passing some type of paper-pencil tests before a person can be fully certified to teach.

☐ Less than half of the 1,287 colleges and universities that train teachers give a test to students completing the teacher education program.[13]

Fortunately this negative cycle appears to be breaking down. The national rededication to excellence in our schools is really, in part, a rededication to teachers. The movement toward a new professionalism is beginning.

A PROPOSAL FOR A NEW PROFESSIONALISM

Teacher union leaders, including the president of the American Federation of Teachers, Albert Shanker, in what appears to be a major shift in policy, have called for a new professionalism. The cornerstone of this new professionalism is a national examination for new teachers, as explained by Shanker in a major speech to the National Press Club:

> First, current exams for new teachers would be considered a joke by any other profession. For the most part, they are minimal competency examinations for teachers. What does minimal competency mean? Well, in a state like Florida, minimal competency for an elementary school teacher in mathematics is measured by passing an examination on a sixth-grade mathematics level. There are similar examinations involving English, involving history, involving the other subjects.
>
> Now, this would be the equivalent of licensing doctors on the basis of an examination in elementary biology or licensing accountants and actuaries on the basis of some type of elementary mathematics examination. I don't wish to criticize the states that have adopted these tests. It was difficult for them to do it. They met a great deal of opposition. In many cases, they met court challenges. What they have done is to take the first step. But it's important to distinguish a necessary first step from an adequate program of testing, which is quite different.
>
> I think the second problem, aside from the nature of the examination, is that we are about to face once again the traditional crunch: the conflict that exists at the state and local level between quantity and quality. We know what's coming. We've seen the statistics. Depending upon whether you take a more or less optimistic projection, it's quite likely that even in fields other than mathematics and science we will be experiencing, within the next five years, a substantial national teacher shortage.
>
> In fields like medicine, if there is a shortage of doctors, you do not find states or hospitals giving anyone a substitute emergency medical license to go out and practice. We don't do it in law or dentistry or in any other field. But our local education agencies will be faced with the usual tough choices as this shortage emerges and grows. They could do the equivalent of what most other professions would do, and do indeed do. That is, after the children come to school and after each teacher's class is full, they could turn to the remaining students and parents and say, "Sorry, there is a shortage of teachers, and those

of you who could not be accommodated this semester will be given the first opportunity to take the first grade next semester or next year.[14]

Shanker suggested that teachers must look beyond collective bargaining to improve their professional status, and proposed the following reforms in addition to a national test to limit entrance into teaching:

☐ A system that would allow students freedom to choose the public schools they attend so that they are no longer "captive clients."
☐ Impartial panels of experienced teachers to evaluate teachers accused of incompetence.
☐ Career ladders that lead to supervision by experienced teachers of the development of novices.
☐ A restructuring of education to encourage bright young people to enter teaching even if only with the intention of remaining five or six years.[15]

Feistritzer agrees that a national test for teachers will contribute to a greater professionalism:

Every occupation that calls itself a profession has national standards. At the entry level, there are selection procedures; on the job, there are standards of excellence and competence.

Teaching will never be truly a profession until it adopts such steps, starting with uniform national standards administered state by state.[16]

However, a standardized test for teachers may be an inadequate response to the problem of eroded teacher professionalism. No written test, no matter how long or well designed, can replace demonstrated competence with learners during carefully supervised practices, such as an internship period. As I have previously stated:

Teaching is a human and social act dealing as much with personality and style as with content. The capacity to inspire, motivate, guide, care, communicate respect, and act as a model—all considered traits associated with superior teachers—is best spotted in the classroom, not in a paper-and-pencil test.

Similarly, the ability to help students aspire, think, imagine, create, and develop is a talent we can judge for ourselves when we see prospective teachers working with children.

The danger in establishing a national teacher licensing test rests with our tendency to overrely on it and to expect that it can do more than it really can. The risk is giving the public the illusion that this test will restore quality to teaching in our schools.

Standardized tests have limits. Test-makers themselves warn us that they are not to be used as absolute standards for judgment, but as one source of information only. Overreliance on standardized tests has resulted in a spotty track record for them. They have been unable to predict future success in many cases, while also labeling other people as losers who later prove to be winners.

If high scores alone on a national test held the key to successful teaching, we would be close to solving our current problem. Robots and computers are able to hold more information and knowledge about more subjects than the best and brightest among us. They would surely score well in a national test and qualify as our future electronic teachers.

Clearly, productive teaching involves more than the mere transmission of information. We need well-rounded human teachers who can use the best that we have, including the new electronic technology, to stimulate students to become all that they are capable of becoming.

No national test can be expected to do that.[17]

As complex as the factors that determine professionalism are, it is clear that merely adding competency testing to the certification process may not have the desired impact on improving teaching. The operational setting in the American public school structure must be radically changed. It is vain to hope that piecemeal school reform initiatives will create the conditions for a renewed sense of teacher professionalism. In fact, any measure short of a totally new image for the teaching profession cannot begin to achieve the level of improvement that the public is demanding for schools.

RENEWING THE TEACHING ENVIRONMENT

Professionalism is a complex issue that goes beyond entrance examinations and certification criteria. Many uncontrollable factors influence the status and prestige of teachers. According to John Goodlad, "The teachers in our sample, on the whole, went into teaching because [of these] inherent professional values. However, they encountered in schools many realities not conducive to professional growth.[18] The nature of the classroom itself, the working conditions in the school, the nature of the community, the various levels of government and policy development—all influence the professional lives of teachers for better or for worse.

Ernest Boyer observes:

Many people think teachers have soft, undemanding jobs. One parent told us, "I'm not sure what they have to complain about. After all, it's an easy life. The hours are good—nine to three—and you get the summer off."

The reality is different. The average high school teacher not only teaches five or six classes a day, but has only 54 minutes of in-school preparation time. . . . Outside the classroom, teachers must review subject matter, prepare lesson plans, correct and grade papers, make out report cards, and counsel students.[19]

The need to restructure the public education system through a comprehensive modernization process is as crucial in the area of teacher professionalism as it is in other areas. The principles and findings examined earlier, including those gleaned from practices in the private sector, are vital in this difficult process. If public education could move away from low wages to proper professional rewards, away from bureaucracy and standardization toward flexibility and decentralization, from a top-down decision-making flow to a bottom-up process, from an over-reliance on schooling to an emphasis on learning and education—such directions might profoundly change the profession.

A COMPREHENSIVE APPROACH TO RENEWAL OF THE PROFESSION

ECONOMIC CONCERNS AND COLLECTIVE BARGAINING
State legislatures need to take over from organized teacher groups the process for improving salary and working conditions. Professional associations are negatively altered when teachers are forced to use them to fight for decent wages and working conditions. Work stoppages and strikes have hurt their public and professional images. Teachers deserve a salary and benefit package commensurate with their responsibilities. Relieved of their economic burden and encouraged to pursue the professional values that brought them into teaching in the first place, teachers can dedicate themselves more fully to their students.[20] There is now ample evidence that state governments are attending to teacher salaries in their particular versions of school reform.

PUBLIC IMAGE OF TEACHERS
Public confidence in teachers seems to have eroded in proportion to the decline in teacher's perceptions of their own professionalism. Perhaps the rebuilding of public confidence will correspond to the rebuilding of professional confidence. Lila Carol and Luvern L. Cunningham of Ohio State University reported that the presence of dedicated, competent teachers was ranked as the number one factor the community used to determine their degree of confidence in individual schools and in a total school district. Tables 8–3, 8–4, and 8–5 illustrate this principle.[21]

Since teachers' dedication and competence are central to the public's positive image of schools, it is the perceived decline of this dedication and competence that contributes to the school's negative image. Their dedication is questioned when they strike.[22] Their competence is questioned when national reports show lowered standards and declining academic test scores.

A Nation at Risk has aimed the charge of mediocrity at public schools and the teaching profession. This criticism, however, is misleading: the inflexibility of a highly standardized school system produces mediocrity by effectively restricting teachers' potential. The charge of mediocrity becomes an indictment of the limitations of the system, not the people working within that system. If the system were restructured to contain a greater degree of built-in flexibility, the varied and individual capabilities of teachers could be more fully utilized.

TABLE 8-3
Ranking of responses leading to confidence at a school district level[21]

Rank	Reasons	No. of Responses
1.5	Dedicated, competent teachers	22
1.5	Special instructional and extracurricular programs	22
3.0	Buildings and grounds	20
4.0	Board/superintendent relations, policies, decisions	19
5.0	Public image	14
7.0	Curriculum	12
8.3	High standards	6
8.3	Student achievement	6
8.3	Success of graduates	6
11.3	Parent participation	4
11.3	Community education	4
11.3	Linkages with other institutions	4
14.0	Communication with parents	3
15.3	Equity	2
15.3	Testing, guidance, counseling programs	2
15.3	Administrator/staff community service	2
18.0	Student honors, awards	1

TEACHERS AS EDUCATIONAL LEADERS OF LEARNING

Restructuring the system would liberate teachers from the constraints of the current bureaucratically standardized school with its prescribed curricula, isolation from other adults, and tedious paperwork. Each teacher would be able to make independent decisions about teaching style, diagnosing student needs, and prescribing specifically tailored programs for students, working with colleagues, and planning alternative learning environments in school and nonschool settings. Freed by the new structure to exercise professional judgment, the teacher would find the work environment more intrinsically rewarding as professionalism is operationally restored. Under the present system, traditional school structure has combined with union-imposed standardization to deprive teachers of their individuality as independent thinking professionals. Breaking the ranks of conformity with either the school structure or the teacher union is often dangerous.

The teacher in the restructured school will be viewed as a community agent linking the school to nonschool learning opportunities. The teacher's responsibilities may include being negotiator with human service agencies, business and industry, and the health agencies to determine the resources available to the learning process; the teacher would serve as coordinator of the learning sequences developed between school and nonschool settings. Teachers would insure that the learning environments in the community are of the highest quality and would provide train-

TABLE 8–4
Ranking of responses leading to confidence at a school building level[21]

Rank	Reasons	No. of Responses
1.5	Dedicated, competent teachers	75
1.5	Special instructional and extracurricular programs	75
3.5	Administrator(s) effectiveness	61
3.5	Buildings and grounds	61
5.0	Student-centered, "caring" atmosphere	51
6.0	Positive attitudes of student/staff	40
7.0	Student discipline	38
8.0	Curriculum	36
9.0	Student achievement	30
10.0	Parent participation	28
11.0	Communication with parents	22
12.0	Public image	22
13.5	High standards, goals, expectations	15
13.5	Board/superintendent relations, policies, decisions	15
15.0	Administrator/staff community service	13
16.0	Courteous office staff	12
17.0	Linkages with other institutions, sectors	11
18.0	Successful graduates	10
19.33	Student awards, honors	9
19.33	Testing, guidance, and counseling programs	9
19.33	Community involvement with school	9
22.0	Adequate funding	5
23.0	Students' dress	4
24.5	Equity	3
24.5	Community education	3

ing when necessary. Thus, an entirely new concept of the teacher emerges. Today's teacher is usually limited to the confines of a classroom (or maximally, a schoolhouse) and is expected to deliver all educational services directly.

Given the knowledge explosion and all its dramatic changes, including new learning tools, the teacher should be the central accountable professional agent facilitating but not always directly providing services. The professional teacher might be responsible for leading educational teams composed of university students acting as tutors, community volunteers including senior citizens, specialists from business and industry or mass media, doctors, nutritionists, artists—all participating as teachers. These community resources can be mobilized into an integrated whole with the key agent being the teacher.

Modest progress in this direction is already evident. Attention to teachers as professionals is now being translated into public policy at different levels of

TABLE 8-5

Preliminary comparative rankings of responses leading to confidence in schools and school districts[21]

Rank	School Reasons	Rank	District Reasons
1.5	Teacher dedication and competence	1.5	Teacher dedication and competence
1.5	Special instructional and extracurricular programs	1.5	Special instructional and extracurricular programs
3.5	Buildings and grounds	3.5	Buildings and grounds
3.5	Administrator effectiveness		
		4.0	Board/Superintendent effectiveness
5.0	Student-centered, "caring" atmosphere	5.0	Administrator effectiveness
6.0	Positive attitudes of students/staff	6.0	Public image
7.0	Student discipline	7.0	Curriculum
8.0	Curriculum	8.3	High standards
		8.3	Student achievement

government. During the 1970s, the federal government sponsored a network of Teacher Centers designed by teachers for teachers. These centers were mostly housed in settings outside the school environment where teachers could gather informally to discuss topics of mutual interest. Recently, as federal aid has diminished, localities, recognizing the importance of these Teacher Centers, have continued to support them.[23] Similarly, in Massachusetts, Governor Michael Dukakis created a Field Center for Teaching and Learning which focuses squarely on teacher needs. It not only has teachers on its governing board but is also entirely committed to teachers' professional development.

CAREER LADDERS FOR TEACHERS

Other plans growing out of state reforms feature career ladders for teachers that create new challenges and rewards. Presently, good teachers are neither rewarded financially or professionally for excellence if they remain in the classroom; their only hope for advancement is to leave teaching for administration. There is currently no way to reward teachers with career aspirations who wish to remain in teaching. The new plans call for advancement through differentiation of professional tasks. Many proposals emphasize the master teacher—someone who has progressed up the professional ladder from novice to experienced teacher to master teacher. Master teachers might assume such responsibilities as curriculum development, coordination of staff development, and supervision of novice teachers while remaining in the classroom in close contact with the students. This career ladder approach might serve as an intermediate step toward professionalism on the way to total modernization.

RESTRUCTURING TEACHER PREPARATION

Clearly, the complexities of teaching in a world rocked by rapidly expanding knowledge justify a new approach to teacher preparation. In the revised pre-service plan, people already holding bachelor's degrees would enter graduate-level programs including both coursework and practical experience through a comprehensive internship program.

A number of education school deans from research universities have formed an ongoing research and discussion group called the "Holmes Group," in memory of Henry W. Holmes.

> Over a half century ago, as dean of Harvard's Graduate School of Education, Holmes invested great energy in attempts to raise the stature and quality of teacher education by urging the nation's leading scholars to take it more seriously. The consortium includes a set of research-intensive institutions whose administrative and faculty leaders are willing to create and adopt new high standards of quality for the initial and continuing education of teachers.[24]

A summary of the Holmes Group's approach to the preparation of teachers as professionals includes the following from the Chronicle of Higher Education.[25]

Goals for the Institutional Environment

☐ The university makes multiple investments in teachers and teaching. Its commitment to more effective schools recognizes excellence in teaching; scholarships for needy, talented students that assure cultural diversity; serious research and development on teaching and learning; and arrangements for teachers' continued education.

☐ The university works with selected school districts to create exemplary school sites for student and faculty learning about teaching excellence. In these "professional development schools," working conditions allow for the very best in teaching practice. Unlike the laboratory schools of old, these are "real world" schools that often include pupils from disadvantaged homes.

☐ The university fosters an interdisciplinary climate in teacher education that reflects diversity, depth, and relatedness to teaching. There is a valuing of collaboration among faculty with different disciplinary expertise that encourages coherent programs of professional preparation.

☐ The university expects an ethos of inquiry to permeate its teacher education programs at the university.

- The university creates significant opportunities for teacher-education students to develop collegial and professional norms. Students have faculty mentors and advisers who remain with them throughout their initial preparation.
- The university assures equitable rights and responsibilities to the academic unit accountable for teacher education. The oversight and governance provisions for teacher education within a college, school, or department are comparable to those of other professional schools.
- The university supports regular improvement of teacher education and participation in a national consortium for ongoing research, development, and program improvement.

Goals for the Faculty

- University faculty members responsible for preparing school teachers are competent and committed. Evaluations by peers at least every two years affect salary, promotion, and professional development.
- The university faculty includes a clinical faculty of practicing school teachers, selected on the basis of exemplary teaching and career status.
- The university faculty contributes regularly to better knowledge and understanding of teaching and schooling.
- The university faculty is made up of strong teacher-scholars designated as "fellows in teacher education" by a national review committee of leading educators.

Goals for Students

- The students matriculating through the phases of study required for career professionals in teaching are academically talented and committed to teaching. Students in the lowest quartile of the college population nationally are denied admission.
- The students reflect our nation's obligation to a multicultural society.
- Students evidence mastery of requisite content knowledge through written examination at various stages of their professional career development. At three points—prior to status as an intern, novice, and career teacher—students must pass components of a Professional Teacher Examination, developed by faculty members from institutions participating in the Holmes Group Consortium (liberal arts, subject area specialists, and professional educators), in cooperation with a major testing firm and practicing professionals.
- Students, as judged by professionals, evidence appropriate ethical commitments and teaching capabilities prior to successful completion of their internship. During the induction year, students are required to successfully complete a teaching internship and continue working toward a master's degree in education.

Goals for a Professional Curriculum

☐ The curriculum for prospective career teachers does not permit a major in education during the baccalaureate years. Instead, undergraduates pursue more serious general/liberal study and a standard academic subject normally taught in schools.

☐ The curriculum requires a master's degree in education and a well-supervised teaching internship over a substantial period of time. Interns, supervised by clinical faculty members, teach children and participate in clinics, action research, and curriculum studies.

☐ The curriculum for elementary career teachers would require study in multiple areas of concentration (each equivalent to a minor) in the subject fields for which teachers assume general teaching authority and responsibility—language and literature, mathematics, science, social science, and the arts.

☐ The curriculum for secondary career teachers would include significant graduate study in their major teaching field and area concentrations in all other subjects they would teach.

During post-baccalaureate study and before being recommended for career status, secondary teachers would be required to successfully complete the equivalent of an advanced specialist degree.

☐ The curriculum for prospective career teachers would include substantial knowledge and skill regarding appropriate policy and practice in teaching students with special needs.

☐ The curriculum required for attainment of career professional status requires advanced study appropriate for specialized work in education with other adult professionals. This advanced study would be in curriculum development, research and evaluation, teacher education, work with special populations, school policy and management, or particular subject fields. The universities also would work with schools to create roles for teachers that combine outstanding teaching of children with outstanding work with adults in education.

Successful completion of such advanced study would carry recognition as a Professional Career Teacher and could lead to a second advanced degree, such as an educational-specialist degree or the doctorate in education.[25]

Already in place at the University of Massachusetts/Amherst is a special teacher preparation program that incorporates much of the current thinking for attracting, retaining, and professionalizing teachers. Designed to alleviate the extreme shortage of math and science teachers, the newly launched Math/Science/Technology Education Project (M/S/TEP) is a partnership linking forty school systems, several leading high tech corporations, and the university. This graduate-level program attracts college graduates who have majored in math or the sciences and are prime candidates for careers in engineering, medicine, and advanced sciences but who have selected teaching as a career instead. These candidates come from the best colleges, have earned good grades, and have scored very high on SAT tests. In brief, they are "the pool" that every national study on education has suggested tapping for future teachers. The point is not just that they represent the best and the brightest, but that this program attracts a different sort of candidate to the teaching profession.

These talented college graduates select this master's level teacher preparation program because it is not a traditional school of education teacher preparation program. Business and industry, partners in this program, provide talent, facilities, and paid internships. Public schools are part of the team. And there is an all-university approach with arts and sciences faculties participating fully. The School of Education at the University of Massachusetts/Amherst acts as the chief coordinator of this multi-pronged training design. The following program description reviews the different components of this model:

Our 14-month plan of study, which began in June 1984, includes
☐ University course work,
☐ Paid teaching internships in secondary schools,
☐ Paid internships in the educational division of one of Massachusetts' leading corporations.

Project participants will
☐ Obtain certification to teach mathematics or one of the sciences at the secondary level;
☐ Earn a master's degree;
☐ Gain knowledge and valuable experience during a corporate internship;
☐ Expand their career options in both teaching and industry.

A COORDINATED DEGREE PROGRAM:

The First Summer (June–August): Students are involved in an intensive series of courses and experiences intended to prepare them for teaching internships. Each student, as a member of a teaching team led by an expert teacher, will work daily with high school students. Familiarity with computer-aided instruction will be developed through hands-on experience with courseware designed to aid the teaching of science and mathematics.

The Academic Year (September–June): The students will be divided into two groups. Group A will spend the first half-year (September–January) as paid teaching interns in schools, and the second half-year (January–June) as paid interns in industry. Group B will reverse the order of these experiences. Each student will therefore spend half of the year teaching and the other half in an educational internship in industry.

During the school-internship semester, interns will teach in a secondary school, with the support and assistance of a Supervising Teacher and university staff. During the industrial-internship semester, interns will work in such situations as

☐ Serving as a member of a team developing computer-based instructional materials;
☐ Developing curriculum for use in the company's staff training;
☐ Helping to evaluate the effectiveness of customer-training programs;
☐ Teaching at the company's training center;
☐ Applying disciplinary skills (e.g., mathematics) to the solution of an industrial-design problem.

In addition, students will be enrolled in courses relevant to their teaching careers and courses designed to place their industry internship into a broader cultural perspective. All coursework will be offered in the late afternoon or evening at a location near the internship sites in the Greater Boston area.

The Second Summer (June–August): Students will complete the coursework for teacher certification (as appropriate), enroll in courses to strengthen their knowledge of mathematics and science, work intensively in the area of educational applications of computers and other new technologies, and complete the requirements for the master's degree. Students will also serve as teaching assistants with the new group of entering interns.

TEACHING COMMITMENT:

Students must make a commitment to teach for a minimum of three years upon completion of the M/S/TEP. This commitment may be fulfilled in a school of the graduate's choice, and is not restricted to school systems which are participants in M/S/TEP or to schools in Massachusetts. (Massachusetts has reciprocity agreements for teacher certification with 30 other states.)[26]

Such model teacher preparation programs based on new partnerships among university, school, and community agencies, including business and industry, add new talent and resources to the task. Arizona State University also has a recruitment and training program, the "Partner Project," combining the cooperative efforts of progressive public school systems and leaders in business and industry with the state university system.[27]

The following state-wide collaborative model for teacher preparation has been proposed as part of Massachusetts' Commonwealth's educational reform efforts. The elements of the new model include

1. *Academic Background*
   All teaching candidates must be college graduates who have majored in an academic subject as undergraduates. Those undergraduates who make an early decision to become teachers would benefit by taking some education courses in the senior year.
2. *Training and Internship*
   After completing a bachelor's degree, teaching candidates enter a training period consisting of an initial summer, an academic year, and a second summer. The first summer session includes training in methods and materials, observation, psychology, and curricular innovation. During the

academic year, candidates intern in schools, taking the place of substitute teachers. Each participating community designates some teaching slots for internships. This paid experience helps aspiring teachers meet the costs of advanced training and relieves the shortage and cost of substitute teachers. Ideally, candidates assist in some curricular design project at their assigned schools during the internship. Candidates would then return for a follow-up summer session, continuing to take courses. This internship year would serve as the provisional period outlined in the current Massachusetts certification laws.

3. *Resident Teachers*

   Those candidates who successfully complete the internship and advanced study period enter a two- to three-year residency period with continued guidance from supervising teachers in participating school systems.

4. *Supervising Teachers*

   A group of experienced teachers, designated by a panel of teachers, parents, and administrators, would take on the responsibility of clinical supervision of interns and resident teachers. School departments would grant these supervisors released time from teaching or extra pay for their responsibilities.[28]

Such state-wide plans make teacher preparation a graduate process, expand the partners who will help prepare future teachers and establish career ladder arrangements. This model is a collaborative modernization effort to achieve professional excellence benefiting both teachers and the communities they serve.

THE PROFESSION AND PRODUCTIVITY

Ultimately, the test of a profession is found in its productivity. For schools and education, this means achieving the goals of the institution. The goal for both education and the profession is nothing less than excellence, and the profession has some distance to travel before reaching productivity. It is critical, however, to set the target and to start the journey. The ground rules are being recast for a profession participating in a major reformation of schooling in the United States.

Educational reform is coming on the heels of major changes being considered in the private sector as it grapples with excellence and productivity. New patterns are emerging in the thinking of corporate management in the United States, stimulated in part by fierce competition from Japan.

The search for a concept of excellence and productivity tied to our own values and culture appears to be in motion. Corporations in the United States are changing the way they do business in much the same way as the schools are. New innovations promise to increase productivity. For example, according to a Conference Board survey of 52 firms, including Hewlett-Packard Company, Northrop Corporation, and Honeywell Inc., new approaches have successfully increased productivity and quality. The following are some of the innovative techniques:

☐ Redesigning jobs to encourage the full ability of workers rather than breaking jobs into specialized tasks.

☐ Creating problem-solving teams and giving them the authority to implement their solutions.

☐ Rewarding workers financially for productivity gains.

☐ Creating union-management programs to improve the working environment.

☐ Building "greenfield plants," plants that are usually small, non-union, and located outside of urban areas (thus, in green fields) and assigning workers based on their ability to work as a team and with minimal supervision.[29]

It can be seen that many of these approaches to increased productivity not only apply to our discussion of education but are already taking place in many reform-oriented school districts.

Clearly, these advances would not be possible without a cooperative willingness among the interested parties to pursue more productive practices. This new willingness to explore, to change if necessary, is part of the new professional spirit essential for progress. The rudimentary beginnings of such a spirit are being fostered by sensitive leadership and appropriate public policy.

STARTING WHERE WE ARE

Change in the profession is inevitably tied to changes in the process of education. Change begins with the present system and those who relate to it. Improvements start where people and their institutions are and move forward from that point. Attempting quantum leaps or pushing prematurely into uncharted directions can backfire. The stakes are too high for such ill-conceived remedies. However, the danger is equally great when a business-as-usual attitude is embraced or politically expedient improvements that treat symptoms and not causes are advocated.

We have advocated a phased approach to reformation—one that begins with the present, builds toward the future and involves the leadership and participation of all parties affected by reforms—not only teachers and their organizations, not only policymakers and school officials, but the community, its agents and its agencies—all who have a fundamental connection to the future of education.

NOTES

1. Marvin Cetron, *Schools of the Future: How American Business and Education Can Cooperate to Save Our Schools* (New York: McGraw-Hill Book Company, 1985); pp. 114–115.

2. Gene I. Maeroff, "Shift in Strategy to Aid Teachers," *The New York Times*, 27 April 1985, 1, 35.

3. "School Teaching Profession in Crisis, New Carnegie Analysis Finds," *Chronicle of Higher Education*, Vol. XXVII, 31 August 1983, 6.

4. Ernest L. Boyer, *High School: A Report on Secondary Education in America*, The Carnegie Foundation for the Advancement of Teaching (New York: Harper and Row, 1983), 155.

5. James Leary, *Educators on Trial* (Farmington, Michigan: Action Inservice, Inc., Publisher, 1981).

6. *Ibid.*, 13.

7. *Ibid.*, 5.

8. Michael Dukakis, Governor of the State of Massachusetts, State Education Policy Seminar, Bank of New England, Boston, 14 February 1985.

9. Dr. David A. Hamburg, President of the Carnegie Corporation of New York and Chairman of the Carnegie Forum on Education and the Economy, *Press Release*, May 1985.

10. "School Teaching Profession in Crisis, New Carnegie Analysis Finds," *Chronicle of Higher Education*, Vol. XXVII, 31 August 1983, 6.

11. *Ibid.*

12. *Ibid.*

13. C. Emily Feistritzer, Guest Columnist, "Opinion," *U.S.A. Today*, 4 September 1984, 10A.

14. Albert Shanker, President of the American Federation of Teachers, National Press Club Speech, 29 January 1985.

15. Gene I. Maeroff, "Shift in Strategy to Aid Teachers," *The New York Times*, 27 April 1985.

16. C. Emily Feistritzer, Guest Columnist, "Opinion," *U.S.A. Today*, 4 September 1984, 10A.

17. Mario D. Fantini, Guest Columnist, "Opinion," *U.S.A. Today*, 4 September 1984, 11.

18. John I. Goodlad, *A Place Called School: Prospects for the Future* (New York: McGraw-Hill Book Company, 1984), 194.

19. Boyer, *High School: A Report on Secondary Education in America*, 155.

20. Mario D. Fantini, *What's Best for the Children* (New York: Anchor Press–Doubleday, 1974).

21. Lila N. Carol and Luvern L. Cunningham, "View of Public Confidence in Education," *Issues in Education*, Vol. II, No. 2, Fall 1984, 113, 119, 118, 120.

22. Fantini, *What's Best for the Children*.

23. R. W. Maloy, S. Germain, R. F. Schilling, Jr., *Teacher Centering: A Resource Book for Planning, Developing and Implementing a Teachers' Center* (Shelburne, Massachusetts: The Teacher/Community SEED Center, with assistance of the Massachusetts Department of Education, 1980).

24. The Holmes Group Consortium, "New Standards for Quality in Teacher Education," A Proposal to the Secretary's Discretionary Program, U.S. Department of Education, The Ford Foundation, The Carnegie Corporation of New York, July 1984.

25. "Summary of Deans' Report. 'Goals for Educating Teachers as Professionals' " *The Chronicle of Higher Education*, Vol. XXX, No. 15, 12 June 1985, 16.

26. Math/Science/Teacher Education Project Brochure, School of Education, University of Massachusetts, Amherst, 1984–1985.

27. "Partner Project," Department of Secondary Education, College of Education, Arizona State University.

28. Mario D. Fantini, Proposal to The Joint Committee on Education of the Massachusetts General Court, 1984.

29. "Insiders: Behind the Scenes in the World of Business," *U.S.A. Today*, 9 July 1984, 2B.

Modernization and Educative Agents   9

The crisis of professionalism threatens not only teachers but all those who perform key roles in public education School board officials, superintendents, principals, and school of education faculty and administrators all need to embrace the values inherent in excellence and gain new leadership for the future.

THE PRINCIPAL

Next to the teacher, the school principal is the agent closest to the learner and the one who has the most authority to make things happen for the better. Almost every study on school effectiveness has reaffirmed the importance of the principal, especially one whose strong leadership leads to organized productivity. Successful schools have a principal who sets goals, maintains discipline, observes classrooms frequently, and gives incentives for learning.[1] In the private sector, strong leadership is a basic key to excellence in successful companies,[2] which is equally applicable to the public sector and to schools.

The principal, however, also suffers from diminished prestige. At one time, the principal, considered better educated and qualified than teachers, taught teachers. However, with increased access to knowledge, teachers gained the same knowledge base as principals and also earned degrees. The notion of the principal's superiority eroded. The principal's authority, once almost absolute, was undermined by collective bargaining and the teachers' increasing concern with power and access to decision making. Consequently, there has been a tug of war between administration and teachers, between the management and labor of education.

As the community began to express its concern about productivity in the schools, especially in urban areas, many parents and other citizens formed their own groups and challenged the school and the principal as manager. These pressures were increased by the principals' position in the system hierarchy: they are ultimately accountable to the central office and to the superintendent.

School reform advocates have recognized the need to restructure the roles of principals and to restore their status. The North Carolina Leadership Institute for Principals and the Harvard (University) Principals' Center were established to provide ongoing training programs for principals. They focus on supplementing the programs available for principals in local school districts and institutions of higher education, offering services to assist building administrators in carrying out the increasing responsibilities and competencies required of them, including field-based services and opportunities for peer learning. National studies by Theodore Sizer[3] and John I. Goodlad[4] advocate a decentralized model whose main features are school-based management, delegation of authority to individual schools or districts, and designation of certain schools as experimental institutions with license to depart from the old model of standardization. This new empowerment gives the principal a renewed sense of the importance of creative leadership, particularly in the allocation of resources during difficult economic times. Principals are learning to assess the common goals of their communities and to direct resources accordingly. As they assume responsibility for new directions for their schools, they take into account the individuality of the school and its community.

Through modernization and the eventual restructuring that will take place, the role of the principal will change dramatically. The principal will become a community agent accountable for good education in the various learning environments, negotiating with managers from business and industry, to share their resources with teachers and students.

The creation of this new structure highlights some remaining structural problems. Many principals are frustrated because they do not have decision-making authority over personnel. They must accept teachers who have been hired by someone else. Budgets are also determined centrally and then given to the individual building principal. Many communities have diverse factions warring over directions and values for the schools. The principal is the person caught in the middle. Teachers, parents, and citizens in the community who should be allies of the principal are not always supportive. Even the central administration may not be compatible with the building principal. The result is often a school administrator whose professional identity is at stake. The North Carolina Leadership Institute for Principals and the Harvard Principals' Center provide hope and assistance to these administrators.

THE SUPERINTENDENT

The superintendent of schools, the public school equivalent of Chief Executive Officer (CEO) in the private sector, has also suffered from diminished prestige. Many assume that the superintendent has most of the power within a school system. However, the superintendent may have power delineated by law or by the school board or school committee. In recent years, increased political awareness of school committees and the rising public concern over productivity in the school has had serious consequences on the superintendent's role.

At one time, superintendents kept their jobs for many years. Recently, the average tenure is slightly more than two years. This foreshortening is a result of the concern that people have over their schools, the pressures that school committees face under the weight of this concern, and the unrealistic assumption that a superintendent can turn a system around within a relatively short time. These expectations indicate a lack of understanding of the system. To expect this is simply to be unaware of how the system works.

With proper support and networking, the superintendent can change the way the system operates. With community and business partnerships, school-based management, and release time for teachers for inservice training, a properly motivated superintendent can make the school system viable.

Public schools belong to the community; they are not independent agencies; they are not isolated from the community. The fundamental reform needed to restore excellence cannot take place without community participation and consent by parents, business, labor unions, government agencies, and retired citizens.

Some superintendents have been able to maintain good relationships with school boards, improve the operation of the present model, and phase in the newer model over a reasonable transition period. In Atlanta and Houston, superintendents willing to invest time have taken failing school systems and turned them into viable school systems, while laying the foundation to support new forms. They have recognized that new models are needed to serve their changing communities.

SCHOOL BOARDS

School boards are the trustees of public education at the local level. They are the counterparts of boards of directors in the private sector. They review the professionals who are to deliver excellence in public education. They monitor educational goals and represent what the public expects and demands.

For many years, the board's most important decision was to select the superintendent—to whom they delegated the responsibility of carrying out school board policies developed by the board with the involvement of the superintendent and staff. At one time, the superintendent had sufficient power to carry out these responsibilities. But as the roles of teachers, principal, and superintendent have changed, so has the role of the school boards. There has been a widespread redistribution of power in the past decade in most areas. New demands for accountability and the expression of diverse points of view from a pluralistic public have eroded professional authority to decide the direction of the schools. This confusion has been compounded by mandates from the states and the courts that make many directions obligatory, even when against the majority sentiment of the local community.

School boards and superintendents, attempting to adhere to court orders, have sometimes been victimized by a public that assumed they could do something other than what was required of them under law. In many cases, community reaction held up progress on those mandates. Many school board members lost elections to dissenting newcomers, who in turn hired new superintendents. There were many communities that wanted certain curricula that the state law restricted. Frustrated communities assumed that power rested with school boards and superintendents, placing school boards and superintendents in a cross fire between the community and the state government.

Increasingly politically significant, school boards now routinely exercise power over institutional direction by forming political coalitions and fighting professionals with the intent of gaining power for their ideology.

Some school boards hire assistant superintendents as well as the superintendent. The more control school boards have over personnel the more power they have to direct the system. At times, this direction contradicts the values of a free and just society and cannot be allowed to go unchallenged. Many dedicated professionals have challenged the motives of school boards or questioned their decisions citing research findings or societal values. The teacher, principal, and superintendent have an obligation to question, to challenge, and to speak out in the interests of the learner.

On the other hand, there are many educationally sound directions that school committees want to take that professionals oppose. These opposing interests need to be balanced. Given the diversity in our society and human variability among learners, uniform impositions by the majority will ultimately result in unequal education. In a pluralistic society, a pluralistic philosophy of education that does not victimize people, does not restrict opportunities, is based on sound educational foundations, accommodates through choice, and offers the best policies for relieving "all or nothing" positions that cause political upheaval in our present school system is needed. A school board must hire the very best superintendent and give that person executive initiative to move the system ahead with a pluralistic policy which keeps the school board posted concerning results.

The only way not to compromise the democratic process is to encourage greater community participation in school board elections. Superintendents and other professionals can encourage this involvement, pointing out the need to insure a balanced educational policy. Unfortunately, it is periods of crisis that produce the most community participation. People who come together to resolve a particular crisis have a vested interest in a particular resolution. There are many citizens who do not understand the issues, do not have time for them, or sit back while others take over. School systems become overly professionalized or politicized when the community reneges on participation—public institutions become less public by default. All power comes from the people: they can recall that power at any time.

One of the current trends to put power back into the community is decentralization—returning authority to the local school level and creating local school community councils made up of teachers, parents, and business and industry. These school-based councils can maximize participation, increase public access, and encourage greater grassroots involvement.

In Massachusetts, a new School Improvement Fund allocates $10 per student annually to local school building-based councils comprised of the principal, three teachers, two parents, and one other community person chosen by the school committee.[5] Grants are distributed to schools as soon as the superintendent certifies to the Commissioner of Education that a council is in place to determine how to spend the funds, subject to a veto of the school committee. Proposals for school-based councils have been strongly opposed by school committees, who see the councils as eroding their authority.

PARENTS

Parents have a vested interest in the education of their children and, therefore, have a primary function as both adjuncts of the school and primary teachers in the home environment. Because these two educative agents are critical to human growth and development, they need to be in close collaboration to identify problems and deal sensitively with issues. If the lines of communication are open and mutual respect is demonstrated, then cooperation follows.

Given the changing nature of the family structure, new lifestyles, and working patterns, the notion that parents can collaborate the same way they did years ago needs revamping. In the old middle-class pattern in which mothers were the primary care-givers and fathers worked outside the home, parent-teacher relationships could be standardized. This is no longer the case. With the advent of telecommunications, many new avenues of communication between teachers and parents are open, but there is no substitute for personal conferences. Teachers must welcome parents into the schools and arrange their schedules to accommodate single parents as well as working parents. Parents must be welcomed as colleagues in their children's education, not as occasional guests. Parents are also consumers and have a right to choose the kind of education that is best for their children.

UPDATING THE MISSION OF SCHOOLS OF EDUCATION

Over the past fifty years, schools of education and higher education have been assigned the responsibility for pre- and in-service preparation of teachers, counselors, school psychologists, and administrators. This brought them into contact with those schools that served as clinical sites for the preparation of educational personnel. During the acute shortage of educational personnel of the post-war period schools of education grew in size and helped support other academic units of universities. Many schools of education helped pay for other services that their universities needed to deliver.

During the 1970s, the boom period ended. With the school-age population declining and the economy suffering severe constraints, schools of education moved into a period of dramatic reduction in the number of teaching candidates. Schools of education then concentrated on graduate in-service education and on continuing education for school personnel. Due to the financial inability of many teachers to take the time off from work to continue their education full time at the university, many schools of education moved faculty into the schools to continue in-service preparation. However, the primary mission for schools and colleges of education remained the pre-service preparation of educational personnel.

Many schools of education were in land-grant colleges and universities that, under the 19th century Morrill Acts, had agreed to provide applied services to the agricultural needs of the society. The land-grant mission expanded to meet the needs of the state in urban, industrial, and high technology areas that affected economic growth and manpower development. Historically, schools of education have been responsive to the socioeconomic structure of the society that created them. Public schools evolved from one-room schoolhouses geared to an agricultural/rural economy to comprehensive schools based on a more industrialized, urban economy, including vocational education among their services. However, the educational model developed to meet the needs of an industrial society is now straining to meet the needs of a post-industrial economic structure as global interdependence replaces the narrowly defined pursuit of national interests.

A new set of realities poses a new set of responsibilities for schools of education, but they are entering this new period with a structure geared to past realities. Schools of education that were previously secure within academic circles because of their financial ability to support the general services of the university, are now faced with cutbacks. The academic standing and scholarly status of schools of education are being questioned and they are criticized for not producing outstanding teachers. Schools of education are currently in the process of redefining their roles, not from a position of strength, but from a position of weakness inside and outside scholastic institutions. On the other hand, this period of change provides significant opportunities for schools of education to assume new leadership roles and to regain status with state government, the public, the schools, and perhaps even within academic circles.

The Southern Regional Education Board's Commission for Educational Quality's report entitled "Access to Quality Undergraduate Education" on the condition of undergraduate education in the United States suggested:

> There is no question that the quality of undergraduate education is unacceptably low and needs to be raised. In the past six months, three independent na-

tional reports reached remarkably similar conclusions on the status of undergraduate education—all pointed to an incoherent curriculum, a lack of rigor in course and degree standards, inadequate methods of assessing student progress, and little consensus within higher education on what knowledge and skills should be emphasized.[6]

Among the evidence cited for this decline was the following:

> Research indicates that the average community college freshman is reading at the 8th grade level and that 60 percent of entering students in community colleges, 35 percent in regional institutions, and 10 percent in universities need further preparation. Recent estimates in Georgia, Florida, Tennessee, Louisiana, and Mississippi show that in all these states approximately 40 percent of the students entering college require remedial education.[7]

These reports are similar to the many reviews calling for reform in precollegiate education, for high standards, and for equal access to quality. What is often missed in these reports, is how higher education delivers its services. The restructuring now being called for in elementary and secondary schools also applies to higher education.

At all levels, education must be responsive to economic growth, to human resource development, and to satisfying the aspirations of the American public in its quest for prosperity and equality. What we seek is an educated society—one that is dynamic, passionate, just, and free. But no society can achieve this goal without a contemporary, first-class system of education. The task of schools of education is to rethink, research, and retool—in short, to modernize—our system of delivering public education. It means moving away from a teaching model to a learning model. It means realigning our system to include potential learning environments outside the four walls of the traditional school. The advent of new educational technology has added new and more powerful tools to supplement print media, classrooms and libraries that must not be ignored.

In this context, schools of education must become leaders in research into learning theory and educational technology. The modernization of public education will require considerably more than just the preparation of educational personnel, as important as that function continues to be. Schools of education must also collaborate closely with public policymakers, with business and industry, with the communities surrounding the schools, and with school systems themselves. Schools of education can become important catalysts in the transformation of the American educational system from a *school* system based on teaching to an *educational* system based on learning.

COLLABORATION WITH STATE GOVERNMENT

One of the new missions of schools of education is to establish close working relationships with state government, especially legislators and local committees that are working on educational policy for elementary, secondary, and higher education. No modernization is possible without a reexamination of educational policy. Schools of education must overcome their traditional disassociation from practical politics. Academics have feared involvement with a political process that might jeopardize objectivity and academic freedom. Many academics have also preferred to communicate their research through scholarly journals, books, and consultations. Their approach has been individualistic rather than systematic, institutional, and collaborative. But if we fail to establish a systematic relationship between knowledge-makers and policymakers in the field of education, schools of education will lose an important opportunity to help formulate sound policies. Schools of education, part of the same public service system as the legislators, must work with legislators, providing the research, scholarship, and information essential to finding answers for the future.

The School of Education at the University of Massachusetts is working through the State Legislature's Joint Committee on Education and with individual policymakers on issues of educational reform. A major symposium co-sponsored by the School of Education and the Joint Committee on Education, entitled "Act and Resolve: Education's Agenda for the 80s," assembled top leaders throughout the state to examine the issues facing public education in the Commonwealth of Massachusetts. The School of Education became a major academic resource for the Joint Committee on Education as it began deliberations on new policy for improving the effectiveness of public education in the state. The collaboration was designed to make the best knowledge available and provide the best review possible on which Massachusetts educational policy could be based. Working with the legislature became a part of the School of Education's service role. Participating faculty were to be rewarded as they would be for publication and other scholarly activity. An academic service corps, arranged through the School of Education, emerged with the resources and expertise of the University coded on a computer and available to the legislature. This resource bank includes not only education, but other fields that are important for improving the quality of life in the Commonwealth.

COLLABORATION WITH THE PRIVATE SECTOR

Schools of education need to collaborate with the private sector, especially business and industry. Schools of education are hesitant to move into the private sector, except as consultants. Faculty fear the private sector's necessary consideration of profits might seriously compromise their academic freedom and objectivity. However, the post-industrial, high tech business community is advancing far more rapidly in the creation of communication and educational tools than the university.

Because the high tech industries have largely been unable to get assistance from the university—historically the place they had looked to for assistance—they were forced to develop their own educational systems. Universities under economic stress failed to keep pace in state-of-the-art technology. However, this alternative system of education is an added business expense that is passed on to consumers.

An improved collaborative model is clearly needed to benefit both universities and businesses. Close relationships, such as between engineering schools and corporations, are classic examples of the mutual benefits of cooperation.

However, the potential exists for broader collaboration. Both schools and universities need to be able to teach such courses as computer literacy if they are going to have a functional relationship with economic development.

This collaboration with corporations need not be based on some notion of compromise. The partnership between the schools and industry should be based on mutual self-interest. Business and industry need a responsive system of education and educated, talented people who can respond to the realities of the technologically-oriented age. At all levels, the education process must contribute directly to economic growth and to the quality of life.

This mutually beneficial relationship might start with the new technology, which is changing so rapidly that no school or university is able to afford new products each time a breakthrough is apparent. Business and industry could make both hardware, software, and experts in their use available to schools.

There is growing concern that shortages of competent math, science, and technology teachers will become acute. This projected shortage would have direct consequences for high tech industries, including such service industries as banks which are becoming dependent upon information systems. Space exploration requires a rigorous competency in mathematical reasoning. As we move into a multi-national global economy with an interdependent network of nations, the need for multilingual/multicultural competency will become increasingly important. All these areas of competency have payoffs for business and industry, the individual learner, and society. If schools of education and the educational community do not provide these competencies, business and industry will have no choice but to continue to develop a parallel educational system, tied to the values of corporate functioning. Many educational professionals have already begun to move into the workplace because they realize that there are more ways to educate the public than the traditional established ways.

PARTICIPATION IN DEVELOPMENT OF NEW EDUCATIONAL TECHNOLOGIES

Traditional learning styles may give way to television, cable, and a host of new technologies that will deliver education and educational services directly to the consumer in a form and shape that will perhaps be more efficient and economical. Most American families now have televisions; computer hardware has become affordable for many; and almost all have telephones. These three elements put together create a telecommunications network capable of delivering education to the home. Competencies attained this way can rival those achieved in any of the more traditional ways. Other new educational environments may range from summer camps to do-it-yourself activities to weekends of concentrated formal learning. If educators are not involved in this process, others will move to fill the vacuum. Universities, with their highly trained people, have an opportunity to move into non-traditional educational environments if they realize the potential of their involvement.

COLLABORATION WITH PUBLIC SCHOOLS

Although schools of education already collaborate with the public schools and their surrounding communities, they have not previously made a specific commitment to assisting school systems in improving the whole range of their services. Rather, schools of education have concentrated on working with the pre-service and in-service preparation of educational personnel. Schools of education need to assist school systems in coping with the changing realities of public education. Curriculum, new technology, the relationship of other agencies in the community, the education of the public—all become very critical issues for schools of education. The campuses must help schools move in new directions. Sizer puts it this way:

> To train people to be good "coaches" for jobs which will not allow them to coach is silly. To train them to "survive"—that is, to accommodate to the system and thus inevitably to teach poorly—is unconscionable. To pretend there isn't a serious problem in the way the high schools are structured and teachers deployed is hypocrisy. Teacher Educators can thus only save their souls by joining with their colleague professionals in the schools in an effort to redesign the ways that students and teachers spend their time in order that effective teaching and thus learning can take place.[8]

Goodlad is assembling a national network of school-university partnerships aimed at improving teacher preparation and the public schools. In preparation for such a network, Goodlad indicated the following:

> There are times when the disjunctures between universities and schools become of more than usual interest, and the rhetoric regarding the need to close the gaps intensifies. One of these times was in the late 1950s and early 1960s following Sputnik. Another is now.
>
> One theme in this rhetoric addresses the disjuncture between elementary and secondary schools and university-based schools of education. The latter group of institutions is criticized because of the failure to produce effective teachers and research relevant to the needs of teachers and administrators. The schools are criticized for failure to provide exemplary models of practice accessible to beginners and, indeed, conditions conducive to supporting effective teachers in their work.
>
> The implication here is that preparing better teachers (counselors, special educators, administrators) requires exposing them to exemplary sites, but creating those sites appears to require university involvement and, particularly, the infusion of relevant knowledge from research. An intimate connection between teacher preparing institutions, particularly their schools or colleges of education, and surrounding schools appears essential.[9]

THE COMMUNITY AS EDUCATOR

Modernization will link school and various community environments into a coordinated and comprehensive system of human learning. The community can be the neighborhood, region, state, nation or world, depending on the frame of reference. Regardless of geographic considerations, community implies a connection among people and their institutions—a combining of efforts to achieve common goals. The common goal is excellence in learning, and the connection is among all the agents, agencies, and settings that educate. Among the most important community educative agents are business, industry, and the workplace; peers; educational associations, including institutions of higher learning; cultural, scientific and agricultural services; legal, civic, and governmental sectors; recreational/leisure services; health and home services; media, travel, and the natural environment.

All of these agents teach by their presence and by people interacting with them. The school and professional educators by assuming a key role in linking these educative sources into a responsive and dynamic new system, exercise their leadership and ultimate accountability for the best interest of each learner. Expertise, which exists in each of these diverse community settings to assist in the delivery of educational services to all people, will require a new orientation for both the professional as well as other educators in the community. Public policy can help by setting in motion legislation that promotes and encourages this type of collaboration.

Larger and richer learning environments, encouraging youth and adults to intermingle and learn from each other, will be created, and many options for lifelong learning will be established.

The concept of community as educator also allows for a more efficient use of resources. Since all the major resources in the community become part of a coordinated education system, the resource base will be significantly increased without adding unnecessary costs. The growing realization that the schools alone cannot deliver all education makes this timely.

Through partnerships, what is dropped from the comprehensive lists of goals of the schools can be taken over by other agencies in the community: driver education by the police or insurance agencies in the community; sex, drug and health education by the medical and health communities; moral development by the clergy; recreational activities, sports, and exercise by the recreation community. Individualization can be achieved through new partnerships with higher education, where students perform community services as part of their graduation requirements. Retirees can also help individualize education programs. Above all, the telecommunications network and new technology can help every child learn the basics at his or her own rate. This use of technology can release teachers to perform new tasks such as monitoring these new partnerships and designing the most powerful learning environments in concert with other educators found in the community.

The community that works together for a common purpose provides an ongoing process for sustaining its own sense of community. Such a community *cares* about the well-being of its members. This personal sense of caring about one another so central to our memory of "the old neighborhood" can be recaptured for modern times through community education.

NOTES

1. Harvey A. Averch, et al., *How Effective Is Schooling? A Rand Educational Policy Study* (Englewood Cliffs, New Jersey, 1974); Ronald Edmonds, "Effective Schools for the Urban Poor," *Educational Leadership*, October 1979, pp. 15–24; Michael Rutter, et al., *Fifteen Thousand Hours: Secondary Schools and Effects on Children* (Cambridge: Harvard University Press, 1970); George Weber, *Inner-City Children Can Be Taught to Read: Four Successful Schools* (Washington, D. C.: Council for Basic Education, 1970), Occasional Papers Number Eighteen; Ross Zerchykov, "School Effectiveness: Public Schools Can Teach All Children," *Citizen Action in Education* (Boston: Institute for Responsive Education), Vol. 8, No. 1, April 1981.

2. Alvin Toffler, *The Adaptive Corporation* (New York: McGraw-Hill Book Company, 1985); Thomas J. Peters and Robert H. Waterman, Jr., *In Search of Excellence: Lessons from America's Best-Run Companies* (New York: Warner Books, Inc., 1984).

3. Theodore Sizer, *Horace's Compromise: The Dilemma of the American High School* (Boston: Houghton-Mifflin Company, 1984).

4. John I. Goodlad, *A Place Called School: Prospects for the Future* (New York: McGraw-Hill Book Company, 1984).

5. Chapter 188 of the Acts of 1985, An Act Improving the Public Schools of the Commonwealth of Massachusetts.

6. "Access to Quality Undergraduate Education: Text of SREB Panel's Report," A Report by the Southern Regional Education Board's Commission for Educational Quality, *The Chronicle of Higher Education*, 3 July 1985, 9.

7. *Ibid.*

8. Sizer, *Horace's Compromise: The Dilemma of the American High School*, 8.

9. John I. Goodlad, "The Education of Educators and the Improvement of Schooling," unpublished document distributed at meeting of The National Network of School and University Partnerships in Chicago, 2 August 1985.

Concluding Words

The last years before the 21st century may well be written in history as the era where the United States rededicated itself to a vision of excellence. It is this vision of excellence as it applies to the field of public education that we have attempted to unfold in the previous pages. In so doing, we trust that the reader will have gained a better understanding and a certain insight into the nature of an emerging definition of excellence in education. It should be apparent that excellence is as much a state of mind as it is a final destination. It is a process of reaching for an *ideal* to replace the real. It is a continuing process with the goal of excellence always being reviewed and being adapted to meet new opportunities and challenges.

We have suggested that excellence as defined in one era may not be appropriate for another. It is, therefore, the responsibility of all Americans to redefine excellence for each generation and the responsibility of all leaders to rededicate their efforts toward that goal. We also hope that the reader will have been encouraged, perhaps inspired, by a quest for excellence in such an important field as public education. Certainly anyone who reads these pages has been exposed to moments of despair and discouragement in association with certain periods in the history of American public education.

Our major agenda for excellence is to modernize the schools, to transform them from a 19th and 20th century model to one suited for the 21st century. Lack of productivity in today's schools, as seen by dropouts, and low teacher morale, is in large part a function of the outmoded system. The old model itself does not have the capacity to do what the changing society expects. Our basically outdated schools need to be transformed into modern operations. This transformation will necessitate a process in which the community is involved until a new model is operational. We estimate that this process will take place over the remainder of this decade and into the next.

We need a phased approach to modernization. We have rejected many reform methods because we believe such efforts merely attempt to add on to or improve an old system in a costly, inefficient way that in the end will not provide the excellence we expect. The problem with developing an action plan is that it must be a staged progression that begins with the old model and those who work within it. Carefully planned activities will create the conditions necessary for change. Already, demographics, technological developments, equal rights activities, and increasingly interdependent economic structures are transforming society. If our educational system can keep pace with such changes, it will have a dramatic influence on the future. All of these changes have recast the importance of education and the need to achieve quality and equality if we are to develop the full talents of the nation.

Perhaps the reader, professional and lay alike, will move from despair to hope, turning what appear to be unsurmountable challenges into viable opportunities. We do hope that the previous pages have revealed that excellence, in whatever form, cannot be achieved without the full participation of each and every person. Excellence is not the domain of any one interested party; we are all interested parties in the achievement of excellence. To be sure, some will have to play more active roles at certain times than others, but we are all players in this important event. We hope all those who interact with our public system of education will have a better view of its significance and its changing state.

For citizens without school-age children, we trust that you see that the public system of education is central to the well-being of our entire society. Without excellence in education, our economic development will be seriously curtailed, as will our search for a better quality of life. Education cultivates the human capital of our society without which no civilization, including ours, can hope to realize its potential.

For parents with school-age children, we hope that you will be inspired to seek new and more dynamic partnerships with the school. You have been and will continue to be the primary teachers of your children. However, we are in an unprecedented period of opportunity to maximize the potential of your child, with you working in concert with school people in a renewed collaboration on behalf of your children.

For teachers, we hope that you will begin to see a new period of professional opportunity in which you count as individuals as well as members of a dignified, dedicated profession. We believe your role is changing, and that you cannot continue to be expected to deliver all services to children in classrooms that were modeled at the turn of this century. Instead, we see you as facilitators of learning in environments that you helped design and tailor to the uniqueness of each and every person both in school and out of school. We hope that you will supervise the new electronic teachers that will become significant tools to enhance these learning environments. You will, in a sense, be supervisors of learning opportunities linking school to nonschool in a comprehensive view of the curriculum.

For school counselors, psychologists, and other support staff, we hope that you see an opportunity to work with teachers, administrators, parents, and the community in the new psychology that comes with embracing prevention rather than cure, encouraging every learner to become all that he or she is capable of becoming. Your job, in essence, is to use your skills to inspire others through the psychology of hope, creating the conditions that promote learning in and out of school with all those who are ultimately the teachers of the young.

For school principals, school administrators, and other leaders, you are the major climate setters for constructive reform. You will open the lines of communication to the school and community in such a way that the goals for which this institution is accountable will be more nearly realized.

For the policymakers, school boards, trustees, and elected officials, you are the enablers through the democratic process of redefining the guidelines by which we unify our efforts and by which the diversity and talents might be harnessed without compromising the ultimate unity.

Excellence is by consensus the goal of all government levels—national, state, regional, and local. This common denominator should warrant as well a bi-partisan approach to its restoration. All branches of government—executive, legislative, and judicial—are likewise unified by commitment to this highest standard. Policies and laws must enable its fuller realization. The chief role of government, therefore, is to use its power and responsibility to keep society and its institutions on a steady course toward excellence. Obviously, this means creating the climate for the citizens themselves to carry out the search. Governments can at best establish the ground rules and set the stage for the action. The action, however, is ultimately carried out by those in the institutions. While we can legislate excellence, we cannot carry it out like those on the front lines of learning.

In the case of schools and education, the search for excellence involves the community itself and all those who interface with schooling and learning. This means, in essence, most of us. We have seen also that government, as a representative of the citizen, can play a monitoring role as an accountant checking the bottom line. When we have strayed from the goal of excellence for whatever reason, government must reorder our priorities. The multiple tasks of implementation occur at the local levels. This is the decentralization that a democratic society demands of its people. But government can assist through policies, incentives, and sanctions.

At present, we appear to be witnessing a massive regrouping of our governmental agencies in this effort. The federal government and the states especially have commenced the exercise of their role. This book is dedicated to helping people of good will in and out of education to carry out their roles in the critical process of regaining excellence in education.

About the author

Mario D. Fantini, Dean of the School of Education at the University of Massachusetts/Amherst, is one of the nation's best-known educational reformers. As a Ford Foundation officer, Dr. Fantini helped initiate some of the most innovative educational programs, many of which are still being implemented throughout the country today. He was also the architect of the controversial school decentralization plan for New York City. An advocate for increasing educational options for students, parents, and teachers and for a public education system that provides quality as well as equal education to all people, Dr. Fantini has been the featured speaker at numerous conferences both here and abroad. Converting our present school system into a comprehensive educational system for the future in which the school becomes an integral part of a community-based, coordinated human service process represents Dr. Fantini's present concern. In addition, he has authored and co-authored many books, including *Public Schools of Choice: A Plan for the Reform of American Education; Alternative Education: A Source Book for Parents, Teachers, Students, and Administrators; Community Control and the Urban School* (with Marilyn Gittell and Richard Magat); *Toward Humanistic Education* (with Gerald Weinstein); *Decentralization: Achieving Reform* (with Marilyn Gittell); *Disadvantaged: Challenge to Education* (with Gerald Weinstein); *Parenting in a Multicultural Society* (with Rene Cardenas); and the recently-released *Education in School and Nonschool Settings* (with Robert L. Sinclair).

Index

A

Aburdene, Patricia, 85
Academic day, length reductions, 96
Academic magnet school, 162
Access to Excellence Bill (Minnesota), 166
"Access to Quality Undergraduate Education" (Southern Regional Education Board), 222-23
Accountability in education, 59, 68, 71, 157-60
Acculturation and socialization of students, 11
Achievement tests, 48, 112
Action in schools, 30-31
Action in the States (Education Commission of the States), 141-47
Action planning for educational excellence, 177-78
Adaptive Corporation, The (Toffler), 28-29
Adler, Mortimer, 49
Administrative structure, reduction of, 34-35
Administrators, 155
  ongoing training, 128
  turnover of, 33
Adopt-a-school programs, 184
Aesthetic literacy, 123-24
Age segregation in schools, 19-20
Agricultural society, 23, 73, 222
Alabama, action for modernization, 144
Alaska, 122
  action for modernization, 144
Alexander, Lamar, 150
Allied Project Athena (Massachusetts Institute of Technology), 167-68

Alternative education movement, 77, 106, 135
American Council of Life Insurance, 184
American Federation of Teachers, 201
American High-School Today, The (Conant), 66
American Psychological Association, 112
A Place Called School: Prospects for the Future (Goodlad), 3
Arizona,
  action for modernization, 144
  school-business partnership, 212
Arkansas, action for modernization, 149-50
Arts education, 93-94, 123-24, 137
Arts magnet school, 161-62
Atlanta, Georgia, urban school reform, 151–57
AT&T Information Systems, 184–85
Authority in schools, 20, 32
Automation, 11–12

B

Baby boom, 18-19, 56
Baltimore Sun, 170-71
Barriers to Excellence: Our Children at Risk (National Coalition of Advocates for Students), 51, 76-77
Basic skills, 122, 138
  teaching strategies for, 125, 126
Behavioral objectives approach to performance standards, 157
Bilingual education, 19
Blanchard, Kenneth, 1, 36
Boards of education, 14

1